Acknowledgments

We commend the authors of the various chapters included in this book. Their convictions about and enthusiasm for using technology to make reading instruction more effective and engaging for students are obvious throughout the book. Each of them could have written more extensively about their incorporation of technology; indeed we hope that these chapters will be springboards to even more writing about their use of technology in literacy instruction. We also wish to thank Kari Gillesse, Kendra Slayton, Rachel Rosolina, Lesley Bolton, and Ed Levy for their generous and continual support, guidance, and encouragement in bringing this book, and its companion, *Using Technology to Enhance Writing: Innovative Approaches to Literacy Instruction,* to print.

Solution Tree Press would like to thank the following reviewers:

Elaine Dondoyano
Technology Teacher and Reading and Math Intervention Specialist
Rainier View Elementary School
Seattle, Washington

Rachael Gabriel
Assistant Professor of Reading Education
University of Connecticut
Storrs, Connecticut

Janice Hinson
Professor and Chair, Department of Reading and Elementary Education
University of North Carolina at Charlotte
Charlotte, North Carolina

Lynn Olson
Director of Elementary Education and Associate Professor of Education
Creighton University
Omaha, Nebraska

Denise Stuart
Professor, Literacy Education, Computer and Information Systems
The University of Akron
Akron, Ohio

Pamela Sullivan
Assistant Professor, Early, Elementary, and Reading Department
James Madison University
Editor, *Reading in Virginia*
Harrisonburg, Virginia

Visit **go.solution-tree.com/technology** to
access materials related to this book.

Using TECHNOLOGY *to Enhance* Reading

Innovative Approaches *to* LITERACY INSTRUCTION

EDITED BY TIMOTHY V. RASINSKI, KRISTINE E. PYTASH, AND RICHARD E. FERDIG

Contributors

Diane Barone, Kaybeth Calabria, Jill Castek, Suzanne Coatoam Chapman, Bridget Dalton, Marie Donnantuono, Bernadette Dwyer, Rachel J. Ebner, Elizabeth A. Edmondson, Lauren Eutsler, Zhihui Fang, Elsa Andreasen Glover, Megan Goss, Dana L. Grisham, Danielle Herro, Carrie E. Hong, Amy C. Hutchison, Rachel Karchmer-Klein, Erin Killeen, William Kist, Lotta Larson, Salika A. Lawrence, Michael L. Manderino, Julie McLeod, J. Gregory McVerry, Geraldine Mongillo, Laura Northrop, W. Ian O'Byrne, Kristine E. Pytash, Yang Qi, Timothy V. Rasinski, Nicole Barrick Renner, Tara Lee Ronzetti, Kimberly McDavid Schmidt, Valerie Harlow Shinas, Linda Smetana, Blaine E. Smith, Kristen Srsen, Katie Stover, Sheri Vasinda, Corrine M. Wickens, Phillip Wilder, Julie B. Wise, Thomas DeVere Wolsey, Lindsay Sheronick Yearta, Chase Young, Jacqueline Love Zeig

Solution Tree | Press

a division of
Solution Tree

555 North Morton Street
Bloomington, IN 47404
800.733.6786 (toll free) / 812.336.7700
FAX: 812.336.7790
email: info@solution-tree.com
solution-tree.com

Visit **go.solution-tree.com/technology** to download the reproducibles in this book.

Printed in the United States of America

19   18   17   16   15   1   2   3   4   5

Library of Congress Cataloging-in-Publication Data

Using technology to enhance reading : innovative approaches to literacy instruction / editors, Timothy V. Rasinski, Kristine E. Pytash, and Richard E. Ferdig ; Contributors, Diane Barone [and others].

    pages cm

  Includes bibliographical references and index.

  ISBN 978-1-936764-99-0 (perfect bound) 1. Reading--Computer-assisted instruction. 2. Reading--Technological innovations. 3. Educational technology. I. Rasinski, Timothy V.

  LB1050.37.U85 2015

  428.40285--dc23

                    2015002213

Solution Tree
Jeffrey C. Jones, CEO
Edmund M. Ackerman, President

Solution Tree Press
President: Douglas M. Rife
Associate Acquisitions Editor: Kari Gillesse
Editorial Director: Lesley Bolton
Managing Production Editor: Caroline Weiss
Production Editor: Rachel Rosolina
Copy Editor: Ashante K. Thomas
Proofreader: Elisabeth Abrams
Text Designer: Laura Kagemann
Compositor: Abigail Bowen
Cover Designer: Rian Anderson, Abigail Bowen

"The people read it and were glad for its encouraging message."
—Acts 15:31 New International Version

"Once you learn to read, you will be forever free."
—Frederick Douglass

Table of Contents

About the Editors xiii

Introduction 1

   How This Book Is Organized 3

   Important Considerations 5

   Conclusion 5

PART I   Reading Foundations 7

Chapter 1   Foundational Reading Competencies Supported With Technology: Phonemic Awareness and Word Recognition 11

By Diane Barone

   What Does the Research Say? 11

   How Do I Do It? 12

   Classroom Example 14

   Your Turn 15

Chapter 2   Rethinking Foundational Reading Skills: Making Room for the Complexities of Digital Texts 17

By Rachel Karchmer-Klein, Valerie Harlow Shinas, and Julie B. Wise

   Foundational Skills for Reading Digital Texts 18

   How Do I Do It? 19

   Classroom Example 21

   Your Turn 21

Chapter 3 Using Tablets to Teach Foundational Skills: Matching Apps to
Student Needs. 25
By Laura Northrop and Erin Killeen
Using Tablets Within a Response to
Intervention Framework 25
How Do I Do It? 26
Classroom Example 31
Your Turn 32

PART II   Reading Fluency. **35**

Chapter 4 Podcasts: Adding Power and New Possibilities to the Readers
Theater Experience 39
By Sheri Vasinda and Julie McLeod
How Do I Do It? 41
Classroom Example 42
Your Turn 43
Conclusion 45

Chapter 5 Student-Produced Movies as Authentic Reading
Fluency Instruction 47
By Chase Young and Timothy V. Rasinski
How Do I Do It? 48
Classroom Example 50
Your Turn 51
Conclusion 51

Chapter 6 Audio-Assisted Reading Builds Reading Fluency 53
By Kaybeth Calabria and Kristine E. Pytash
How Do I Do It? 54
Classroom Example 57
Your Turn 59
Conclusion 59

PART III   Reading Vocabulary **61**

Chapter 7 Post-Reading Vocabulary Development Through VSSPlus. 65
By Dana L. Grisham, Linda Smetana, and Thomas DeVere Wolsey
The Role of Technology. 66
How Do I Do It? 66
Classroom Example 68
Your Turn 69
Conclusion 71

Chapter 8 Bringing Words to Life Through Student-Created
Vocabulary Videos. 73
By Bridget Dalton and Kimberly McDavid Schmidt .73
How Do I Do It? 75
Classroom Example 76

Your Turn 77
Conclusion 78

Chapter 9 Self-Regulated Vocabulary Learning on the Internet 81
By Rachel J. Ebner
How Do I Do It? 83
Classroom Example 85
Your Turn 86
Conclusion 88

PART IV   Comprehension of Informational Texts **89**

Chapter 10 Using the Multimodal Explanatory Composition Strategy to
Respond to Informational Texts 93
By Amy C. Hutchison
How Do I Do It? 94
Classroom Example 96
Your Turn 99

Chapter 11 Annotation Apps: Supporting Middle School Students'
Interpretation of Science Texts 101
By Jill Castek and Megan Goss
How Do I Do It? 102
Classroom Example 105
Your Turn 108
Conclusion 109

Chapter 12 Online Research and Media Skills:
An Instructional Model for Online Informational Texts 111
By W. Ian O'Byrne and J. Gregory McVerry
How Do I Do It? 113
Classroom Example 114
Your Turn 115
Conclusion 116

PART V   Comprehension of Literary Texts **117**

Chapter 13 Digging Deeper With Reader Response: Using Digital Tools to
Support Comprehension of Literary Texts in Online
Learning Environments 121
By Lotta Larson and Bernadette Dwyer
How Do I Do It? 122
Classroom Example 127
Your Turn 128
Conclusion 129

Chapter 14 Coding and Connecting Complex Literature 131
By J. Gregory McVerry and W. Ian O'Byrne
Purposeful Analysis of Text 132

How Do I Do It? 133
Classroom Example 133
Your Turn 134
Conclusion 135

Chapter 15 Linking Through Literature: Exploring Complex Texts Through
Hypertext Literary Analysis. 137
By Blaine E. Smith and Nicole Barrick Renner
How Do I Do It? 138
Classroom Example 140
Your Turn 141

PART VI   Reading Across Disciplines. **145**

Chapter 16 Classroom Blogging to Develop Disciplinary Literacy. 149
By Michael L. Manderino, Corrine M. Wickens, and Elsa Andreasen Glover
How Do I Do It? 150
Classroom Example 151
Your Turn 154
Conclusion 154

Chapter 17 Using eReaders to Enhance Literacy Instruction in the
Content Areas. 157
By Zhihui Fang, Lauren Eutsler, Suzanne Coatoam Chapman, and Yang Qi
How Do I Do It? 159
Classroom Example 159
Your Turn 162
Conclusion 163

Chapter 18 Supporting Inquiry With Digital Texts in School Disciplines. 165
By Phillip Wilder and Danielle Herro
How Do I Do It? 166
Classroom Example 167
Your Turn 169
Conclusion 170

PART VII   Motivation for Reading. **171**

Chapter 19 "I Wanted to Film, So I Read the Book": Filmmaking in the
English Classroom. 175
By Kristen Srsen and William Kist
How Do I Do It? 177
Classroom Example 183
Your Turn 184
Conclusion 186

Chapter 20 eBooks and eReaders: Removing Obstacles, Improving Motivation 189
By Elizabeth A. Edmondson
How Do I Do It? 191

Classroom Example 192

Your Turn 194

Chapter 21 Using Literacy iPad Apps for Reading Motivation 197

By Salika A. Lawrence, Carrie E. Hong, Marie Donnantuono, and Geraldine Mongillo

How Do I Do It? 199

Classroom Example 200

Your Turn 201

Conclusion 202

PART VIII   Reading Assessment **203**

Chapter 22 Literacy Assessments in the Digital Age 207

By Jacqueline Love Zeig and Tara Lee Ronzetti

How Do I Do It? 208

Classroom Example 209

Your Turn 212

Conclusion 213

Chapter 23 Developing and Assessing Fluency Through Web 2.0 Digital Tools . .215

By Jacqueline Love Zeig

How Do I Do It? 218

Classroom Example 218

Your Turn 219

Conclusion 220

Chapter 24 Using Blogs as Formative Assessment of Reading Comprehension . 223

By Katie Stover and Lindsay Sheronick Yearta

How Do I Do It? 224

Classroom Example 225

Your Turn 229

Conclusion 231

References and Resources 233

Index 253

About the Editors

Timothy V. Rasinski, PhD, is a professor of literacy education at Kent State University. As a researcher, author, consultant, and presenter, he focuses on reading fluency and word study, reading in the elementary and middle grades, and readers who struggle. His research on reading has been cited by the National Reading Panel and published in *Reading Research Quarterly*, *The Reading Teacher*, *Reading Psychology*, and the *The Journal of Educational Research*. He has also taught literacy education at the University of Georgia and was an elementary and middle school classroom and literacy intervention teacher in Nebraska for several years.

Tim served a three-year term on the board of directors of the International Reading Association and for seven years was coeditor of *The Reading Teacher*, the world's most widely read journal of literacy education. He has also served as coeditor of the *Journal of Literacy Research*. Tim is former president of the College Reading Association, and he has won the A. B. Herr and Laureate awards from the College Reading Association for his scholarly contributions to literacy education. In 2010, he was inducted into the International Reading Hall of Fame.

Tim has written more than two hundred articles and authored, coauthored, or edited over fifty books or curriculum programs on reading education, including the best-selling *The Fluent Reader*. To learn more about Tim's work, visit www.timrasinski .com or follow @TimRasinski1 on Twitter.

Kristine E. Pytash is an assistant professor in teaching, learning, and curriculum studies at Kent State University's College of Education, Health, and Human Services, where she codirects the secondary Integrated Language Arts Teacher Preparation Program. She is a former high school English teacher. Kristy's research focuses on using disciplinary writing, understanding the literacy practices of youth in alternative schools and juvenile detention facilities, and preparing teachers to teach writing. Her work has appeared in the *Journal of Adolescent and Adult Literacy, English Journal, Voices From the Middle*, and *Middle School Journal*. To learn more about Kristy's work, visit www.literacyspaces.com or follow @kpytash on Twitter.

Richard E. Ferdig, PhD, is the Summit Professor of Learning Technologies and is professor of instructional technology at Kent State University, where he works in the Research Center for Educational Technology and the School of Lifespan Development and Educational Sciences. He has served as researcher and instructor at Michigan State University, the University of Florida, the Wyższa Szkoła Pedagogiczna (Krakow, Poland), and the Università degli studi di Modena e Reggio Emilia (Italy). At Kent State, his research, teaching, and service focus on combining cutting-edge technologies with current pedagogic theory to create innovative learning environments. His research interests include online education, educational games and simulations, and what he labels a deeper psychology of technology. In addition to publishing and presenting in the United States and internationally, Rick has also been funded to study the impact of emerging technologies, such as K–12 virtual schools.

Rick is the founding editor-in-chief of the *International Journal of Gaming and Computer-Mediated Simulations*. He is the editor-in-chief of the *Journal of Technology and Teacher Education*, serves as a consulting editor for the development editorial board of *Educational Technology Research and Development*, and is on the review panel of the *British Journal of Educational Technology*. Rick earned his doctorate in educational psychology from Michigan State University. To learn more about Rick's work, visit www.ferdig.com or follow @rickferdig on Twitter.

To book Timothy V. Rasinski, Kristine E. Pytash, or Richard E. Ferdig for professional development, contact pd@solution-tree.com.

Introduction

Here we sit in the middle of the second decade of the 21st century. Isn't it amazing how some things have changed since we ushered in the new millennium? Shifts in technology and our use of technology have been breathtaking to say the least. We have seen the introduction and widespread use of online bookstores, social media applications, interactive whiteboards, smartphones, tablets, and other devices and applications that allow us to communicate, take and share photos and videos, play sophisticated games, access and search the Internet, and perform many other tasks. No longer are we tied to a computer workstation in our office or classroom. More changes are sure to follow in the coming years, leading to both a feeling of excitement and a slight sense of being overwhelmed. Just when we have mastered one application or device, a new one emerges.

At the same time, it is interesting to note what has not changed. One of these is reading achievement among our elementary, middle, and secondary students. Despite significant investments of money and other resources by the federal, state, and local governments, student achievement levels in the United States have hardly budged. Take, for example, Reading First—President George W. Bush's reading initiative that was supposed to raise reading achievement of third-grade students in the United States. Reading First was based on state-of-the-art effective reading instruction, as reported by the National Institute of Child Health and Human Development (NICHD; 2000). Yet, the results of Reading First were hardly encouraging. Reading achievement among U.S. students has remained largely stagnant, and Reading First produced no statistically noticeable effects on reading achievement when compared with non-Reading First schools (Gamse et al., 2008).

Clearly we need new solutions for and new ways of thinking about the problems of literacy education. In a world that is becoming increasingly competitive, maintaining the status quo simply will not cut it. However, even maintaining the status quo has become a challenge. Since the financial crisis of 2008, budgets for schools have been reduced, class sizes have increased, and curricular demands have expanded. "Do more with less" seems to be the current policy mantra.

Technology may offer some solutions to the problems we confront in literacy education. We would never suggest that computers could or should replace good teachers, but we do think technology can be a multiplier—it can allow teachers to create new methods of instruction and cover more content than they could without technology. Essentially, technology provides teachers with tools for developing novel approaches for engaging students and effective instruction for literacy learners. Moreover, it is becoming increasingly clear that technology is changing how we read, what we read, and how we respond to what we read. In this age of reading education, technology cannot be avoided.

Despite the ever-expanding influence of technology on reading and reading instruction, many teachers simply do not feel completely comfortable embracing technology for teaching reading. They may be so overwhelmed with the growing curricular demands (for example, changing curriculum and instruction to align with the Common Core State Standards [CCSS] or other state standards) that there is not enough time or expertise to consider how technology can impact their teaching of reading. The rapidly changing technology environment may sway some teachers to hold off on implementing technology solutions in their reading classrooms. Regardless of the reason, we cannot stand still when it comes to technology and the teaching of reading. For our sake, and our students' sakes, it is imperative that we begin to explore ways teachers can make good use of technology to improve their literacy teaching and students' reading outcomes.

That is what this book is all about. We have brought together many thought leaders on the subject to offer practical insights into how they have used technology to improve their literacy instruction. Our contributors range from classroom teachers who put technology to work daily, to college professors who have explored the power and potential of using technology to solve many of the problems in literacy education. Our hope in developing this book and its companion volume, *Using Technology to Enhance Writing: Innovative Approaches to Literacy Instruction,* is to provide you, the classroom teacher or literacy interventionist, with practical reading instruction strategies that you can easily implement or adapt today in your own instructional environment. Additionally, we hope that this book will inspire you to think outside the box and begin creating your own technology-oriented approaches for reading instruction.

We want to emphasize that this book is not about technology per se; rather, it is about how reading instruction at all levels can be made more effective and engaging through the thoughtful and intentional employment of technology. Reading is the heart and soul of this book; technology is simply one way to improve reading.

How This Book Is Organized

Research has identified essential factors or competencies associated with success in learning to read. If teachers help students develop mastery in these areas, students are likely to become proficient readers. We have organized our book, then, around several of these key reading competencies, which have been identified by the National Reading Panel (NICHD, 2000), the Common Core State Standards (National Governors Association Center for Best Practices [NGA] & Council of Chief State School Officers [CCSSO], 2010), *Handbook of Reading Research, Volume IV* (Kamil, Pearson, Moje, & Afflerbach, 2011), and other scholarly reports. We group the chapters into the following eight parts.

    I.   Reading Foundations

   II.   Reading Fluency

  III.   Reading Vocabulary

  IV.   Comprehension of Informational Texts

   V.   Comprehension of Literary Texts

  VI.   Reading Across Disciplines

 VII.   Motivation for Reading

VIII.   Reading Assessment

Each part focuses on existing, research-based instructional practices that have been adapted with technology applications or novel strategies to take advantage of currently available technological features. Although specific chapters may focus on a particular range of grade levels, we feel that readers should be able to easily adapt the strategies for any grade level or audience.

Each part begins with a brief introduction written by the editors to provide background information. Following each introduction are three chapters that emphasize instructional approaches for teaching the focal competency or topic of the part. For example, after the introduction to Reading Foundations, you will find chapters that explore how technology can be applied to teaching phonemic awareness, phonics, and other related competencies to emerging readers. We wish to emphasize that the instructional approaches and technological tools presented in each chapter could fit into other parts or span across multiple parts or grade levels. Thus, we challenge you, the reader, to adapt the presentations in the individual chapters to create instructional applications that address the specific needs of your students.

Each chapter focuses on a specific pedagogical practice implemented with technology or digital tools. As we mentioned earlier, the chapters have been written by exemplary educators and scholars who have used the technology with students, conducted research related to the technological application, made professional development presentations and presentations at professional organizations on their topic, or have written in professional journals about their particular use of technology in reading. The authors have published in leading literacy journals such as *The Reading Teacher* and the *Journal of Adolescent and Adult Literacy*. Moreover, these authors have worked extensively in real classrooms with students and teachers. The chapters provide first-hand accounts of how particular instructional approaches work and include specific suggestions to adapt and implement them in other instructional settings.

Each chapter is organized in a similar manner so that you can more easily negotiate the various topics and look broadly and comparatively at the variety of approaches for reading instruction. We hope you will be able to analyze the instructional practices across multiple contexts and populations. After an overview of the theoretical perspectives and research bases for the particular instructional approach presented, each chapter is structured more or less as follows.

1. **How Do I Do It?:** The authors provide a rich description of the pedagogical practice.

2. **Classroom Example:** Specific examples from the authors' personal experiences highlight how the instructional approach works and how it advanced students' reading and knowledge and use of technology.

3. **Your Turn:** The authors invite you to explore how you might adapt the particular pedagogical practice for your own classrooms.

We commend the chapter authors for their enthusiasm and dedication in sharing their knowledge of reading instruction and technology. Each of the authors could easily have written more extensively about their classroom experiences; however, they worked to provide a succinct presentation of some of the most promising research-based, pedagogical strategies. We also commend you for choosing this book. Teaching is tough, and there are many books that claim to improve how teachers teach reading. We truly believe that this book has great potential for transforming the way you look at technology and literacy and, more importantly, how you use technology to benefit your students' literacy development.

Important Considerations

The best reading instruction is both an art and a science. We have organized this book around essential reading competencies and critical pedagogical topics in the teaching of reading. These are areas that have been identified through scientific thought and inquiry as essential for successful literacy instruction. Of course, effective reading instruction cannot be artificially separated into these distinct areas. Just as the purpose of this book is to explore how technology can be integrated into reading instruction, we challenge our readers to consider how the competencies and topics can be integrated into their own reading curriculum. This is the art of teaching reading. We hope that you will allow the artist in you to consider ways that the content of the various parts and chapters can be adapted for use in your own instructional situation and total reading curriculum.

Conclusion

In order to effectively teach reading with technology, teachers must have conceptual knowledge of the reading process and factors associated with proficient reading, pedagogical knowledge about the teaching of reading, and knowledge about how technology can facilitate students' growth and development in reading. This leaves teachers with much to know and consider. As students engage in using technology on their own to learn about the world and communicate with one another, teachers must continue to explore what these new forms and formats mean for the teaching of reading. Moreover, as the tools students use continue to evolve, teachers must have an extensive knowledge of why certain tools might promote certain instructional approaches. We hope this book provides you with a deeper understanding of the theoretical perspectives and research base, as well as the practical implications of how to implement these instructional approaches in the reading classroom.

PART I | Reading Foundations

To build a strong, enduring structure, you need a solid foundation. Similarly, students must have a solid reading foundation to become proficient, thoughtful, and lifelong readers. Part I deals with developing that reading foundation in two different ways.

First, *foundation* refers to the principles that should guide the application of technology in the teaching and assessment of early reading. Teachers and school administrators must be aware of these principles, developed through scholarly inquiry, which will lead to the most effective use of technology.

Second, foundation can also be interpreted in terms of the specific literacy competencies that make up the building blocks for future success in reading. The Common Core State Standards, very likely to be the guiding force for literacy instruction in the United States for the foreseeable future, have identified foundational literacy competencies that must be mastered early in students' reading lives and that are necessary to help students move to proficient college- and career-ready reading. These foundational competencies include phonemic awareness, word recognition or phonics, and ultimately sight word development. (Reading fluency is also identified as a foundational skill. It is addressed specifically in part II of the book.) *Phonemic awareness* refers to students' ability to perceive discrete speech sounds (phonemes) and manipulate those sounds in various ways (segment spoken words into individual sounds, blend sounds into words, and so on). *Phonics*, of course, refers to the ability to translate written symbols (letters and letter combinations) into their corresponding sounds and words. Sight word recognition refers to the ability of proficient readers to recognize words in print automatically and effortlessly on sight. Clearly, these are skills required for any type of conventional reading.

For adults, technology can sometimes be challenging. Children just beginning school, however, are what the authors call *digital natives*. Technology has become an integral part of their lives. As educators, we need to be willing and able to create reading instruction that allows students to take advantage of their interest in and experience with technology.

First, Diane Barone demonstrates how to use technology to adapt traditional early literacy practices such as language experience and a morning message to the digital classroom. Next, Rachel Karchmer-Klein, Valerie Harlow Shinas, and Julie B. Wise explore the principles of multimodality, reading path, and the language of digital texts that will help teachers bridge early reading instruction beyond print. With the increasing proliferation of computer tablets and the continual development of computer applications, Laura Northrop and Erin Killeen discuss how matching the right app to the skill to be taught and applying the gradual release of responsibility model of instruction can lead to early reading instruction that is not only effective but also highly engaging.

 **Diane Barone** is a foundation professor of literacy at the University of Nevada, Reno. Her research focuses on children's literacy development and instruction in high-poverty schools. She collaborates with teachers in public schools to enhance student learning in literacy, and she has mentored teachers seeking National Board Certification. She served as the editor of *Reading Research Quarterly* and was a board member of the International Reading Association and the Literacy Research Association. She is currently editor of *The Reading Teacher* with Marla Mallette. She is a member of the Reading Hall of Fame and will serve as president of the International Reading Association in 2015.

CHAPTER 1

Foundational Reading Competencies Supported With Technology: Phonemic Awareness and Word Recognition

By Diane Barone

With the increased use of technology in everyday practice and the simultaneous increase in the use of technology by young children, early childhood and literacy educators are seriously considering the use of technology for instruction (Beschorner & Hutchison, 2013). New technological innovations like smartphones and tablets confirm that literacy acquisition is more than a print-based endeavor (Wohlwend, 2010). Clearly, as educators, we know that technology is not going away, so we must ask, "What research is centered on early literacy skill development, and what might it look like in practice?"

What Does the Research Say?

Before focusing on literacy, it is important to consider student technology use. One of the earliest criticisms of the use of technology was that young children were not able to use it (Glaubke, 2007), but Rosemary Luckin, Daniel Connolly, Lydia Plowman, and Sharon Airey (2003) argue that young children could interact with a screen and a toy (such as Webkinz). Additionally, young children are engaging in Internet use as they see older siblings and their parents using devices like smartphones and tablets, and they are eager to play too (Barone, 2012). For instance, children younger than twelve are one of the fastest growing groups using mobile technology

(Shuler, 2009). Frequently, young children engage with print-based materials and then quickly explore a website that features the characters in a book (for instance, children might read a book by Lauren Child featuring Charlie and Lola and then visit www .milkmonitor.com to interact with these characters)—at least they can at home.

The research on early literacy instruction is consistent in that experts suggest the following elements are necessary for students' literacy growth (NICHD, 2000): explicit instruction in phonemic awareness, phonics, vocabulary, fluency, and com-prehension. In contrast, the research on infusing technology with this instruction and environment is not as clear (Paterson, Henry, O'Quin, Ceprano, & Blue, 2003; Tracey & Young, 2007). Surprisingly, many of the integrated programs typically bought by school districts have not received extensive research. In these programs, each student is placed at his or her level of knowledge for further instruction in a particular literacy area, such as decoding. Although research has acknowledged that students are more engaged with this instructional support, there are few studies that document increased student achievement (Paterson et al., 2003).

Even though the research is limited, there is support for the use of technology with literacy skill acquisition. Marguerite Hillman and Terry Moore (2004) and Paul Attewell, Belkis Suazo-Garcia, and Juan Battle (2003) find that students who used a computer performed better on phonics, phonemic awareness, letter-word recognition, and comprehension. Peter Albion (2008) suggests that early literacy and technology are enhanced with the use of tablets, as very young students can touch a word or letter and get immediate feedback.

How Do I Do It?

This section focuses on infusing technology into basic literacy instruction by shar-ing functions for ebooks, apps, and computers. I narrowed this section to technology that is easy to implement, as teachers don't have time to be frustrated with setting up technology or recognizing the connections to literacy learning. Additionally, the technology support is focused on skill development, not on comprehension or other sophisticated reading applications.

eBooks ·

Electronic books support the idea of students being read to and able to listen to it without direct adult support (Korat & Shamir, 2008). The research on ebooks demonstrates that students gain word knowledge (de Jong & Bus, 2002) and phono-logical awareness (Chera & Wood, 2003). Tricia Zucker, Amelia Moody, and Michael McKenna (2009) suggest that ebooks reduce the cognitive load on young students;

rather than being derailed by limited word knowledge when they are unable to read a word, the book will read it for them, allowing them to continue the story.

eBooks are easily available for teachers and are often free of cost. Sites like Gizmo's Freeware (www.techsupportalert.com; mr6n8, 2013) help teachers select appropriate books for young students. Starfall (www.starfall.com) also has ebooks grouped by categories such as the alphabet, decodable books for learning to read, and rhymes. I selected Starfall's *A* alphabet book, and the first page has a capital *A* and a lowercase *a* being brought to the screen by ants; the letter name is read as this action occurs. When you press the arrow, the sound of a short *a* is heard. On the next page there is an *a* and an apple; when a student clicks on the *a*, the short sound is heard, and the letter moves to the beginning spot in the word *apple*, allowing students to hear the sound, associate it with a letter, and then see it placed into a word. The book continues with other words that begin with *a*, such as *alligator* and *astronaut*. This book and others on this site are easy for young students to navigate on their own, and they allow for extensive practice, as they are engaging.

In books with text, a student can read alone or click the word to have it read to him or her. When I read *Canada Goose*, also on Starfall, the words were read by syllable and then the whole word was read smoothly, modeling fluent decoding. Students can easily hear each discrete part and then listen as the word is decoded. This book also offers limited hot spots for animation, which allows students to focus on the words, not the actions of the goose.

Apps

Apps (short for *applications*) and ebooks can overlap, as there are apps filled with ebooks, such as FarFaria (www.farfaria.com). Similar to ebooks, apps allow students to hear sounds and have support for unknown words (Northrop & Killeen, 2013). In addition, many familiar authors have shared their books as apps. For example, search "Dr. Seuss's ABC book" on YouTube to see how it is reconfigured as an app. In general, apps are more interactive than ebooks. For instance, the app iWriteWords allows students to write letters with their fingers as they learn about them.

As tablets become more available in schools, their use with young students will grow, as they are immediately engaging and familiar. As with the iWriteWords app, students can use their fingers to navigate rather than controlling a pencil, which is an easier process with a direct response on a screen. With site licenses, teachers can download apps to a set of tablets so that a group of students can easily use them. Generally, teachers request that the principal or technology specialist obtain a site license, and then the app is downloaded to each tablet.

Computers

Linda Labbo (2005) offers two ways to use computer technology to support foundational literacy skills. Both of these strategies include the teacher as a model and recorder and can be completed in whole-group, small-group, or one-on-one settings. The first strategy is *digital language experience*, built from the ideas of Russell Stauffer (1970), where a student dictated a story to his or her teacher and the teacher recorded the story on paper. In the digital language experience, the teacher places digital photos of students or images that students have created in software like PowerPoint. The students dictate a caption for each image that the teacher then types on the slide. Students read the captions multiple times by moving through the PowerPoint. Through this process, students develop knowledge of foundational print concepts such as directionality, sound-symbol relationships, and word knowledge.

A second strategy is shifting to a *digital morning message*. If the teacher has a SMART Board or projection device, he or she can write a message about the day, and students watch the message being written letter by letter and word by word. Students can participate by pressing a letter key, like a *T* for *Today's Message*. Digital morning messages can be read with a voice synthesizer, allowing the voice to be changed, which increases the students' engagement. Similar to digital language experience, students learn about sound-symbol relationships and sight words as they see the message written and as they read it or listen to it.

Classroom Example

On a visit to a kindergarten classroom, I watched as small groups of students moved through an iPad station. Students at this station were working with the abc PocketPhonics app. Each student was investigating beginning and ending consonants and short vowels to build and blend CVC (consonant, vowel, consonant) words.

I asked the teacher what she had done to engage these students so well while she was working with another small group of students. Here is a summary of the guidelines she offered:

> We talked about the iPads as a class and how we were to use them before I expected small-group work. Each student practiced taking the iPad out of the cart, turning it on, and touching the app they were to use. I had a parent volunteer work with the students until each one could do this.
>
> I modeled the app we were using, abc PocketPhonics, with the whole class. I had students demonstrate what to do. I had already taught the

alphabet and simple blending without the iPad app, so students knew these skills, although they were still developing automaticity.

Students rotated into the station and worked with the app. Either a parent or I rotated through the center to keep students on task at first. Quickly we were able to just watch students engage with the app, as there were no behavior issues. Students loved to show one another what words they created, and I was pleased with the social interaction as students individually interacted with the technology.

Just before it was time to rotate, I had the students write one word on a piece of paper that they had explored on the app. I wanted them to see the connection between electronic writing and writing on paper.

Her conversation demonstrates the careful planning that occurred so that students interacted with the iPad in ways that were expected and supported their learning.

Your Turn

Complementing traditional instruction of phonemic awareness and word recognition with technology is not that difficult to do, especially with the introduction of tablets. The important thing is that teachers teach the literacy concept first so that students are able to engage independently with an ebook, app, or computer program, thus ensuring they are familiar with the skills necessary to be successful. When students attend school, it is critical that teachers build on the literacy experiences that the students have had at home, and today these experiences increasingly include technology for learning to read and write.

Rachel Karchmer-Klein, PhD, is an associate professor of literacy education and educational technology at the University of Delaware, where she teaches a wide range of classes on topics such as the assessment and instruction of literacy skills, differentiating instruction, reading and writing in digital environments, and technology integration in inclusive educational settings. Her research focuses on the relationships between Internet technologies and reading and writing, with particular emphasis on the practical implications of technology use in K–12 education. Rachel's work has been published in literacy and educational technology journals such as *Reading Research Quarterly, Journal of Research on Technology in Education, Reading Research and Instruction, The Reading Teacher*, and *Journal of Research on Technology in Education*. Visit https://sites.google.com/a/udel .edu/rachelkarchmerklein to learn more about Rachel's work.

Valerie Harlow Shinas, PhD, is an assistant professor in the Graduate School of Education at Lesley University, where she teaches literacy methods and reading research courses. Her research interests include digital literacies, adolescent literacy, and the changing nature of reading and writing in response to multimodal digital texts that take advantage of the affordances of new tools and technologies. Valerie has a deep interest in the ways teacher educators prepare their students to integrate technology in K–12 classrooms. Much of her research is focused on the relationship between preservice teachers' technological pedagogical content knowledge (TPACK) and teacher preparation programs. Visit www .lesley.edu/faculty/valerie-harlow-shinas to learn more about Valerie's work.

Julie B. Wise has been in education for twenty years. Beginning her career as an elementary school teacher, she taught third grade before earning her master's degree as a reading specialist and focusing her efforts on supporting K–12 struggling readers. Currently, she is a doctoral student at the University of Delaware. Her research focuses on student-created digital documentaries in K–12 social studies classrooms. Visit www.myreadingsecrets.com to learn more about Julie's work.

CHAPTER 2

Rethinking Foundational Reading Skills: Making Room for the Complexities of Digital Texts

By Rachel Karchmer-Klein, Valerie Harlow Shinas, and Julie B. Wise

When we were asked to write this chapter, we began by reflecting on our early experiences with technology. Valerie, the digital dinosaur of the group, explained technology use was limited to her father's electric typewriter and the cassette recorder she received for her twelfth birthday. She recalls spending summer days writing a neighborhood newspaper with friends, generating multiple pages of each edition with carbon paper, and capturing audio recordings of family sporting events. Available technologies were few, but learning to use the tools was easy when there were adults to watch and mimic.

Julie shared her memories of the small television in the corner of the family room. It sported two silver antennae on top and offered just thirteen channels. She also remembers her first college computer. It was equipped with a modem, allowing her access to the library's card catalog from the comfort of her dorm room. Using her dot-matrix printer was a bit of a chore though—she had to be careful to line up the holes on either side of the paper feed so the text would not be misaligned on the page.

Rachel's earliest technology experiences revolved around the Atari video system her parents bought her in 1981. She spent hours playing games, trying to maneuver characters with the now-antiquated joysticks and paddles. She also has vivid memories of her father bringing home new games; each time, he opened the wrapped box, took out the directions, and began to read them aloud. Meanwhile, Rachel would grab the cartridge out of the box, jam it into the system, and start playing. Her father would always ask the same question: "How are you going to know how to play the game if you haven't read the directions?" Each time, Rachel offered the same response: "I'll figure it out!" And she did. The technology was simplistic enough that one could easily navigate the environment by making sense of flashing lights, sound effects, and other visual and audio features that led to beating an opponent and winning the game.

All three of us grew up with technology, albeit less sophisticated than the iPads, personal computers, and smartphones available today. Still, we played video games, watched movies on a VCR, begged to use the family's cell phone, and wrote school reports using electronic tools of one type or another. Overall, each of us was relatively tech-savvy given the available technologies of the time.

Today, we refer to tech-savvy students born after 1980 as digital natives (Prensky, 2005). Their experiences with technology are unlike those of any earlier generation, due primarily to their immersion in the rapidly changing digital landscape. Specifically, they tend to have ready access to computers, the Internet, cell phones, texting, and social networking. Moreover, they utilize each of these to read, write, and communicate for a variety of purposes. Many assume that because of access, all digital natives are skilled technology users who easily take on the skills necessary to engage with information and communication technologies, perpetuating the notion these students can figure them out. However, there is no evidence indicating that unlimited access to technology equates to deep understanding of how to read and write effectively with digital texts. Additionally, there is the challenge of keeping up with the constantly evolving nature of technology. This, in turn, results in viewing literacy "as a moving target, continually changing its meaning depending on what society expects literate individuals to do" (Leu, Kinzer, Coiro, & Cammack, 2004, p. 1584).

Foundational Skills for Reading Digital Texts

The Common Core State Standards Initiative (NGA & CCSSO, 2010) makes clear that in order to be college and career ready in the 21st century, students must be able to read and interpret digital texts and media. Upon close examination of the standards, we found both explicit and implicit references to reading digital text. For example, anchor standard seven for reading states, "Integrate and evaluate content presented in diverse media and formats, including visually and quantitatively, as well as in words" (CCRA.R.7; NGA & CCSSO, 2010). This anchor standard acknowledges the multiple formats available in digital environments.

A more implicit reference can be seen in anchor standard one for reading: "Read closely to determine what the text says explicitly and to make logical inferences from it; cite specific textual evidence when writing or speaking to support conclusions drawn from the text" (CCRA.R.1; NGA & CCSSO, 2010). This anchor standard does not explicitly refer to media or technology text forms, but it does infer that to master this skill, one must think deeply about digital text features and how they work together to convey meaning.

We are very glad to see digital reading represented in the CCSS. Teachers are more apt to integrate technology when a clear connection between its use and curriculum standards has been made (Karchmer-Klein & Layton, 2006). Yet, we cannot help but wonder how teachers make the leap to critical reading of digital texts when the foundational skills necessary to acquire them are largely ignored.

The CCSS define foundational skills as "necessary and important components of an effective, comprehensive reading program designed to develop in proficient readers the capacity to comprehend texts across a range of types and disciplines" (NGA & CCSSO, 2010). Early literacy instruction focuses on skills such as concept of print, directionality, phonemic awareness, and the alphabetic principle to prepare young children to make connections between sounds and symbols and the culturally constructed rules of reading (Snow, Burns, & Griffin, 1998). However, digital environments increase the complexity of reading by incorporating multimodality and nonlinear directionality, together transforming the reader from passive consumer to co-designer of meaning (Kress, 2010; Reinking, Labbo, & McKenna, 1997). Additionally, students must understand the metalanguage associated with reading online (Unsworth, 2009). Despite urgent recommendations that today's students must be prepared to read and write in digital environments (International Reading Association [IRA], 2009; NGA & CCSSO, 2010), we continue to teach foundational reading skills as they relate only to printed books. Instead, we must teach skills that reflect the digital nature of text.

How Do I Do It?

Students must be aware of the characteristics of digital texts so they may effectively navigate and comprehend their meanings. Therefore, skills typically taught in later grades need to be introduced earlier so students have opportunities to build on and refine them throughout their K–12 schooling. Fortunately, there is a growing body of literature informing our understanding of why an expanded set of foundational reading skills is needed in order to navigate and construct meaning from digital texts (Jewitt, 2011; Karchmer-Klein & Shinas, 2012a; Unsworth, 2009). Three of these important skills are (1) multimodality, (2) reading path, and (3) common language.

Multimodality

Multimodality is the understanding that modes other than written language can convey meaning. Modes are signs and symbols that carry meaning, such as written and oral language and visual, audio, gestural, and spatial representations (Kalantzis, Cope, & Cloonan, 2010; Kress, 2003). Modes may be represented in different ways. For instance, oral language may convey different meanings depending on pitch, volume, and pace. Many texts, particularly those written for young children, comprise multiple modes (Hassett & Curwood, 2009). As teachers engage students with these texts, there is typically talk about the ways in which words and images work together to convey meaning. This discourse must extend to reading digital texts so students recognize two critical points. First, words are not the only mode in digital texts. Second, nonlinguistic modes may carry much of the meaning (Kress, 2010). Just as traditional literacy instruction focuses on breaking the code of alphanumeric symbols, we must teach students to take into account images, sound effects, music, and any other modes present to make meaning of an alternative coding system (Walsh, 2006).

Reading Path

A reading path is the sequence a reader follows while engaged with a text. In a traditional print-bound book, the reading path tends to follow a top-to-bottom, left-to-right trajectory. Traditional literacy instruction reinforces this perception. In contrast, the reading path in a digital environment can take multiple forms, co-constructed by the author's intent and reader's knowledge of digital text, making this a complex task (Karchmer-Klein & Shinas, 2012a). As Maryanne Wolf and Mirit Barzillai (2009) remind us, "comprehension is not simple, nor does it develop overnight" (p. 34). Thus, explicitly teaching young readers how to approach a digital page will prepare them for the sophisticated texts they will undoubtedly encounter in the later grades (Zammit, 2007).

Common Language

The goal of the CCSS is to develop a common understanding of what K–12 students should know and be able to do for college and career readiness (NGA & CCSSO, 2010). Similarly, in direct reference to literacy, there are common definitions of reading-related terms and skills. For example, the National Reading Panel (NICHD, 2000) defines *phonemes*, *phonemic awareness*, *systematic phonics instruction*, and *reading comprehension*. Unfortunately, there is no common language when discussing reading in digital environments, despite calls for such an initiative. The purpose would be to "provide the labels and tools with which teachers and students can explicitly describe and talk about the various texts" (Zammit & Downes, 2002,

p. 29). For example, in order to have a conversation about how we make meaning from digital text, students and teachers must share an understanding of a reading path and how to construct one. They must be able to recognize modes beyond written language and talk about how and why they attend to them.

Classroom Example

Inanimate Alice (Pullinger & Joseph, 2012) is a digital novel that tells the story of a young girl through the modes of written language, images, and audio. It also requires readers to solve puzzles and games to progress through the story. When reading this text with eighth graders, Valerie Harlow Shinas (2012) found students' reading paths were influenced by two actions performed in tandem. They scanned the page to determine which modes were present (such as written language, moving or static images, or music) and then used prior experience with digital reading to determine which modes carried the most meaning. However, all students did not identify the same modes as important, thus creating different reading paths. For example, most students felt the words on the screen carried the meaning of the story so they focused on them and paid little attention to the moving images and music. Conversely, a few students reportedly ignored the written language, instead focusing on the images and music. Follow-up retellings indicated that although all students comprehended the text at a literal level, there was variance in their depth of understanding, possibly due to variations in reading paths.

Similar behaviors have been observed when young students read digital texts. Shirley Lefever-Davis and Cathy Pearman (2005), for instance, found that digital modes can distract first graders. One student in particular was captivated by embedded images; however, this stalled his reading path, causing him to focus on a mode that did not always convey the story's intended meaning. Thus, an effective reading path is a precursor to a deeper understanding of digital texts.

Your Turn

We encourage you, the true change agents of the classroom, to recognize two approaches to technology integration in early reading instruction. First, and perhaps most widely acknowledged, is using technology to *support* traditional foundational reading skills. For years researchers have studied the effects of software programs on phonemic awareness (Foster, Erickson, Foster, Brinkman, & Torgeson, 1994), phonics (Lefever-Davis & Pearman, 2005), and fluency (McKenna, 1998). Moreover, teachers have provided informative insights about their experiences using technological tools in the reading classroom (Aitken & Dewey, 2013; Karchmer, Mallette, Kara-Soteriou, & Leu, 2005; Zucker & Invernizzi, 2008). We understand the value of this approach because it can help you differentiate instruction and provide additional practice for students. However, this alone does not adequately prepare students to read in the 21st century.

We feel a second approach is necessary, one that conceptualizes reading to *extend* beyond skills associated with traditionally printed text. In this way, you can instruct students in the expanded set of reading skills needed to navigate and construct meaning from digital texts. One way to begin this process is to identify a working vocabulary that makes sense to them instead of waiting for literacy researchers to come to agreement. Bridget Dalton (2012/2013) suggests inviting students into the process as well by allowing them to develop their own terms, giving them a sense of agency. As a school or district, this will ensure continuity across grade levels so students and teachers are on the same page when discussing the complexities of digital text and the skills required to read them.

By incorporating multimodality, reading path, and the common language of digital texts in beginning reading instruction, we can provide students with the stepping stones necessary to become proficient readers of the increasingly wide range of texts available.

Laura Northrop is an adjunct instructor of education at John Carroll University and a doctoral student in educational policy at the University of Pittsburgh. Laura previously taught middle school and currently teaches K–12 students through school and university-based reading intervention clinics. Her research interests include reading intervention at the middle school level, as well as policy analysis using large-scale national and international datasets.

Erin Killeen is a literacy specialist for Stow-Munroe Falls City Schools in Stow, Ohio. Previously, she taught fourth grade and first grade. She is also an adjunct instructor of courses in literacy education at John Carroll University in Cleveland, Ohio. To learn more about Erin's work, follow @EK4literacy on Twitter.

CHAPTER 3

Using Tablets to Teach Foundational Skills: Matching Apps to Student Needs

By Laura Northrop and Erin Killeen

Since the technology has been available, many school districts have added iPads or other tablets to the resources teachers have in their primary classrooms. In our experience, we have often seen elementary teachers using these devices during choice time or independent work time. While it is clear that students are engaged and motivated to use the technology, what is less evident is whether students are learning skills they need or working on tasks that are appropriate for their level of instruction. This chapter will offer guidance on how to match students to the most appropriate apps based on their individual learning needs and how to implement tablet-based learning in a response to intervention (RTI) framework.

Using Tablets Within a Response to Intervention Framework

Response to intervention provides a way for teachers and schools to provide instruction at multiple tiers of service (Fuchs & Fuchs, 2009). At Tier 1, teachers implement high-quality core instruction to all students. At Tier 2, students who are not meeting district or state benchmarks are provided small-group interventions, often by the classroom teacher. Students who do not make progress toward meeting their individualized goals may also be provided more intense, individualized interventions at Tier 3.

Integrating tablets into instruction at all three tiers can provide a motivating and engaging way for students to continue to practice and develop their skills in phonological awareness, phonics, and word identification. Because many foundational skills develop gradually, and on a predictable continuum (Bear, Invernizzi, Templeton, & Johnston, 2012; Ganske, 2000; Snow et al., 1998), elementary teachers should not adopt a one-size-fits-all approach to teach these concepts. We recommend teachers use diagnostic assessment data to gain an understanding of where on the developmental continuum a student falls to determine individual student goals at all three tiers of instruction.

When determining individual student goals, we recommend providing instruction within the zone of proximal development (Vygotsky, 1978), the area of development in which students can be successful with the help of adult guidance and feedback. This provides for instruction that is neither too easy nor too hard. Additionally, we suggest that instructional decisions be grounded in developmentally appropriate practice (Copple & Bredekamp, 2009), where teachers meet students at their level and provide intentionally designed learning experiences that help them stretch to the next level of development. Intentionally matching students to apps can help teachers maximize the time students are working at their instructional level.

How Do I Do It?

We recommend a five-step process to integrate tablets into foundational skills instruction.

1.   Review student assessment data, and identify areas of need.

2.   Choose a target skill.

3.   Match target skill to an appropriate app.

4.   Use the gradual release of responsibility framework to introduce both the target skill and the app.

5.   Use student or teacher reflection sheets to track progress and evidence of learning.

Correctly matching apps to student needs begins with reviewing assessment data to identify areas of strengths and weaknesses across three foundational areas: (1) phonological awareness (including syllables, rhymes, and phonemic awareness), (2) phonics, and (3) sight word identification. Use the assessment results to determine skills that a student has mastered and skills that a student still needs to develop. Then choose a target skill for each student or small groups of students.

Once a target skill is chosen, select an appropriate app that offers the right type of practice for the student. The tasks in the app should not only match the skills needed by the student but should also provide activities that are most effective for helping the student develop the skills. Many apps offer practice with foundational skills using the following types of instructional activities: listening, tracing, matching, fill in the blank, multiple choice, sorting, and quizzes. When choosing an app, you should also be aware of the level of difficulty in thinking the instructional activity within the app requires. For example, apps that rely on students listening to explanations or watching examples or videos require very little student thinking, whereas apps that require students to sort words utilize complex thinking processes such as comparing, contrasting, and analyzing. Students who are new to a concept or skill may benefit from starting with an app that requires a lower level of thinking and input; however, as students partially master the skill, they would benefit from being challenged by apps that require higher levels of cognitive input. Unfortunately, we have found very few apps that require students to use complex thinking to generate their own original answers.

After identifying the target skill and choosing an app that is at a student's instructional level, both in regard to the content of the app and the level of thinking required by the instructional activity, you should ensure that the student is successful when utilizing the app during independent work time. First introduce the targeted skill without the use of technology and then model using the app with a think-aloud (Northrop & Killeen, 2013). Because many apps require students to use multiple skills at once, or have several different games for the same content area, modeling the appropriate way to use the app helps ensure that the student works productively with the targeted literacy skill. The gradual release of responsibility framework (Duke & Pearson, 2002; Pearson & Gallagher, 1983) allows you time to provide feedback and guidance prior to the student engaging in the activity independently.

Using apps at different tiers requires different techniques. At Tier 1, for instance, we recommend that you introduce the app during small-group reading time or during a whole-class minilesson and then allow students to do independent practice with the app during choice time. Tiers 2 and 3 require higher levels of teacher support and greater amounts of teacher feedback. When using tablets as part of an intervention program, have students use the app during intervention time so you can provide additional modeling and allow more time for guided practice with teacher feedback.

Finally, try to incorporate a way to track progress toward mastery of the targeted skill. At Tier 1, have students complete a reflection sheet that tracks which app they used during choice time and how they felt about their learning that day. A student reflection sheet (see figure 3.1, page 28) allows you to keep track of what skills students are working on during independent work or choice time.

App Record Sheet

Directions: Mark the box each day for the app you used during choice time. Then, think about how easy or hard it was for you.

App	Mon	Tue	Wed	Thurs	Fri	Reflection
iWriteWords						Too Easy Just Right Too Hard
WordConnex						Too Easy Just Right Too Hard
Fry Words						Too Easy Just Right Too Hard
Starfall ABCs						Too Easy Just Right Too Hard
Word Wizard						Too Easy Just Right Too Hard

Figure 3.1: Example of a Tier 1 student reflection.

Visit **go.solution-tree.com/technology** for a reproducible version of this figure.

Tracking progress at Tiers 2 and 3 requires greater teacher involvement; when providing intervention, it is beneficial to collect more specific data about how a student is progressing toward specific learning goals. For example, if a student is working on letter identification, you should monitor progress by keeping track of which specific letters the student can identify, not just whether or not the student used an app that teaches letters. At Tiers 2 and 3, we suggest that you track individual performance each time a student uses the app. Some apps come with built-in ways to track progress, but many do not, so use additional scoring sheets like the one in figure 3.2 to record student progress.

Student Information	Skill Information	Intervention Information
Name:	Skill:	_____ Tier 2
	_____ Uppercase letter identification	_____ Tier 3
Teacher:	_____ Lowercase letter identification	App:
Grade:	_____ Letter sounds (short vowels)	Time, Week, or Both:
	_____ Letter sounds (long vowels)	
	_____ Letter sounds (short and long vowels)	

Letter	Week 1	Week 2	Week 3	Week 4	Week 5	Week 6	Week 7	Week 8
A								
B								
C								
D								
E								
F								
G								
H								
I								
J								
K								
L								
M								
N								

Figure 3.2: Sample Tier 2 or 3 progress-monitoring record for letter identification or letter sounds.

Continued on next page →

Letter	Week 1	Week 2	Week 3	Week 4	Week 5	Week 6	Week 7	Week 8
O								
P								
Q								
R								
S								
T								
U								
V								
W								
X								
Y								
Z								
Total	/26	/26	/26	/26	/26	/26	/26	/26

Visit *go.solution-tree.com/technology* for a reproducible version of this figure.

Some of our favorite apps to use for letter identification and letter sounds include the following.

- iWriteWords
- Little Matchups ABC
- Starfall ABCs
- Super Why!
- Touch and Write Phonics

For phonics practice, we recommend:

- Starfall Learn to Read
- abc PocketPhonics
- Montessori Crosswords
- VocabularySpellingCity

To teach sight words, Fry Words and Sight Words have premade lists of sight words. They also allow you to customize word lists. Students can play in flash card mode or quiz mode. Another option, Bob Books, takes students through four levels that start with letter matching and ends with spelling simple CVC words. Two apps that allow for more customized learning include iCardSort, in which you can create your own word sorts, and Word Wizard, which has a movable alphabet and allows the student to practice spelling words while simultaneously hearing the letter sound and how that letter blends with the other letters chosen. Visit **go.solution-tree.com /technology** for more app recommendations.

Classroom Example

Kevin, a kindergartener referred for intervention instruction, needed to develop better awareness of letter sounds. According to his teacher, Kevin's assessment data showed that he scored well below the benchmark for letter sound fluency and was receiving intervention at the Tier 2 level in this area. During intervention time, Erin Killeen used the app Starfall ABCs to practice specific letter sounds that Kevin had not yet learned. She chose this app because it provides several different ways for students to practice identifying and providing letter sounds, and she was able to choose the specific letters to practice, enabling her to match the activity to Kevin's specific needs.

She used alphabet letter cards to start—naming the letters and their sounds with pictures as key words. Then she demonstrated how to do the activity on the app for two letters. The activity included naming each letter, clicking on the letter to hear its sound, repeating the sound, and then naming an animated picture of an object that begins with that sound. Kevin was able to perform each task after Erin's demonstration, but he did get confused twice when looking for the button to click on for a new letter. She had to repeatedly remind him that the glowing arrow was the one to touch.

The tasks were effective in helping Kevin develop better awareness of letter sounds, and they were developmentally appropriate to his area of need. However, without teacher guidance for at least a few minutes of his work time, he may have gotten lost in the activity.

Erin also worked with Holly, a first grader who needed to improve her understanding of short vowels. Assessment data showed that Holly scored just below the district's benchmark for decoding words with short vowels and had not received any intervention to date. Erin chose the app Montessori Crosswords because it offers practice with onsets and rimes and blending CVC sounds into words. Erin knew that in class, students had practiced blending onsets and rimes, so Holly was familiar with these features. With this app, Erin was able to choose specific vowels to work on, again targeting practice to Holly's individual learning needs.

Tasks involved clicking on a picture of an object, then clicking on empty boxes (similar to Elkonin boxes) to hear each sound in the word. Students then click on letters to hear their sounds and match a letter to the sound in each empty box. When each box is filled in correctly, the word is spoken out loud. The word also glows, and a screen appears with magical floating objects.

Erin demonstrated these tasks with two words, then guided Holly on the third word. She needed a reminder about what to click on first but did very well after that. She was able to go on and practice on her own without any difficulty. The tasks and activities were appropriate for her skills, and she was able to complete the tasks and navigate through the app with minimal guidance.

For both students, Erin carefully considered their skills and learning needs, chose apps with tasks that matched their needs, and spent time demonstrating the activities. Kevin needed more support than Holly to complete the tasks, illustrating the necessity of differentiated teacher prompting, guidance, and feedback while students are working with apps. Though Kevin experienced some confusion trying to navigate through the app, he did show improvements in matching letters to sounds as he worked through the tasks. Holly was able to correctly spell and decode all ten of the short vowel words she practiced. Using the gradual release of responsibility framework to demonstrate the tasks, provide guidance, and allow independent practice proved effective in helping these two students strengthen their skills.

Your Turn

Choosing the appropriate app can be a hard decision. There are so many options! To help you sort through them all, we've provided table 3.1, which includes specific guidance on choosing apps and progress-monitoring tools based on student needs and the Common Core State Standards. Because apps change frequently and new ones are created daily, it's especially important for teachers to be familiar with the content being taught in the app. We recommend spending time exploring the app and understanding the different levels and features of the app before assigning it to students.

In addition, to help integrate tablets into foundational skills instruction, we have created guiding questions for you.

1. **Review student assessment data to determine student areas of need:** What does the student already know? Which skills does the student need to learn? Can I group the students by similar areas of need?

Table 3.1: Matching Apps to Student Needs

If your student has trouble with . . .	Then look for an app that includes . . .	And monitor progress at Tier 2 and Tier 3 by . . .
Identifying letters Standard: RF.K.1.D	Letter matching Letter tracing	The number of upper- and lowercase letters identified
Letter sounds Standard: RF.K.3.A	Matching letters to sounds Matching pictures to sounds	The number of letter sounds identified
Rhyme Standard: RF.K.2.A	Onset-rimes Picture rhymes Rhyming pairs	The number of correctly identified pairs of rhyming words
Blending phonemes Standard: RF.K.2.C Standard: RF.1.2.B	Onset-rimes Movable letters that manipulate sounds Fill-in-the-blank words	The number of CVC words blended correctly
Short vowels Standard: RF.K.3.B Standard: RF.1.3.B	Word families Fill-in-the-blank words Word sorts	Correct words spelled with that vowel pattern from a target list of words
Sight words Standard: RF.K.3.C Standard: RF.1.3.G Standard: RF.2.3.F	Sight word matching Sight word games (such as Bingo)	The number of sight words read correctly from a target list of words (such as Dolch or Fry)
Long vowels Standard: RF.K.3.B Standard: RF.1.3.C Standard: RF.2.3.A	Matching pictures to vowel sounds Fill-in-the-blank words Word sorts	Correct vowel sounds identified Correct words spelled with long vowel patterns

Source: NGA & CCSSO, 2010.

2.   **Select a target skill for instruction:** According to a developmentally appropriate sequence of instruction, what is the next skill that this student needs to learn? Which Common Core State Standard is this skill aligned with? Which students need to be taught this skill?

3. **Match the targeted skill to an app:** Does this app teach the targeted skill? Does this app teach other skills that may confuse the student? Does this app require skills or knowledge that my student does not have yet? Does the app require lower-level or higher-level thinking to complete the activity? How many practice items are there for the targeted skill?

4. **Use the gradual release of responsibility framework to guide student use of the app:** How can I model the literacy content of the app? How can I model the technological aspects of the app? If implementing at Tier 1, will my students be able to use this app during independent work time? If implementing at Tier 2 or 3, what kind of feedback can I provide during guided practice?

5. **Track progress with reflection sheets:** What data do I need to collect to have evidence of student learning? Does the app collect that information already, or do I need to use an alternate assessment or tracking sheet?

Following these steps will ensure that student use of technology in the form of tablets and apps will be not only engaging but also productive in moving your students toward improved reading. It certainly has for us!

PART II | Reading Fluency

Despite research that identifies reading fluency as critical for student success in reading (Rasinski, Reutzel, Chard, & Linan-Thompson, 2011), reading scholars consider it a topic that is "not hot" (Cassidy & Grote-Garcia, 2013, p. 11). We feel that this lack of enthusiasm is due to the way many commercial curricular programs and approaches have addressed reading fluency. Because fluency is often measured by oral reading rate or speed, fluency instruction in these approaches becomes a matter of having students read orally with the primary goal of improving their reading rate or speed. We think this is a corruption of the notion of fluency.

In our opinion, fluency should be a hot topic, and that is why we have included it in the book. Fluency comprises two separate constructs. The first is automaticity in word recognition. Fluent readers are able to decode and understand words in text so easily, effortlessly, and efficiently that they can devote most of their finite cognitive resources to the critical goal in reading—comprehension. Students who are not sufficiently fluent use an excessive amount of their cognitive resources for word recognition (these are readers who read slowly and laboriously) and thus have reduced cognitive capacity for making meaning from the text. The second construct of fluency is prosody or expression. Fluent readers are able to read orally with appropriate expression that reflects the meaning of the text. In a sense, fluency is a bridge between word-recognition mastery and reading comprehension. Research has demonstrated that readers who are automatic in their word recognition and expressive in their oral reading tend to have the highest levels of comprehension in silent and oral reading (Rasinski et al., 2011). However, as students exhibit decreases in their fluency, their comprehension similarly declines.

Two of the most important, research-proven methods to improve fluency are through practice in and assistance while reading. Practice can take two forms. The most common is wide reading, where students read a text once, respond to the reading in some way, and then move on to a new passage. This is a common practice in schools. The other form of practice is deep or repeated reading. It involves students reading a text several times to the point that they read the text fluently, demonstrating ease in word recognition and appropriate expression. The problem with repeated reading is how to find authentic ways to engage students in repeated reading. Two of the chapters in this part deal with this issue of authentic approaches to repeated reading using technology to allow for performance. If students are to perform a text, they will have to rehearse in advance. Rehearsal is an authentic form of repeated reading. In their chapter, Sheri Vasinda and Julie McLeod describe how podcasting can be a powerful vehicle for allowing students to perform texts they have rehearsed. Chase Young and Timothy V. Rasinski's chapter focuses on the possibilities and potential of student-produced movies to move students into repeated readings—rehearsal that is aimed at expressive and meaningful reading, not speed.

Assisted reading involves students reading a text while hearing it read to them fluently by a more proficient reader. Assisted reading often takes the form of a student reading with a more fluent partner, often a teacher or aide. The problem here is that a teacher reading with one student may not be the most efficient use of the teacher's time. One solution is to use technology as the partner reader. Kaybeth Calabria and Kristine E. Pytash describe how digitally recorded texts can be an optimal tool for providing the assistance that less fluent readers need. We hope that the ideas presented in these chapters are springboards for creating your own technology-oriented approach for developing reading fluency.

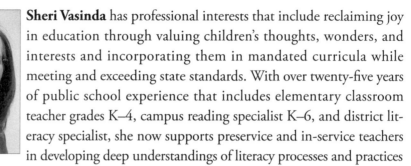 **Sheri Vasinda** has professional interests that include reclaiming joy in education through valuing children's thoughts, wonders, and interests and incorporating them in mandated curricula while meeting and exceeding state standards. With over twenty-five years of public school experience that includes elementary classroom teacher grades K–4, campus reading specialist K–6, and district literacy specialist, she now supports preservice and in-service teachers in developing deep understandings of literacy processes and practices at Oklahoma State University. She is passionate about supporting struggling readers and writers through purposeful and powerful pairings of new technology tools with strong traditional literacy strategies to amplify the effects of both. She continues to discover ways that technology affords authentic self-assessment opportunities and is exploring frameworks of thinking about the technology integration and pedagogy as well as new literacies. To learn more about Sheri's work, visit www.sherivasinda .weebly.com or follow @svasinda on Twitter.

 **Julie McLeod, PhD,** is an avid proponent for powerful student work and deep-thinking teachers. With a rich background in educational technology, Julie has created technology-rich learning experiences for students from first grade through graduate school. She currently serves as the director of technology at Good Shepherd Episcopal School in Dallas, Texas, as well as teaching graduate courses in educational technology at the George Washington University and Texas A&M University-Commerce. She also leads faculty professional learning sessions that help teachers discern, implement, and reflect on meaningful technology integration. Julie's research interests include exploring students' curiosity, power, and motivation as they use technology to learn. She has also published book chapters and journal articles that discuss powerful ways to integrate technology by purposefully matching a proven learning strategy with the affordances of the technology, creating a learning experience not possible without the technology. To learn more about Julie's work, visit www.juliemcleod.org or follow @juliemcleod on Twitter.

CHAPTER 4

Podcasts: Adding Power and New Possibilities to the Readers Theater Experience

By Sheri Vasinda and Julie McLeod

There's something powerful about hearing your own voice as a podcast of a reading piece posted to the Internet. After the initial giggles and comments—"I don't sound like that!" or "That's not me!"—performing readers move past the sound of their own voice to the quality of their reading. Without prompting, they notice and critique their expression, phrasing, smoothness, pacing, and volume.

Performance reading, or readers theater, has a long-standing history and research base for building both reading fluency and comprehension (Griffith & Rasinski, 2004; Martinez, Roser, & Strecker, 1998/1999). Miriam Martinez, Nancy Roser, and Susan Strecker (1998/1999) define *readers theater* as an interpretive, voice-only performance. Performing readers use their voices to bring the characters to life without sets, costumes, props, or memorized lines, the inclusion of which would change this work from readers theater to more traditional stage drama. In readers theater, the readers' goal is to expressively read a text so that the audience can visualize the story (Martinez et al., 1998/1999). Teachers and researchers studying the practice of readers theater find that in a ten-week period of daily repeated reading and weekly live performances, struggling students make an average of one year's growth in reading comprehension while increasing their reading fluency (Griffith & Rasinski, 2004; Martinez et al., 1998/1999; Vasinda & McLeod, 2011).

In our work to thoughtfully and purposefully integrate the digital richness that many students find outside of school into the classroom, we look for ways to pair appropriate digital tools with strong practices that engage students and amplify the effects of traditional strategies or work. One purposeful and powerful pairing is auditory digital tools with readers theater. We wondered if digitally recording the performances, rather than performing for a live audience, would have the same effect on reading comprehension and fluency.

Although the easy access and capability for audio recording has been available since cassette tape recorders, the fragile nature of cassettes themselves—as well as the switching of tapes for each student and finding specific spots on recorded tapes—made that 20th century technology a bit unwieldy. A digital recording, on the other hand, can be recorded and stored as individual events with the added benefit of easy global sharing. Because of the pervasiveness of iPods, to which the masses began downloading music, the term *podcast* was coined to combine the words *iPod* and *broadcast*. That said, you don't need an iPod to listen to (or create) a podcast. A podcast is simply a digital audio recording that is stored, retrieved, and heard from the Internet, usually in an MP3 format. You can listen directly from the computer or download it to any MP3 player or smartphone as part of a playlist.

We find the same remarkable gains in reading comprehension and fluency when readers record and create podcasts of their reading performances as did the teachers and researchers using live performances, but we also find some important additional benefits. One of the advantages of these audio recordings is that they provide a permanent record of the performance that affords self-evaluation and self-determined goals for improvement (Vasinda & McLeod, 2011, 2013). A live performance of a readers theater script provides the perception of how it sounded, but once performed, it is but a memory. When readers can hear themselves, they naturally evaluate their performance and set goals for the next performance. This opportunity to listen to and critique themselves from school, home, or on the go, heightens the performers' sense of a wider audience. When interviewed, these performing readers remarked on their potential reach of "thousands of listeners" (Vasinda & McLeod, 2011, p. 493). They understood that their audience is real and has an unlimited reach. Therefore, students were self-motivated to work hard to improve their readers theater podcasts (Vasinda & McLeod, 2011, 2013).

However, these benefits are not just for the most technology savvy teachers or even the ones who work in one-on-one interventions. As digital tools become easier to use and more ubiquitous, the benefits of podcasting readers theater can be enjoyed by all!

How Do I Do It?

Readers theater podcasts fit well into classroom rhythms and are achievable with limited technology. Teachers need only a single classroom computer, mobile tablet device, or their own smartphone along with free recording software or apps to support a fluency-building practice (Vasinda & McLeod, 2011, 2013). Some teachers include readers theater as a regular and continuing practice year round.

The basic classroom structure of readers theater that we recommend is as follows.

1. **Monday:** New scripts are given to groups, parts are assigned, and students read them on their own, asking questions and getting help as needed.

2. **Tuesday through Thursday:** Students practice (rehearse) their scripts in their small groups. During this practice time, the teacher might model prosodic or expressive reading of various parts and monitor practice sessions, but most often the groups practice on their own while the teacher meets with small groups for targeted instruction.

3. **Friday:** Each group records its performance reading and creates the MP3 file. Some classes do this with the teacher as a small-group activity, while the rest of the class quietly works on other literacy activities, such as independent reading, independent writing, or word work. In other classes, performance day is a celebration of the work—each small group performs, the teacher records, and the nonperforming classmates participate as the audience.

While we advocate heterogeneous groupings because we believe the fluent readers in each group provide great models for emergent and transitional readers, we have also used this process with alternate scheduling and with homogeneous groups of striving readers in Tier 2 and Tier 3 RTI groups. Following a within-the-school-day, small-group intervention structure, students were in literacy intervention or enrichment groups three days per week and mathematics intervention or enrichment groups two days per week, so we worked on a two-week readers theater cycle. During the forty-five-minute intervention, fifteen minutes were devoted to repeated readings (rehearsal) of a readers theater script chosen at an instructional level for these small groups. The rest of the intervention block was divided into guided reading or strategy instruction and word work. The performances were podcasted and posted every two weeks rather than weekly.

Classroom Example

We have been directly involved with students of various ages and reading abilities. In this chapter we focus on sixth graders. For other examples of this approach to readers theater, including younger students and striving readers, see our other publications (Vasinda & McLeod, 2011, 2013).

The sixth-grade students in a Title I elementary school in Texas were reading on grade level but still appreciated the benefits of podcasting readers theater. While students needing reading intervention received RTI targeted instruction during grade-level intervention time two days each week, the Tier 1 students participated in reading enrichment. Though two days a week is not ideal, the structure worked for these students. Generally, the students were ready to record after four days of practice—so it took two weeks before students were ready to perform. We then posted the podcasts online using our classroom blog.

We found that students were highly engaged in choosing their own scripts and groupings. Initially, this age group tended to select their script based on a group composed of their friends rather than the content of the script. We did not worry about the difficulty of the reading level for the scripts; all scripts seemed to have one or more words that students would either ask how to pronounce or what it meant. Some scripts were quite long, so we divided those into smaller sections to record episodes of the story rather than the entire script. On recording day, the students recorded and listened carefully to themselves. Then they usually wanted to re-record to improve their performance.

After a few rounds of practice, recording, and posting online, students began to discuss the scripts differently. They became more interested in the content of the script, sometimes even selecting group members based on content rather than their friends. They also became more interested in the characters and the plot lines. When the story did not work out the way they thought it should, students began to ask if they could rewrite the ending. The first time students asked to create a different ending, it was the recording day on the last episode of their script. We asked them to record, since they had been practicing that script. However, we offered them the opportunity on the following two-week cycle to write and record an alternate ending and post that new ending alongside the original ending. This really excited the group, and other groups immediately jumped in to write and record alternate endings. A few groups were satisfied with the scripts they had used and wanted to continue with another script instead of writing and recording alternate endings. Ultimately, because groupings were changing constantly, all students ended up in groups that did rewrites of the endings without the need for us to force the issue.

We found that these fluent readers were deeply engaged in the process of podcasting readers theater in several ways. In addition to working to improve their prosodic reading, students began using their literary analysis skills to critique the scripts, which led to revisions resulting in more multidimensional and satisfying work. Students found a greater sense of agency in this performance and revision process.

This classroom example represents the broad possibilities that arise when students are offered the opportunity to do important work that they value as much as (or more than) the adults around them. Benefits such as increased fluency and comprehension happen naturally alongside authentic reasons to write and publish. Importantly, many of these benefits happen because the technology brings something qualitatively different to the learning experience and environment. With its permanency and wide audience, students intuitively know they are doing work that has importance and value. Thus, they naturally invest themselves deeply with powerful results.

Your Turn

Podcasting is a nice first step into technology integrations that have a more public potential. Audio recordings are easy to make and have no visuals, other than sound waves, so technology-shy teachers and families find this a nonthreatening entrance into authentic audiences beyond the classroom walls. Posting these performances online opens the doors of your classroom practice to parents and extended family and friends who cannot attend live performances during the school day.

The first step to realizing all the benefits of readers theater in your classroom is to find scripts. Some teachers choose favorite children's books to adapt into scripts, and there are hundreds of free scripts online. By searching the phrase "free readers theater scripts," we find many sites with many scripts. We look for scripts that result in performances between five to eight minutes and no longer than ten minutes. We also look for script sources that grant permissions for classroom and non-profit use. Because podcasting these performances is becoming more common, some free script providers—such as Aaron Shepard—provide permission release directions on each script. The only restriction Aaron Shepard has is posting the actual script (A. Shepard, personal communication, January 2, 2015), but live and podcasted performances are encouraged. (Visit www.aaronshep.com/rt/RTE.html for more information.) Also, just as with music, public domain works can be used without permissions. Public domain stories for children include the Wizard of Oz series, Sherlock Holmes stories, and fairy tales and folk tales. (Older students can take these old classics, break them up into smaller segments, and determine places that end with great cliffhangers, leaving the audience waiting for the next installment.) Public domain stories can be found on many websites, such as the Oklahoma Department of Libraries Online (www.odl.state .ok.us/kids/century/century.htm). For stories not in the public domain, we ask our script authors to grant permission for non-profit podcasted readers theater performances. Readers can then podcast their performance reading for a wider audience to enjoy! Additionally, students often want to change the endings of scripts or author their own (Miner, 2013).

Of course, once the scripts are selected, students need to practice. This practice should be daily, but it does not have to be extended. Our work included only ten to fifteen minutes of practice each day. You might be tempted to ask older students to practice for homework. Consider the social nature of readers theater before you assign the practice as homework. While students will likely want to work on their parts at home, which we encourage, it is important to have class time and group time. This will give your students the accountability and purpose they need to maintain their practice and will also make the recording times run more smoothly.

On recording day, ensure you have good-quality microphones. Microphones do not have to be expensive. Most devices (such as laptops, tablets, and smartphones) have built-in microphones. These vary in quality depending on the device and the students' voices, so test it out and decide with your students if you will need an external microphone. A handheld microphone is preferable over the integrated microphone or headphone, because students will need to pass the microphone around as they read their parts. We have had great success in clarity and volume with handheld USB microphones priced between ten to twenty dollars. We prefer the ones that sit on a stand so they can be part of our computer set-up and are easily accessible to the students.

You will also need some type of software to save the recording. If you are using desktops or laptops, download free software such as Audacity to record the podcast (http://audacity.sourceforge.net). This software is simple enough that our groups of third graders used it independently, but it also offers enough options that older students will be able to add music and effects to enhance their podcasts and make them sound professional (see Vasinda & McLeod, 2011, for a full description of this process).

Remember that if you are posting the audio file online, it should be an MP3 file in order for it to play seamlessly on all devices and in all browsers. If you are using a tablet or smartphone, be aware that many of the standard apps that come on the devices will not save the audio in MP3 format, which can cause playback issues for your audience. Move the files to your computer and convert them to MP3 files using a free web-based tool, or use other free apps and services that will save the files in the correct format. For example, Pocket WavePad, a free app, has an option to save the files as MP3 files. Then email the file to yourself. Another option is a web-based audio service such as SoundCloud that has an accompanying free app. By using a web-based audio service, the file is automatically saved in the proper format for Internet listening. It also alleviates the need to email audio files to yourself. No matter the technology set up, the main consideration for a good podcast is a quiet environment so that there is minimal background noise.

Finally, post the MP3 audio file online. In many districts, the teacher website providers have podcast options. In a simple step-by-step process within your system, upload each podcast as an MP3 file. Another option is to use a free, online podcasting or blogging site to post the audio file, such as Edublogs (www.edublog.org), a site designed specifically for teachers and students. Our sample site was made with Edublogs; visit http://drvasinda.edublogs.org to listen to podcasts. (For more information on Edublogs and blogging, visit http://edublogs.org/curriculum-corner -using-a-blog-with-students). Most allow you to post an audio file much like you would attach a file to an email. These sites also allow your followers to subscribe so that they get the latest podcasts automatically. They usually include moderated commenting features as well so that your listeners can cheer on your students!

Conclusion

We continue to find that the tools available for making voice recordings are getting easier and more convenient to use. Additionally, we've found that the integration of podcasts into instruction offers more benefits to students than we initially anticipated. When we started, students were spontaneously self-assessing. They were not satisfied with their recordings, as they considered the potential vastness of their audience. We have witnessed disengaged readers find their voice and, spontaneously and willingly, engage in the repeated readings, leading to improved fluency and comprehension. As we continue trying this approach in a variety of settings with new and updated tools, we see students taking on more and more responsibility for production—not just with technology but with the scripts as well. As students find their voices as readers, they are also finding their voices as revisers and authors. Additionally, families appreciate the opportunity to participate as the listening audience for readers theater podcast performances. This technology integration is one way to share student work and progress with families whether they live across the street from the school or across the country. Go ahead! Grab a microphone, and explore the possibilities!

Chase Young, PhD, joined the Department of Educational Leadership, Curriculum and Instruction at Texas A&M University-Corpus Christi in the fall of 2013. Chase received his doctorate in reading education from the University of North Texas. His primary research interests include reading fluency, supporting struggling readers, and integrating technology in elementary literacy instruction. In 2014, Chase was the recipient of the Jerry Johns Promising Research Award presented by the Association of Literacy Educators and Researchers. He is currently the editor of the *Journal of Teacher Action Research*. Previously, he taught in the primary grades and served as a literacy coach in public schools. Visit www.thebestclass.org to learn more about Chase's work.

Timothy V. Rasinski, PhD, is a professor of literacy education at Kent State University. His scholarly interests include reading fluency and word study, reading in the elementary and middle grades, readers who struggle, and parental involvement. His research on reading has been cited by the National Reading Panel and has been published in journals such as *Reading Research Quarterly, The Reading Teacher, Reading Psychology*, and *The Journal of Educational Research*.

Tim served on the board of directors of the International Reading Association. He has also served as coeditor of *The Reading Teacher* and the *Journal of Literacy Research*. In 2010, Tim was elected to the International Reading Hall of Fame.

Prior to coming to Kent State, Tim taught literacy education at the University of Georgia. He also taught for several years as an elementary and middle school classroom and Title I teacher in Nebraska. To learn more about Tim's work, visit www.timrasinski.com or follow @TimRasinski1 on Twitter.

CHAPTER 5

Student-Produced Movies as Authentic Reading Fluency Instruction

By Chase Young and Timothy V. Rasinski

When Chase was a kid, he made movies all the time. Here's his story: I went through those little tapes faster than my parents could hide them. Sure, I may have taped over a few family vacations and a piano recital or three, but I felt that my movies were more deserving of preservation, despite my parents' emphatic disagreement. In fact, I was grounded from the video camera on several occasions, but imagine if I walked to school only to find out we were making movies! Yeah, that never happened, but because of technology's widespread availability today, it could happen tomorrow.

Most teachers have embraced the call for innovative and technologically enhanced literacy instruction (Kist, 2000; Lapp, Moss, & Rowsell, 2012; Leu et al., 2004). This chapter presents an approach for improving students' reading fluency and fostering other literacy competencies all while complying with the Common Core's directive to integrate technology into language arts (NGA & CCSSO, 2010).

Historically, researchers sought effective and efficient methods to increase students' reading fluency. The search identified several means to increase reading fluency, ranging from teacher-controlled read-alouds (Farrell, 1966) to more student-centered approaches like repeated readings (Samuels, 1979). Although repeated readings consistently produce positive results (Chard, Vaughn, & Tyler, 2002; Rasinski, 1990; Rasinski et al., 2011; Samuels, 1979), a teacher may become weary of the practice due to the lack of authenticity in the experience as students read repeatedly for the purpose of increasing their reading speed. Literacy scholars have investigated more authentic methods of repeated readings—such as readers theater (Griffith & Rasinski, 2004; Martinez et al., 1998/1999; Young & Rasinski, 2009) and poetry slams (Wilfong, 2008)—and found that such activities still generate positive results on students' reading fluency. Other scholars add a podcasting component to enhance readers theater technologically (Vasinda & McLeod, 2011). The following strategy also adds a technology component by shifting from the readers theater stage to the big screen as students produce motion pictures based on children's literature (Young & Rasinski, 2013).

In the early stages of this strategy, students consider their reading preferences (Pachtman & Wilson, 2006) and decide on a preferred genre (Risko, Walker-Dalhouse, Bridges, & Wilson, 2011). During the preproduction stages, students visually represent sequences of the selected mentor text (Naughton, 2008), compose summaries (NICHD, 2000), and transform texts into dialogue ideal for movie production (Culham, 2011; Dorfman & Cappelli, 2007; Smith, 1994; Young & Rasinski, 2011).

Later in the process, students focus on rehearsing their scripts until they achieve sufficient automaticity in their reading. After word recognition becomes automatic, the students focus on expressiveness (prosody) and adjust their elocution to appropriately match and expand on the meaning of the story (Kleiman, Winograd, & Humphrey, 1979). Rehearsing for prosody helps students master the skill needed for the acting phase. The now well-prepared actors and actresses record their movies and upload the footage in order to edit and produce their movies. The strategy takes about two weeks, working approximately fifteen to twenty minutes per day.

How Do I Do It?

In this strategy, students produce movies based on mentor texts. The students use a complex technology-based process consisting of eight steps that deepen their understanding of the mentor text (Young & Rasinski, 2013) and lead to improvements in reading fluency, which is a critical reading competency that is not sufficiently developed in many students. Here are the eight steps, as told by Chase.

Step 1: Students Divide Into Groups

I prefer to allow my students to choose their own groups. The students choose their groups based on their genre preferences—they reflect on their preferences and begin the somewhat chaotic configuration process. Assemble those who possess similar genre interests in a group. I stay available to guide students who are experiencing difficulty finding a group. I also encourage students to discuss the overall vision and determine if the group is a good fit.

Step 2: Students Develop an Idea

I ask the students to reminisce about favorite books (or a segment of a favorite story) related to their chosen genre and choose one. The students then approach me with their idea. I think carefully about whether the book would work well with the activity and either approve the idea or ask them to select another text. For example, some books are too long or too nebulous, making it hard to turn them into movies.

Step 3: Students Create a Script Treatment

Students complete what's called a *script treatment* by writing a summary of their future production. I also require them to include a list of characters and students that are cast for each role. Students can recruit additional cast members from other groups if needed. In addition to casting, students assume roles such as camera person and director. It is not necessary to have these set in stone, but I believe filling these two roles with responsible and organized students makes the process go more smoothly. Then, I review their summaries and determine whether the group should proceed to the next step.

Step 4: Students Create Storyboards

I provide the students with a storyboard template (figure 5.1, page 50). The primary function of the storyboard is to display the cinematic view. The students draw the scene from the camera's view. The storyboard also contains the essentials of each scene, such as characters, materials, and the filming location. It is critical that we only allow students to move forward if they have a high probability of successful completion. I always ensure that students can obtain the materials and that we can access the proposed filming locations.

Step 5: Students Transform the Text Into a Script

Developing a script can be a difficult process, so I ensure that students get plenty of experience scripting. Students read and reread their texts to complete this complex process. Students are required to think about how to incorporate existing dialogue, as well as how to make the voice of the narrator come alive. This can be done through acting, set design, or insertion of new dialogue.

Step 6: Students Meet With the Teacher

I carefully review their scripts and storyboards, and I converse with the production group to understand their vision. I also provide any insight or creative suggestions I may have. At first I thought I should hold back, but then I realized that I am their teacher, and it's my job to help turn the impossible into the possible. We also discuss a filming schedule; I typically plan for one day with several filming sessions spread out through the day.

Step 7: Students Film the Movie

We usually complete the filming in a single day. Students are instructed to bring all their materials on the selected filming date. I post the filming schedule on the board.

Movie Title: _____   Scene: _____

Camera View:

Additional Information:

Characters:	Materials:	Filming Location:

Figure 5.1: Sample storyboard.

I try to film about three scenes at a time in between other instructional activities. This helps break up the day, and it prevents the audience (the rest of the class) from getting bored while they watch the movie-making process. The director instructs the actors and actresses and carries the storyboard. They frequently make mistakes, so it often requires multiple takes (I always make a bloopers reel for the end of the year).

Step 8: Students Engage in Postproduction

In this step, the students upload their footage to a computer and edit it with movie editing software—most operating systems come with free editing software (such as iMovie on a Mac or Windows Movie Maker on a PC). After a quick minilesson, the students are ready to master the art of video production. They select the best takes, put them in order, trim the clips, add transitions, create title and credit sequences, and polish the final production with a soundtrack.

Classroom Example

Two students in my classroom of second graders formed a group based on their desire to produce a scary movie. The young horror enthusiasts immediately reached for Alvin Schwartz's (1981) *Scary Stories to Tell in the Dark* series. After reading through a few short stories, the duo decided on "The Bad News." After I approved their idea and script treatment, they began to storyboard the movie.

After the storyboarding, the students wrote the script. It was a bit difficult because most of the short story was narrated; thus, the students had to support the narration with the props, the set, and acting. The rest of the narration had to be creatively transposed into dialogue. Clearly, students had to have a good understanding of the original text in order to develop dialogue that represented and extended the meaning of the original. After the little production team successfully scripted the movie, they filmed, edited, and uploaded their movie (for video, see Young, 2013).

In the movie, two baseball players ponder the afterlife and wonder if people play baseball in heaven. Eventually, one of the friends makes it to heaven, returns to his friend, and shares the good news that baseball does indeed exist in heaven. However, he also shares some bad news; his living friend was scheduled to pitch the following day!

Your Turn

Before you begin, make sure you have access to the technology required for the project. The students need a video-recording device (such as an iPad, digital video camera, and so on) to film the movies. For the editing process, students need movie editing software, such as the free applications that are typically installed on a Mac or a PC. After securing the necessary technology, you are ready to guide the students through the eight steps of movie production.

After all the movies are complete, invite parents and students to attend the big premiere, a time when all the students can introduce and play their movies. The students are proud of their productions after persisting through the complex process of producing a movie.

Conclusion

While the students typically think about the fun they had, I usually reflect on the many literate processes students used to create their technological masterpieces. Students' writing was positively affected as they transformed a mentor text (story or portion of a story) into a script (Culham, 2011). In order to *summarize* and then *create* a new representation of the original text, they had to read closely for the author's intended meaning and the meaning they intended to convey in their movie (Krathwohl, 2002). Finally, the rehearsal of the script, where the purpose of the rehearsal was the improvement of automatic word recognition *and* prosody (expression), had a positive and authentic impact on the foundational reading fluency competencies. The fact that the students (and I) thoroughly enjoyed making movies was an added bonus!

 **Kaybeth Calabria, PhD,** has worked in the field of special education for forty years. Her varied career includes working as an early intervention teacher, serving adults with disabilities in sheltered workshops and group homes, providing services as a school psychologist, and developing and teaching a community-based classroom for high school students with severe disabilities. In 1998, Kaybeth was presented with the Franklin B. Walter Outstanding Educator Award. She also enjoyed coaching high school swimming and track. For the past eight years, she has had the privilege of teaching at Franciscan University. The role of a college professor has allowed her to engage in researching, writing, and presenting on topics of special education, teacher education, and literacy.

 **Kristine E. Pytash** is an assistant professor in teaching, learning, and curriculum studies at Kent State University's College of Education, Health, and Human Services, where she codirects the secondary Integrated Language Arts Teacher Preparation Program. She is a former high school English teacher. Kristy's research focuses on using disciplinary writing, understanding the literacy practices of youth in alternative schools and juvenile detention facilities, and preparing teachers to teach writing. Her work has appeared in the *Journal of Adolescent and Adult Literacy, English Journal, Voices From the Middle,* and *Middle School Journal.* To learn more about Kristy's work, visit www.literacyspaces .com or follow @kpytash on Twitter.

CHAPTER 6

Audio-Assisted Reading Builds Reading Fluency

By Kaybeth Calabria and Kristine E. Pytash

At the beginning of every competitive swim season, high school freshmen with little background and few swimming skills would join our rural high school team. Despite their lack of experience, these students could quickly become successful in the water with the use of long black fins, which helped them feel more balanced and fluid. The fins assisted the new swimmers in gaining the sensation of a more effortless swimming stroke—they were able to get the gist of fluent swimming. Similar to the use of fins, we have found that reading along with an audio recording of a fluent and expressive reader helps students better understand the end goal. The support of listening to a fluent and expressive reader of a challenging text can help high school students get the gist of reading fluently.

Comprehension of text is the end goal of any high school teacher when assigning a book or chapter. Highlighting vocabulary, summarizing the text, and analyzing the structure of the text are common ways that teachers scaffold instruction to meet this goal. However, Nell Duke, Michael Pressley, and Katherine Hilden (2004) conclude that 75 to 90 percent of students with comprehension difficulties have reading fluency problems that are a significant cause of the comprehension difficulties. Students who cannot read fluently will make word-recognition errors, struggle to smoothly read phrases, fail to notice key semantic and syntactic features of the text, and read without meaningful expression; thus the understanding of the text is compromised

(Rasinski et al., 2011). Fluency and comprehension seem to form a reciprocal relationship; readers with good expression enhance their understanding of the text, and comprehension of a text leads to improvements in oral fluency (Paige, Rasinski, & Magpuri-Lavell, 2012). Difficulty with reading fluency can be a sign of a struggling reader with a history of reading difficulties, but it can also signal a proficient reader who has encountered a particularly difficult passage—for instance, when presented with the unfamiliar dialect and language patterns found in John Steinbeck's (1937) *Of Mice and Men*. Adding audio-assisted reading to a teacher-supported close reading of the text can benefit students with diverse reading skills.

Assisted reading or reading while listening has long been found to increase the fluent reading and comprehension of text (Chomsky, 1976; Schreiber, 1980). When reading a text several times while listening to fluent reading, students begin to use the expressive qualities of oral speech that reflect the meaning of the text, such as the beginning and ending of phrases, sentences that are statements, or those that ask a question. Moreover, the improvements made on the assisted text transfer to new, previously unread texts. The automatic and expressive reading of text serves as an important scaffold for constructing meaning (Rasinski, 2003). Fluency practice that uses various types of technology—such as iPods, ereaders, closed-captioned television, audio tapes, compact discs, and computers—has proven beneficial for developing students' reading fluency (Rasinski et al., 2011). We have found that using this technology to provide assisted reading can support high school students who face unfamiliar text types with difficult structures and abstract content.

How Do I Do It?

Our first step when implementing audio-assisted reading is to inventory the technology available to create an audio-assisted listening center. We look for items such as computers, iPods, iPads, tape recorders, compact disc players, and earbuds or headphones. We tend not to use ereaders, because the voices on ereaders are accurate but can be robotic and do not model the rich, expressive reading we want our students to model.

Asking for donations of older technology, such as tape recorders and compact disc players, has helped us create a learning center. Often students will want to use their own iPads, iPods, and earbuds. The lack of wires or need for electrical outlets helps free up space in the classroom. In addition, with the use of an interactive whiteboard, document camera, or LCD projector, the texts can be projected; students can then participate in choral readings or whisper read while listening to the audiotape.

To prepare for using audio-assisted reading, we try to locate available audiobooks to match or complement the core text we are using in class. The following websites are excellent resources for the high school classroom (visit **go.solution-tree.com /technology** to access links found in this book).

- Ambling Books (www.amblingbooks.com), which maintains a site of 1,500 books and LibriVox (https://librivox.org), is an online publisher of public domain audiobooks read by volunteers where teachers can find classics such as *The Adventures of Sherlock Holmes*, *Pride and Prejudice*, and *Anne of Green Gables* on this site.

- Lit2Go (http://etc.usf.edu/lit2go) is a site maintained by the University of South Florida. Use this site to find text and audio versions of classics in the public domain. This site is easy to navigate because you can search by author, book, genre, collection, and best of all, readability level. Passages are reported as Flesch-Kincaid grade levels to help you match the readability of a book or poem to a reader from first grade to twelfth grade.

- Folger Shakespeare Library (www.folger.edu) is a repository of teaching resources on William Shakespeare. The online teaching resources include audio and video podcasts of his plays and poems.

Once a passage has been selected, we ask the students to listen to it as they follow along with the text projected on a screen or as they read formatted text on a page. As the text is being read, we stop the recording and highlight specific features of fluent reading—for example, how the reader paused after different phrases, or how the reader raised his or her voice when asking a question or changed voices at various parts. After doing a whole-class close reading of the text while simultaneously listening to the passage, the students quietly reread the selected passage while listening and using headphones or earbuds. Students can also use just one earbud so that they can monitor the volume of their voice.

Teachers can produce recordings of fluent readers in your classrooms on tape or within a PowerPoint slide presentation. Poems, songs, and other types of short text can be easily copied into a PowerPoint presentation. Using the record feature in PowerPoint, a fluent reader can record the text written on each slide. VoiceThread (www.voicethread.com) is an online application that can also be used to record audio to accompany text and pictures. By creating our own library of recordings, we can adjust the speed of the reading so that students can read along with the text.

To assist students in noticing the elements of fluency in their reading, we have created a rubric (figure 6.1, page 56). Each time students practice, they complete the log and rate their reading of the passage. The rubric is based on the dimensions of fluency (Rasinski, 2003).

Audio-Assisted Reading Log and Self-Evaluation

Student: _____

Date: _____

Text: _____

Minutes Read: _____

After listening to the tape, read five to ten lines of text independently. Rate your own oral reading in each category.

	Fair	**Good**	**Outstanding**
Expression and Volume	I focused on making sure I pronounced each word correctly. I read quietly.	For the most part, I read as if I was carrying on a conversation; at times, I could tell my voice did not vary in expression or volume.	I read as if I was carrying on an interesting conversation; my reading had varied volume and expression.
Phrasing	Sometimes my reading was word by word. I tried to read in two- to three-word phrases.	I sometimes read in phrases and sentence units, but sometimes I could not tell when to end or begin a phrase in this passage. Many times, I could hear my inflection change as I read the passage.	I read with phrasing by reading in clause and sentence units. I could hear my inflection change as I read the passage.
Smoothness	I hesitated as I read, and I sometimes had to repeat or sound out words.	Sometimes I had difficulty pronouncing words or reading a sentence, but I could correct my errors, and keep reading.	My reading was smooth. On occasion, I hesitated or made an error, but I corrected my errors without too much difficulty and kept reading.

	Fair	**Good**	**Outstanding**
Pace	My reading was moderately slow. I generally read the passage at this pace.	I mixed up the pace as I read depending on the vocabulary and sentence structure of the text; sometimes I read fast and other times slowly.	I consistently read at a conversational level. My pace was even throughout the text and appropriate to the meaning of the text.

Figure 6.1: Elements of fluency rubric.

Classroom Example

Joe Vermillion, a high school English teacher, is concerned about the varied reading abilities of his sophomore class. He knows that several students have fluency problems, often due to the lengthy and complicated texts required in high school classes. Some of his students still struggle with decoding, others with the phrasing of text, and many read slowly and deliberately, although accurately. Joe selects audiobooks to support the reading of classic fiction in his class.

Shakespeare's *Julius Caesar* is a challenging unit. This play has archaic, complex vocabulary; understanding its tone and dialogue is difficult, yet critical, since students must understand not only what is being said, but also the characters' emotional states. Some of his colleagues require students to read Shakespeare independently and silently. Others assign students a character and have them read the play in a round-robin style. Joe tried these approaches but did not find them effective or beneficial to students.

Using the Folger Shakespeare Library (www.folger.edu), Joe finds podcasts and audio recordings of *Julius Caesar*. He asks each student to select one excerpt from the play, a part they found particularly meaningful or important. Students become fluent readers and speakers of Shakespeare by repeatedly reading and hearing one speech or passage. On the first day, he puts Mark Antony's famous speech on the whiteboard. The students listen to the speech three times. During the second reading, he stops the recording to highlight specific features of the speech, saying, "I am going to mark the iambic pentameter. I want you to watch what I am doing and make my markings on your copy as well."

Students gain an understanding, not only of the content, but also of how the plays were written, for example, noticing meter and iambic pentameter. The audio assistance provides students with explicit and meaningful modeling so they can closely read and understand the content and structure of the passage.

Next, Joe plays the recording one more time and asks students to note how the recorded reader used tone and repetition to emphasize particular words. He explains, "I want you to pay attention to the repetition of the word *honorable*."

He then highlights the word *honorable* throughout the speech.

He continues, saying, "Now we are going to listen to the first three lines. I want you to pay attention to the reader's tone."

Joe then shares his own thinking about the speech: "As I am listening to this, I notice the reader's tone shifts when he uses the word *honorable*. People want to be known as honorable, yet, as a reader I noticed he keeps repeating the word, and he is very sarcastic. This makes me think that he is actually saying Brutus isn't honorable."

Joe explains to the students that they will be doing a similar exercise tomorrow in class with their self-selected passages. He gives students the rest of the class to select their passages, and he has them printed for the following day.

The next day in class, Joe reminds students: "Listen to your speech or passage at least three times before you do anything. Then start to listen specifically for rhythm and actually mark the iambic pentameter on your printed version of the passage. Also note if there are any words repeated throughout. What is the tone? For example, is the speaker happy, somber, inquisitive, or angry?"

As students read and listen, Joe circulates the classroom to assist. He stops by Stephen's desk.

"OK, Stephen, what passage did you select?" Joe asks.

Stephen replies, "I picked a speech by Cassius. I thought it was important, because afterward, Brutus starts thinking that maybe Caesar shouldn't have so much power and that maybe the conspirators were right."

Joe says, "Good. OK, I see you have started your annotations. Tell me what you have done."

Stephen says, "Well, I marked the iambic pentameter. Then I noticed he says, 'What is in a name' and then keeps repeating Caesar's name. When I listen to the recording, it sounds like he is mad at Caesar."

After reading and marking the text, students begin rehearsing with the audio recordings. Joe notes that the repeated readings make his students fluent readers of Shakespeare, while increasing their comprehension of *Julius Caesar*. Once the students feel they have sufficiently practiced, they create podcasts of their own readings. Using tools such as Audacity, students record their speeches and share them with classmates by uploading them to the class website.

Your Turn

After completing a quick inventory of available old and new technology in your classroom, think about the text passages that seem to create comprehension difficulties for your students. As you read these texts, highlight phrasing, difficult vocabulary, and intonation patterns that may be problematic for a reader. Search the suggested websites or your library for books on compact disc or audiotape. Listen to the passages you selected for a close reading. Determine if the reading rate is appropriate for your students, and if so, have students do a close reading of the text and then a reading with the audio. If the reading rate of the passage is too fast for your students to read along, record an expressive, but slower reading of a passage within Audacity, VoiceThread, PowerPoint, or on a tape recorder. Select students who enjoy reading aloud and read with those expressive qualities that other students can model. Students who are expressive readers can work together to create a dialogic reading of a play or novel. By eliciting their help, you can use your class website to share podcasts and create your own library of audio-assisted books and passages. Having a large library of audio-assisted books and passages will increase your ability to differentiate instruction for each student in your classroom.

Using an interactive SMART Board is an efficient and effective way to begin instruction. In this format you can work on the text, listen to the fluent reading of the text, and highlight aspects of fluency when you introduce the rubric. By practicing the use of the rubric to rate examples of fluent reading and less fluent reading, students will learn how to use the rubric independently and judge the quality of their own reading.

Conclusion

As students engage in audio-assisted reading of passages that you specifically recommend, they will try to match their reading to the fluent and expressive reading of a peer or a professional actor or actress. When the students complete this co-reading, they will be able to analyze the dimensions of fluency in their own reading: expression and volume, phrasing, smoothness, and pace. This self-assessment provides you and the student feedback. Therefore, reading aloud with a proficient model provides the student practice in gaining reading fluency, an important scaffold for constructing the meaning of text (Rasinski, 2003).

PART III | Reading Vocabulary

It's not enough for readers to be able to sound out the words they encounter in print. They also need to know what the words mean. Meaning cannot be accessed if readers do not have understanding of the individual words in the passage. Knowledge of word meanings, or vocabulary, has long been recognized as essential for success in reading.

Despite recognition of the importance of vocabulary, developing students' vocabularies has continually been a challenge for teachers. One reason is that the English language contains more words than nearly any other language. Moreover, new words are constantly being added to English—often words that are related to various academic areas. This means that teachers not only have a lot of words to teach, they also need to be selective in the words they choose. To complicate matters even more, words in English can have more than one meaning, including nuanced or implied meanings, and multiple words can have the same or very similar meanings. Clearly, because of these and other factors, teaching and learning the meaning of English words is no small task.

Traditional approaches to vocabulary instruction also hamper teachers. For example, students in too many classrooms are assigned a list of ten to twenty words for which they have to look up, write the definition, and then memorize both the spelling and meaning for a test every Friday. By the following Monday, the words are often forgotten. Not only does such a rote-memory approach have questionable value for word learning, it is also one of the reasons that students come to hate and avoid the study of words.

Part III highlights new approaches to teaching words through the use of technology. Three innovative approaches are offered in this part. First, Dana L. Grisham, Linda Smetana, and Thomas DeVere Wolsey present their Vocabulary Self-Collection Strategy Plus, which combines many of the methods we know work in vocabulary learning—such as multiple exposures to words, multiple readings of texts, and collaboration—with others in a novel learning process. Next, Bridget Dalton and Kimberly McDavid Schmidt's vocabulary videos have students create short video skits to help them demonstrate and share meanings of important vocabulary words. Finally, Rachel J. Ebner presents a research-based and classroom-tested method for students doing Internet searches to find information on targeted words. Hopefully, the instructional strategies in this part will inspire you to make the rote-memorization wordlist approach a distant memory. Word study and vocabulary instruction can and should be fun and engaging! Technology can help make it that way.

Dana L. Grisham, PhD, is certified core adjunct faculty at National University. She retired as a full professor from California State University in 2010 and is noted for her research on teaching, particularly the intersection of literacy and technology. She received the Distinguished Teacher Educator Award from the California Council on Teacher Education in 2008 and the Computers in Reading Research Award from the International Reading Association's Technology in Literacy Education group in 2013. She is a noted scholar with over eighty publications in national and international journals and chapters in books. Her most recent book with T. D. Wolsey provides professional development for teachers in techniques for integrating writing with web 2.0 technologies. Currently, Dana serves as editor of *Reading and Writing Quarterly*.

Linda Smetana is professor of educational psychology at California State University, East Bay, where she teaches graduate courses in the teacher preparation, special education teacher preparation, and graduate reading programs. In addition to her work at CSU East Bay, she has thirty years of public school teaching experience from preschool through continuation high school. Linda currently maintains a connection with teachers and students in her role as a literacy and learning specialist in an urban school district. The public school setting provides opportunities for action research. Her interest in technology stems from a desire to provide additional instructional strategies for teachers to use with students who often find learning core content difficult. Linda has published numerous articles in the areas of literacy, teacher preparation, response to intervention, and technology. She is a recipient of the Outstanding Article of the Year from the *Journal of Reading Education* for her article (with Dana Grisham) on generative technology.

Thomas DeVere Wolsey, PhD, is the board chairman and chief executive officer of the Institute to Advance International Education. He teaches graduate literacy courses online at the University of Central Florida. He worked in public schools for twenty years teaching English and social studies. Prior to working with IAIE, he served as program director for all graduate literacy programs at a large midwestern university. Currently, his publications appear in the *Journal of Educational Administration*, *Literacy Research and Instruction*, and others. His books are published by Pearson, Corwin Press, Guilford Press, and Holcomb Hathaway. Two new books featuring graphic organizers as literacy learning tools were released in October 2014 with coauthors Diane Lapp, Karen Wood, and Kelly Johnson. He served as coeditor (with Dana Grisham) of *The California Reader*, and he guest-edited issues of the *Journal of Educational Administration* and *Teacher Education Quarterly* with colleagues. Visit http://tdwolsey.com to learn more about Wolsey's work.

CHAPTER 7

Post-Reading Vocabulary Development Through VSSPlus

By Dana L. Grisham, Linda Smetana, and Thomas DeVere Wolsey

As one teacher told us, "I love how differently we can approach vocabulary than merely giving students a list and asking them to memorize it. Teaching vocabulary is really about inviting students into a realm of authentic exploration and discovery that will afford greater retention" (E. Danysh, personal communication, 2013). The need for breadth and depth of vocabulary accelerates through the grades as students encounter more challenging academic texts in print and on the Internet (NGA & CCSSO, 2010). Improving students' vocabularies is critical if students are to develop the advanced literacy proficiencies required for success in school, higher education, and the workplace (Biancarosa & Snow, 2006; Graves & Watts-Taffe, 2008; Lubliner & Grisham, 2012).

To be effective, vocabulary instruction takes intense, interactive teaching over time, but research indicates that not much current classroom time is dedicated to vocabulary instruction (Blachowicz & Fisher, 2000). Often, vocabulary is addressed superficially in the form of mentioning and assigning (Scott, Jamieson-Noel, & Asselin, 2003), rather than robust teaching with opportunities for students to engage deeply with word meanings before they read, as they read, and after they read (Marzano, 2004).

Research suggests that students with well-developed vocabularies learn many more words indirectly through reading than from instruction (Cunningham & Stanovich,

1998). If wide reading promotes vocabulary development, then having conversations about reading with adults and peers can also strengthen students' word learning (Biemiller & Boote, 2006). Similarly, some writing tasks may engage students in choosing precise, academic vocabulary as they compose (Wolsey, 2010). The goal of effective vocabulary instruction is to promote a lively interest in words through student expression and participation in a learning community that enjoys playing with words, builds on individual interests as well as curriculum needs, and emphasizes self-efficacy (Beck, McKeown, & Kucan, 2013; Graves & Watts-Taffe, 2008; Marzano, 2004).

The Role of Technology

Within the realm of vocabulary development, the impact of technology needs to be considered (Castek, Dalton, & Grisham, 2012). In other contexts, we have suggested that technology integration should be *generative* in the sense that learners should use technology to satisfy their curiosity and to generate products that demonstrate and extend their learning (Grisham & Smetana, 2011). For this chapter, however, we chose a research-based strategy and employed generative technology to capitalize on the learning affordances of the technology. There is some evidence that linking images and linguistic information in the brain magnifies learning (for instance, see Sadoski & Paivio, 2007). In our digital version of the Vocabulary Self-Collection Strategy or VSSPlus, images form the basis for powerful word study and word learning.

VSSPlus occurs after a selection has been read. It is based on the principles of VSS (Haggard, 1982), a researched-based strategy that captures the essence of vocabulary learning: multiple exposures to a word, multiple readings of a text, collaboration between students and teacher, oral discussions and presentations, and selection of words that are important to know. In the original VSS, after the word selection, nomination, and discussion, a class wordlist was formed, and students continued to do activities surrounding the vocabulary words, such as completing a vocabulary journal. For VSSPlus, we decided to incorporate technology: writing a script and recording an audio podcast that highlight important aspects of the word, conducting an Internet search for illustrations of the word, and building semantic webs around the word. VSSPlus accomplishes the exploration of words electronically, rather than with pencil and paper. The goal is additional and meaningful work to deepen word (and concept) learning.

How Do I Do It?

VSSPlus is an instructional structure that helps students become more independent over time. The VSSPlus process can take one to two weeks, and we suggest you use texts that have interesting or unknown words, have figurative language, or are dense with academic language. Collaboration and peer learning are essential. It can take more time in the beginning as teachers and students get used to the technology, timing, and process, so be sure to allow for this.

Consider fifth-grade students who completed a science textbook selection on states of matter. After they were introduced to VSSPlus, the table groups selected an important word from the chapter they had just finished reading, read aloud the sentence it appeared in, defined it in their own words, and provided a rationale for why the word was important to know. After classroom presentations on each group's important word, students went to the computer lab, where they worked in the same table groups to generate e-dictionary pages for the words on a class website that can expand throughout the academic year and beyond. Their teacher noted that the students were very enthusiastic about their projects and talked constantly about how they remembered the words and their meanings.

Formatting for the e-dictionary should appear in the following order.

1. Word and written definition

2. Image selection from the Internet, photos, illustrations, or student drawings (if a scanner is available)

3. Semantic web (we used WordSift)

4. Student audio-recording about the word (critical thinking about word learning)

5. Arrangement of the information in PowerPoint, ThingLink, or other program

6. Posting of pages to the website (classroom e-dictionary)

PowerPoint and ThingLink (www.thinglink.com) are two ways to construct the classroom e-dictionary. You can use these in combination or separately, depending on your preferences. Following are directions for PowerPoint:

1. Students place the teacher-approved definition on the header of the PowerPoint slide.

2. Students place scanned images or drawings on the e-dictionary page.

3. (Optional) Students place a word web (we used WordSift) on the e-dictionary page.

4. Teacher records the students' voices as they talk about the word chosen to be included on the PowerPoint slide. PowerPoint has

narration tools embedded in the software, but we used digital audio recorders and attached the recording separately as MP3 files.

5.   Students orally present their e-dictionary word and show the final PowerPoint slide or slide show to the whole class. (Visit **go.solution-tree.com/technology** for alternatives.)

ThingLink is a more integrated method. To use ThingLink, use the following directions:

1.   Students select and create the media they wish to use to illustrate their word. They may select the appropriate definition from an online or print source—including a link or attribution—but the teacher must approve it.

2.   Using the editing tools in ThingLink, students insert the definition and the link to the definition. They may insert various icons into the image to fulfill the requirements of definition, rationale, and podcast.

3.   Teachers should encourage students to find and include additional media to insert.

4.   Students create an audio file or podcast (we uploaded ours to Podbean), include their rationale for choosing the word, and link the podcast to the ThingLink image.

5.   The ThingLink is made unlisted so that only students can access the site. Do note that several other sites are also well suited to the task, such as VoiceThread, Prezi, and Glogster.

Visit **go.solution-tree.com/technology** to find more detailed directions for using ThingLink, as well as directions for inserting podcasts into presentations. Other tools are also available—a cursory Internet search will provide several options.

Classroom Example

The thirty-three students in Eric Danysh's fifth-grade classroom were placed into eight collaborative groups. We worked with Eric and his students in the computer lab (each group had access to two computers). The students had already chosen science content words as part of the VSSPlus instruction, defined them, and researched them, so that morning they worked to generate PowerPoint pages and ThingLink presentations. Here we provide an example of a PowerPoint slide (figure 7.1). Groups were assigned the names Madera 1–8 to avoid using student names.

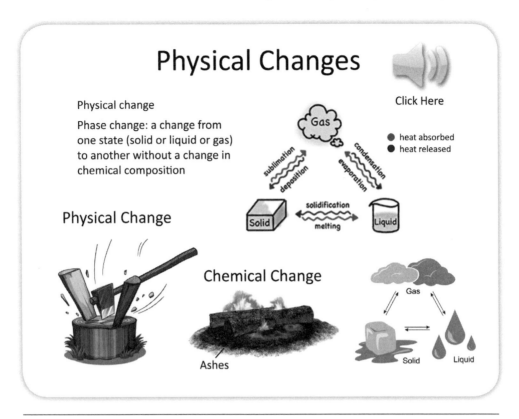

Figure 7.1: PowerPoint slide of physical changes.

In the PowerPoint, the students also wrote and recorded an audio podcast that addressed their chosen term. (Visit http://youtu.be/wq9ZdBnMGos to see a collection of VSSPlus examples.)

During observations of the students' work, we were each struck by the level of engagement (and enjoyment) of the students as they grappled with both the content (vocabulary) and the procedures (technology). We observed that students worked together well, helped each other solve problems, and went beyond our expectations of their learning of complex scientific vocabulary.

Your Turn

The Common Core State Standards (NGA & CCSSO, 2010) require that technology be integrated into instructional and independent learning sequences. In this post-reading vocabulary assignment, you will use several forms of technology to increase student interest in vocabulary. You'll also use VSSPlus to engage students in more robust vocabulary learning.

First, you need to divide your class into working collaborative groups of no more than three to four students who will read the same content area or literary text.

Teach some vocabulary before students read the identified section, and proceed with normal reading instruction for the text. We suggest that you review the Directed Reading-Thinking Activity strategy (Stauffer, 1969) by dividing the text into sections and discussing each section before proceeding to the next.

After reading the text, use a think-aloud protocol to model VSSPlus. Present a nominated word to the class, and provide suggested answers to the following questions. In the demonstration, you will speak for a pretend team or select several students you have prepared to model responses to the questions (in a fishbowl style).

1. Where is the word found in the text? (List the page number and read the sentence aloud.)

2. What do the team members think the word means? (List the definition.)

3. Why did the team think the class should learn more about the word? (List the rationale.)

Students can begin using the strategy on their own once the process has been modeled and the student questions have been answered. Students go back to the text and discuss it, collaboratively deciding on three words of interest or those essential to comprehending the text selection.

A spokesperson for each team then identifies the nominated word and responds to the three questions. During the team presentations, you facilitate the discussion, write the nominated words on the board with their projected meanings, and invite class members to contribute additional clarifications of the words. At this point, class members vote on words to go into the e-dictionary. There should be enough words to allocate one to a team. You may also suggest a word.

Next, allocate the words to each team (we recommend that the teams make the choices). You should also model the e-dictionary process for the students, using an example already prepared for the lesson. In our work with fifth graders, students actively monitored each group's conversation to avoid duplicating words other teams near them had selected.

Team members then use the Internet to locate images and definitions for the target word. Teams must collaborate to determine which of the images and definitions best fits their prediction and context of the word meaning. With this information, students construct an e-dictionary page for their word using either PowerPoint or ThingLink.

Presentations of this material can be very flexible, as you can adjust any requirements or supporting materials based on the needs of your students, the Common Core or other standards, and your students' course of study in any discipline. For example, a mathematics e-dictionary would be useful to students. You could also source words from a text the students are reading as a part of their English language arts program. Remember that fair use must apply for all images found (for more information on fair use and copyright, see Media Education Lab, n.d., 2012). Finally, post the students' completed slides to the classroom e-dictionary, which may be kept on a classroom website, on the ThingLink site, in a wiki, or in a file on the classroom computer.

Throughout the academic year, when students encounter the same words in different contexts (much of English is polysemous), they may access the e-dictionary to remind themselves of the meaning or add to the definitions, either through VSSPlus or as individual contributions. The e-dictionary may be archived or used for multiple academic years.

Conclusion

We have used VSSPlus in the upper-elementary grades with remarkable success. Our first attempt took three hours, and students worked willingly to complete the e-dictionary pages, using both PowerPoint and ThingLink options. Our student teachers also used VSSPlus with success, reporting that their students at upper elementary and secondary grade levels learned content area vocabulary more deeply and with greater engagement. VSSPlus helps students connect images, discussion, research, writing, and technology to define and extend their learning of vocabulary and conceptual knowledge.

Bridget Dalton, EdD, is an associate professor in literacy studies at the University of Colorado Boulder. Her research focuses on the design and use of scaffolded digital reading and composing environments, with special attention to the needs and interests of students who are experiencing literacy difficulties. Bridget previously taught at the University of Guam and Vanderbilt University and served as chief literacy and technology officer at the Center for Applied Special Technology. She has published widely on digital literacies, codeveloped the award-winning reading program *Thinking Reader*, and was coeditor of the International Reading Association's electronic journal, *Reading Online*. With colleagues, Bridget blogs about literacy and technology at www.literacybeat .com. Bridget earned her doctorate in reading, language, and learning disabilities at Harvard University. Visit www.colorado.edu/education/people/bridget-dalton to learn more about Bridget's work.

Kimberly McDavid Schmidt is a doctoral candidate at the University of Colorado Boulder studying critical literacies and multimodal composition. She is a research assistant on the Collaborative Strategic Reading Project and the Multimodal Reading and Composing Project at the university. She previously taught in elementary school at the pre-kindergarten through second grade levels and worked with elementary teachers as a professional development specialist and coach.

CHAPTER 8

Bringing Words to Life Through Student-Created Vocabulary Videos

By Bridget Dalton and Kimberly McDavid Schmidt

What do *boycott* and *dystopia* have in common? Both words were the subject of vocabulary videos that students created to develop and express their understanding of key words from texts they were reading in class. Third graders read a biography of civil rights activist Rosa Parks and then videotaped themselves acting out a bus boycott, while high school students dramatized a dystopia in response to their class novel, *The Hunger Games* (Collins, 2008). In this chapter, we present a rationale for the use of digital vocabulary videos, describe how to apply this strategy in your classroom, and provide examples.

To read for understanding is to know words—lots of words (or if we want to power up our word choice—a plethora of words)! Studies have shown that vocabulary knowledge is highly correlated with comprehension, ranging from a correlation of 0.6 to 0.8 (Kame'enui & Baumann, 2012). Academic vocabulary is especially challenging for students, since it involves specialized terminology and knowledge that goes beyond students' everyday experiences (Fang, Schleppegrell, & Cox, 2006). Although the third graders who were learning about the 1960s civil rights movement began the unit with some understanding of the concept of *boycott* (every child knows the power of refusing to do something in order to get what they want), they did not know the academic term or understand its use in historical or modern contexts of civic protest. For the teens learning *dystopia*, it was both an unfamiliar concept and term.

Vocabulary knowledge is incremental and multilayered. We develop word knowledge on a continuum from "I've never seen the word before" to "I know this word well and could flexibly use it in multiple contexts" (Beck, McKeown, & Kucan, 2008). In addition to developing students' vocabulary breadth (how many different words they know), we also develop vocabulary depth (how well they know the multiple meanings of the word and its relationships with other words). In effect, we construct webs of meaning that are interrelated. Vocabulary videos require this contextual use of words while simultaneously helping students demonstrate a range of use. For example, one group of third graders acted out a protest march with signs proclaiming "No more bullying!" and "Take care of our planet!," while a different group acted out a scenario protesting to their teacher about too much homework.

A wealth of vocabulary instruction research highlights the importance of teaching vocabulary so that students are actively engaged in the process, including expressing their word knowledge through different modes such as speech, writing, drawing, and drama (Beck et al., 2008). We also know that successful vocabulary instruction incites students' curiosity about words and develops a love of (or at least an interest in) words (Graves & Watts-Taffe, 2008). There is fairly strong evidence that multimedia, such as images and animation, improves students' word learning as well (Dalton, Proctor, Uccelli, Mo, & Snow, 2011; Mayer, 2001). In addition, students with diverse literacy needs benefit from creating multimedia vocabulary hypertexts and video (Pritchard & O'Hara, 2009; Xin & Rieth, 2001).

The popularity of youth-created video on the Internet has extended to the creation of vocabulary videos. In October 2013, the *New York Times*'s Learning Network held a student contest for fifteen-second vocabulary videos (Schulten, 2013a). When introducing the contest on her blog, Katherine Schulten shared several vocabulary videos illustrating a range of approaches. For example, Mr. Felazzo's bilingual students used still images and audio narration to express *problem* in an Instagram video, while others used live-action video. We encourage you to check out the winning videos (see Schulten, 2013b).

Here, we will focus on Bridget Dalton's vocabulary-video instructional strategy, a six-step approach that we find works well for students across grade levels (Dalton, Smith, & Renner, 2012). However, we encourage you to experiment with different methods to learn what works best for your students and to take advantage of the digital media and tools available at your school.

How Do I Do It?

Vocabulary videos are brief fifteen- to forty-five-second skits that illustrate the meaning of a word. The videos tell a quick story and are designed to be somewhat improvisational so that the emphasis is on expressing the meaning of the word within a short time frame and with just a video camera. The process does not involve script writing or use of a video-editing tool (although this could be an option). Briefly, here is an overview of this six-step process.

First, students select a word for their video. Often, we provide a list drawn from a curriculum topic or text and ask students to select from the list. Allowing students some choice is important, especially at the beginning when you are building word interest.

Second, students explore the meaning of the word using print or digital resources. For example, they may consult a dictionary, an online thesaurus, or a digital tool like Visual Thesaurus, which displays an interactive word web. Students may also want to reexamine the word within a passage from a text they are reading to explore its meaning in that context. We use a word web to guide students' investigation, prompting them to add related words and phrases and to brainstorm where the word might be used, who might use the word and why, and how the word makes them feel. Visit **go.solution-tree.com/technology** for a generic word web and a character-traits word web. Students then create a large sign with their word on one side, and the definition on the other side. At the end of the video, they will show the word and provide a definition to connect the use of the word in the skit with a formal definition.

Third, students briefly brainstorm different scenarios for illustrating the word. The goal is to create a video that will help their classmates remember the word. The teams also decide on roles: video director, actors, and word-card person (the latter can be one of the actors, if needed).

Fourth, students record their skit two or three times, quickly gathering after each shoot to view the video and provide feedback to improve it. The focus is on making it more appealing (Is it dramatic? Funny?) and impactful (Did we use related words to help illustrate the meaning? How do our actions, voice, and facial expressions reinforce the meaning?). In addition, technical quality is checked (Can everyone be heard? Can the actors be seen clearly?). Then students select their best video to share and delete the other videos.

Fifth, students present their video. How they accomplish this depends on the tools you are using. For example, when using digital cameras and smartphones, it is efficient to hook each device to a class laptop or tablet and then download the videos into a folder. Each team can then present their vocabulary video to the class, projecting onto a large screen or whiteboard. Following their video presentation, each team asks for feedback on the design of their video and clarification questions about the word meaning (all of the students know that they are going to be responsible for knowing each other's words, so this is a meaningful activity).

Finally, students publish their videos. Vocabulary videos are a valuable learning resource and should be available for students to access easily. A key decision is how public the videos will be, given concerns about student privacy. There are options to create a YouTube account, blog, or wiki that is restricted to your students and their families. You may also save the videos onto selected classroom computers and laptops, in specially marked folders. You may want to email one vocabulary video each week to students and parents to view and discuss together.

Classroom Example

Vocabulary videos address several Common Core State Standards. Most important, students demonstrate their understanding of words and learn how to use vocabulary reference tools. In addition, they develop narrative skills and technology skills as they compose and critically evaluate vocabulary videos. Finally, they learn how to work in a team. The following two examples show different types of videos and highlight possible extensions.

Character-Trait Vocabulary Videos

In one fourth-grade class, students have been exploring character traits as they read and respond to a novel and short stories. The teacher leads them in creating a large chart listing various traits, such as *curious*, *bossy*, and *shy*. They discuss evidence from the text and their own life experiences to describe certain kinds of traits. To delve more deeply into the meaning of various traits, the students divide into six teams of four or five students and go through the vocabulary video process described previously, selecting their word from a list of character traits.

A team of four students selects the word *rich*. One student takes the role of video director and films the group as it tries out its skit over several iterations. In the final version, three students walk up the stairs, chatting about how they are "so rich." One student describes how he is so rich that he can travel anywhere—to Mexico, to France, and to the mall; a second exclaims that she is so rich that she can give lots of money away and still have plenty to spend; and the third gushes about the beautiful jewels and clothes she could buy. Their voices and gestures convey how pleased they are with their rich status. This concept of material richness is an easy one for this age group to understand. An interesting extension would be to create a second video illustrating wealth not based on money. Having multiple meanings and examples is essential to developing vocabulary depth.

The Hunger Games *Vocabulary Videos*

A high school teacher uses vocabulary videos to develop academic vocabulary encountered in the reading of the novel *The Hunger Games*. Every few chapters, student teams are given a list of words from the novel (Dalton et al., 2012). They are randomly assigned a word to express in a video, following the same general procedure described previously. Students then research the remainder of the words and add them to their vocabulary journals. After their vocabulary-video presentations, students complete a vocabulary quiz for each set of words.

One team creates a video for the word *alter*. Although the word is used in the novel to describe how individuals alter their looks to conform to societal expectations of beauty, the students choose to focus on another context of use, altering clothing for better fit, effectively using related words such as *modify*, *tailor*, and *change*. In the first scene, a student (the tailor) examines the back of the dress. She says, "Do you need me to tailor it? Do you need me to modify it? Do you need me to change it?" (*laughs*) "Do you need me to make it fit better?"

The second student (the customer) turns to face the tailor and says, "Um, yes I do."

Finally, the third holds up a word card, which reads, "*Alter*, to change."

Their video raises a question about how language use is situated in practice. In this case, the meaning of *alter* is the same (to change or modify) for both beauty and clothing. However, one has a very specific and concrete meaning, while the other opens opportunities for deeper discussions of beauty and the extent to which people are willing to transform themselves. One extension that would encourage connections between these two contexts would be to ask students to elaborate on their definition at the end of the video to make the different uses in the novel and their video explicit, such as: "*Alter*, to change. In our video, a dress was being altered. In *The Hunger Games*, people altered their physical appearance. This said something about their society and how they felt about themselves."

Your Turn

So, how much is enough? The goal of the vocabulary-video experience is broader than helping students learn individual words; we believe that the process also builds students' word-learning strategies and generates interest in words. Thus, we recommend that you integrate these videos strategically so that you realize the benefits without it being too time intensive. One option is to designate periodic vocabulary-video sessions for the entire class, dividing students into five or six teams to create and present their videos. A second option is to feature a weekly vocabulary video, with a different team creating and presenting its video each week. A third option would be to rotate teams so that each day during the literacy block, one team's daily vocabulary video is shown.

To begin, we recommend that you involve the entire class in creating vocabulary videos, either through a classwide video that you direct or through student teams exploring different words. This will both generate excitement and help students understand the process. The first session always takes the longest. As students become more adept at the process, the time will shorten. We find that twenty to thirty minutes to research the word and video is typical at the beginning; we like to reduce this to approximately fifteen minutes with practice.

Regarding necessary equipment, each team needs its own video camera so it can operate efficiently. Digital cameras, tablets, and smartphones are all good options. In addition, you will want to project the videos for the class presentation and store them on a device that students can access. Provide construction paper and markers for the word signs as well, and ensure you have access to print or digital vocabulary reference tools.

It's important that students have some choice in selecting words. That said, it makes sense to constrain their choices so they select words that are important in the curriculum, including academic vocabulary. Review your list to make sure the words lend themselves to dramatic play and that some words are easier than others. Limit the team's time to choose their word to one minute so they quickly move on to researching their word. To help get everyone started, visit **go.solution-tree.com /technology** for a reproducible student guide sheet.

Conclusion

To close, we offer you some additional implementation recommendations.

- **Create your own model vocabulary video:** Recruit a couple of colleagues to create a vocabulary video or two that you can share as models for your students. You will have a better understanding of the process, and students will enjoy seeing you acting! In addition, there are student-created vocabulary videos online you could use as models.

- **Demonstrate how to use the camera:** Provide a camera tip sheet outlining how to record, zoom, set volume, preview, save, and delete. Designate certain students as video experts and distribute them across the teams. Alert students to two main pitfalls: (1) students are speaking softly or looking away from the camera and can't be heard clearly, and (2) the camera is shooting into the sunlight and the actors can't be seen clearly. As students gain experience, they can share their own shooting techniques.

- **Guide students in providing feedback:** Help students praise and critique one another on the content of the videos (What did I learn about this word? How does the video story help me learn it?), as well as the video design (What makes this video appealing?).

- **Assess:** Once students have experience creating vocabulary videos, collaborate with them to create a self-assessment rubric, which they will use to evaluate the quality of their content and design, as well as how effectively their team worked together (visit **go.solution-tree .com/technology** for a sample rubric). Students can also create a quiz question for their word to be used in a class quiz.

Multimedia has an important role to play in developing students' vocabulary knowledge. Vocabulary videos require students to investigate word meaning, situate it in a particular context of use, and communicate it through an appealing video story that they share through presentations and publication to class blogs, wikis, or a classroom desktop. Strategically integrated into your curriculum, vocabulary videos can help develop engaged and knowledgeable word users.

 **Rachel J. Ebner, PhD,** is an educational psychologist who specializes in developing and researching innovative ways to advance student learning and assessment. She serves as director of student learning assessment and as clinical assistant professor of psychology at Yeshiva University in New York City. She holds master's degrees from the Harvard Graduate School of Education and Columbia University's Teachers College, as well as a doctorate in educational psychology from the City University of New York's Graduate Center.

CHAPTER 9

Self-Regulated Vocabulary Learning on the Internet

By Rachel J. Ebner

Vocabulary is a key building block for students' literacy achievement and overall academic success. Technology, especially the Internet, can serve as a powerful vocabulary-building tool. Its vast resources, easily accessible through search engines, provide students with instant access to multisensory (visual and auditory) experiences with words in different contexts. The incremental theory of word knowledge suggests that learning the meaning of a word is not all-or-nothing but instead a matter of degree that requires multiple and varied encounters with the word (Nagy & Scott, 2000). Using the Internet for vocabulary development is an efficient and effective way to build incremental word knowledge.

The Internet, however, may also be a significant source of distraction, making it difficult for many students to remain focused while learning online. This is because Internet learning is self-directed and affords users the autonomy to direct their own learning paths (Leu et al., 2004). Students attempting to learn vocabulary online can go astray when they encounter layer upon layer of hyperlinks, which often lead to websites containing irrelevant, outdated, or erroneous information. For this reason, effectively engaging in self-regulated learning is essential for online learning success (see Artino, 2008; Coiro & Dobler, 2007; Greene & Land, 2000). Self-regulated learning is defined "as the degree to which students are metacognitively, motivationally, and behaviorally active participants in their own learning process" (Zimmerman, 2008, p. 2).

My empirical research not only finds promising support for using the Internet to develop vocabulary, it also reveals that online vocabulary learning is more effective for students trained in self-regulated learning techniques. I have completed three online vocabulary-learning studies in which college students used the Internet to learn the meanings of particular terms contained within a Wikipedia article (Ebner & Ehri, 2012, 2013, 2014). Results show that by interacting with Internet tools and resources, students significantly increased their knowledge of each term's general meaning, grammatical usage, and meaning within the context of the online article. That said, the extent of word-knowledge gains on these dimensions varied (Ebner & Ehri, 2012, 2013).

My second study (Ebner & Ehri, 2013) examines the effects of a structured think-aloud procedure to help students self-regulate their online vocabulary learning. A think-aloud requires a student to voice his or her thoughts during a learning task. This has been found to be beneficial not only for gaining insight into processes for comprehending printed text (Pressley & Afflerbach, 1995) but also for online comprehension (Coiro & Dobler, 2007). My design and use of a *structured* think-aloud procedure for online vocabulary learning was unique: in addition to revealing online learners' thought processes, it actually enabled students to self-regulate those processes while engaging in a specific online vocabulary-learning task. By requiring students to repeatedly remind themselves of their vocabulary-learning goals and to engage in step-by-step planning and evaluation of their online actions in relation to achieving those goals, my procedure helps students remain focused on both their online learning goals and the online actions they took to pursue those goals.

The study's results reveal that structured think-aloud participants demonstrate significantly greater vocabulary gains, both overall and within specific dimensions of word knowledge (such as declarative knowledge, sentence writing, and relation to the learning topic) compared to a control group that was required to think aloud but not in any particular way. Both quantitative and qualitative analyses suggest that differences between conditions in vocabulary gains were attributable to structured think-aloud participants' greater metacognitive focus on the task.

My 2014 study (Ebner & Ehri, 2014) examines the effects of alternative, more practical, structured thinking procedures in order to extend our previous findings on the benefits of using a structured think-aloud procedure when learning vocabulary online. More specifically, we were interested in (1) whether using a structured think-aloud procedure that did not require the presence of a coach or prompting or (2) whether using a structured think-to-yourself procedure that did not require prompting would be as effective in encouraging students to self-regulate their online vocabulary learning as a structured think-aloud procedure with a coach. Both of the coachless procedures are more practical applications, since online learning is typically a self-directed, independent activity. The results also reveal that both were equally effective, and both were as effective as a structured think-aloud with a coach in enabling college students to gain more word knowledge online. These results further support the benefits of using structured thinking procedures to scaffold students' self-regulated vocabulary learning on the Internet, thereby making learning more effective (Ebner & Ehri, 2014).

How Do I Do It?

Begin by explaining to students that they will use the Internet to learn a list of vocabulary words related to the unit topic. Provide oral and written instructions indicating that for each word, the students' goal will be to use the Internet to learn how to pronounce it, define it, use it in a sentence, and describe what it means in relation to the unit topic. Then instruct students to perform any online action they wish in order to learn about the terms. For example, they can read about the words in the context of an online article, click on the words if they are hyperlinked to other websites, visit online dictionaries, or conduct other Internet searches in order to learn about each word.

Next, tell students that to help them avoid online distractions and stay focused on their word-learning goals, they will be using a structured think-aloud procedure. Explain that this procedure requires a student to continually answer the following two questions for each online action the student takes to learn about a word.

1. **Before I act:** "How will this help me reach my goal?"

2. **While or after I act:** "Is this helping me, or did that help me, reach my goal?"

In addition, explain to students that they will be using a printed checklist to indicate each time they believe they have reached one of the vocabulary-learning goals for each word. Figure 9.1 (page 84) is an example of such a checklist for a unit on earthquakes.

Students should practice this procedure by continually thinking aloud about and answering the two structured-thought questions as they use the Internet to learn assigned vocabulary terms. A student can practice thinking aloud either to a classmate or to the teacher. For example, if students work in pairs, the online vocabulary learner should think aloud about the two structured-thought questions while researching the assigned words and also read aloud anything that he is reviewing in order to help learn about a word. Or consider a student researching the word *epicenter*.

Student's Name: _____

Directions

1. Remember your goal. For each term, learn how to:
   - Pronounce it
   - Define it
   - Use it in a sentence
   - Explain its meaning in relation to the topic of earthquakes

2. As you learn about the terms online, continuously think aloud or to yourself:
   - Before I act—"How will this help me reach my goal?"
   - While or after I act—"Is this helping me, or did that help me, reach my goal?"

3. For each term on the vocabulary list, make a checkmark when you have reached each learning goal:

Term	Pronounce it	Define it	Use it in a sentence	Explain its meaning in relation to the topic of earthquakes
fault				
seismic				
epicenter				
magnitude				
landslide				
tsunami				

Source: Adapted from Ebner & Ehri, 2013.

Figure 9.1: Sample online vocabulary learning checklist.

She could think aloud that she is going to read about the term in the context of a Wikipedia article on earthquakes in order to obtain contextual information about the word. Or, the student may decide to go to Google Images to see pictures of what an epicenter looks like. Before engaging in either of those online actions, she should think aloud how that action will help her reach the goal of defining the word, using it in a sentence, or explaining its meaning in relation to the target topic. Then, after doing the online action, the student should think aloud whether or not it was helpful in reaching one of the vocabulary goals. The student's partner or teacher should act as coach by directing and reminding her to continuously read aloud, think aloud the two structured-thought questions, and mark the checklist each time the learner feels that he or she has attained one of the vocabulary-learning goals.

After students have practiced using the procedure by thinking aloud, have them begin using the procedure on their own. Instruct students to continually ask themselves the two structured-thought questions and to use the checklist each time they believe they have reached a vocabulary-learning goal for a word.

Classroom Example

I have used the structured think-aloud procedure successfully with students in both research and classroom settings. In connection with my research, I worked one on one with college students, instructing and coaching them on how to use the structured think-aloud procedure when using the Internet to learn about ten hyperlinked terms contained in a Wikipedia article on religion in ancient Greece. After explaining the goals for each term and how to use the Internet to research the terms, I explained the structured think-aloud procedure. In particular, I asked the students to read aloud anything they chose in order to learn about the words. I also gave them oral and written instructions to think aloud about the two structured-thought questions.

I sat alongside each student while he or she performed this learning task, and if the student forgot to read aloud or think aloud, I would remind him or her to do so. If a student simply plugged one of the words into an online dictionary without reading the article, I would remind the student to think aloud about the goal of learning the meaning of the word in relation to the article topic. The students who were instructed to use this structured-thinking procedure gained significantly more word knowledge than students who were asked to read aloud and think aloud while performing the task without the benefit of the two structured-thought questions.

I have found the structured think-aloud procedure to be easily adaptable for elementary and secondary students. For example, I instructed third-grade students on how to use the structured think-aloud procedure when performing Internet research on a history project. Students worked in pairs, with one student reading and thinking aloud as he or she conducted online research, while the other student coached the reader to think the two structured-thought questions aloud. At the end of the activity, I asked students to write down what they liked most about the online activity. Students indicated that using the procedure not only helped them become less distracted, but in some cases even helped them realize how easily they otherwise become distracted.

It's important to note that students using the alternative procedures—using the structured think-to-yourself procedure without a coach or partner—should be first trained using the structured think-aloud procedure so they understand the process well enough to complete it alone. They should also use the type of checklist illustrated in figure 9.1 (page 84) to structure and monitor their vocabulary learning.

I have also tried the structured think-to-yourself procedure with a sixth-grade student. After having him practice with the structured think-aloud procedure, I asked him to think the two structured-thought questions to himself when learning vocabulary words about religion in ancient Greece. I also asked him to use the checklist to indicate that the vocabulary-learning goal for each word had been reached. I observed that this technique helped him stay on task and complete the assignment much more effectively and efficiently than when he was previously conducting online research without using the procedure. For example, when he was not using the procedure, the student got sidetracked by websites that had little to nothing to do with what he was supposed to learn in connection with ancient Greek religion. In another adaptation of my structured think-to-yourself procedure, I provided students in grades 3–5 with a worksheet that illustrated possible online actions that they could use while conducting their research. (See figure 9.2.)

The worksheet also asks students to record each of their online actions and to indicate whether each action was helpful in reaching their learning goal by circling either a thumbs up or thumbs down.

My observations, along with those of classroom teachers, and my interviews with students at the conclusion of the exercise suggest that it was an effective way to help students stay focused on using the Internet productively as a learning tool. For example, one fourth-grade student said that it helped him "know which things to click on and which things not to click on."

Your Turn

Generate a list of vocabulary words for students to research online in connection with a unit topic, or ask students to produce their own list of words. Explain to students that in this activity, they will be using the Internet to learn about each of the target words, including how to pronounce it, define it, use it in a sentence, and explain its meaning in relation to the topic of interest. Next, introduce the structured think-aloud procedure. In particular, explain to students that it is a way to help them avoid online distractions and stay focused on their goal of learning about the vocabulary words.

After explaining the procedure, model it for students using a few sample words. Do this by asking and answering the structured questions aloud as you use the Internet to learn about a word. For example, show students that *before* you click on a hyperlinked word in an online article, you ask yourself, "How will this help me reach my goal of learning how to define this word?" Then show that you answer

Name:

Directions:

Please answer this question:

Look for the answer on the computer. Write down each thing you did. Circle whether it helped you or did not help you find the answer.

Look at the box below for some strategies you can use.

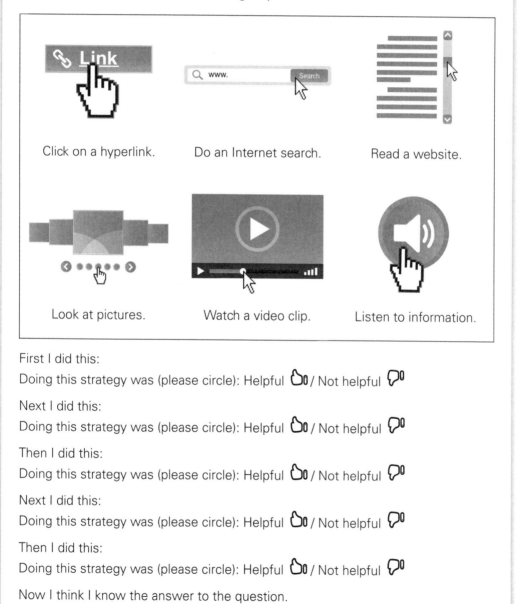

First I did this:

Doing this strategy was (please circle): Helpful 👍 / Not helpful 👎

Next I did this:

Doing this strategy was (please circle): Helpful 👍 / Not helpful 👎

Then I did this:

Doing this strategy was (please circle): Helpful 👍 / Not helpful 👎

Next I did this:

Doing this strategy was (please circle): Helpful 👍 / Not helpful 👎

Then I did this:

Doing this strategy was (please circle): Helpful 👍 / Not helpful 👎

Now I think I know the answer to the question.

It is:

Figure 9.2: Sample worksheet for possible online actions.

this question by thinking, "Clicking on this hyperlink may give me a more detailed explanation of the word's meaning." Finally, demonstrate that *after* you click on the hyperlink, you ask yourself, "Did this help me reach my goal of learning how to define the word?" Also show them you answer this question by indicating to yourself whether it helped, why it helped, and what you are going to do next to reach more of your online vocabulary-learning goals.

Once you have modeled the procedure several times, ask students to choose a partner to practice using the learning procedure with. After each partner has had a chance to practice, have all students come up with their own list of words from a webpage or online article. Then have them work on their own. Tell each student that instead of thinking the two questions aloud, he or she should think them silently, as well as fill in a blank word-learning checklist that you provide.

Conclusion

The Internet serves as an ideal platform for students to efficiently expand the multidimensional word knowledge, but avoiding online distractions and staying focused on learning goals can be a challenge. The structured think-aloud procedure described in this chapter is an effective way to help students self-regulate their online learning so they stay focused on their learning goals and, in turn, fully reap the benefits of using the Internet to learn vocabulary.

PART IV | Comprehension of Informational Texts

There has been a growing conversation among reading scholars and educational policymakers about the importance of informational texts. As teachers consider the ways to make informational texts a more integral part of their classroom instruction, it is worth exploring how technology can aid and support students' comprehension of such material.

Across grade bands, researchers and educators agree that students can benefit from explicit comprehension strategy instruction (Beers, 2003; Kamil et al., 2008). Kylene Beers (2003) notes that while we spend ample time assessing comprehension, we do not always teach students how to comprehend. Yet researchers agree that explicit instruction can develop students' reading comprehension (Beers, 2003; Kamil et al., 2008).

The gradual release of responsibility model (Pearson & Gallagher, 1983) is an evidence-based approach for introducing students to a new learning task. This model can be particularly useful when teaching students strategies for comprehending informational texts. Teachers begin by explaining the purpose of the strategy and how it will assist readers. During this time, teachers actually implement and model the specific strategy while, at the same time, discussing with students the features of the strategy that can aid comprehension as well as features of the text that may make the reading comprehension difficult or challenging. Next, students should have many opportunities to practice the strategy under the guidance and support of the teacher and classmates. Finally, students use the strategy independently in their reading.

The chapters in part IV highlight the ways technology is integral for students' reading and comprehension of informational text. Amy C. Hutchison's chapter explores the Multimodal Explanatory Composition strategy, in which students use multiple modes of response to demonstrate and deepen their understanding of a text, such as through a combination of audio, images, drawings, writing, and color. Jill Castek and Megan Goss show how apps, such as DocAS and Diigo, can help students thoughtfully annotate their texts, furthering their comprehension. Finally, W. Ian O'Byrne and J. Gregory McVerry present the Online Research and Media Skills model, which utilizes technology for collaborative inquiry, comprehension, and content construction. Comprehension of informational texts is going to become an increasing priority in the years to come. Technology can add instructional tools for helping students navigate these texts.

**Amy C. Hutchison** is an assistant professor of literacy at Iowa State University. Her interests include the study of the new skills, strategies, and dispositions required to read, write, and communicate with digital technology and how to best prepare teachers for the integration of literacy and technology. To learn more about Amy's work, visit http://tipcycle.wix.com/tech-integration or follow @HutchisonAmy on Twitter.

CHAPTER 10

Using the Multimodal Explanatory Composition Strategy to Respond to Informational Texts

By Amy C. Hutchison

Encounters with informational text should be common in classrooms today due to the influence of the Common Core State Standards on reading and understanding informational texts (NGA & CCSSO, 2010), as well as the prevalence of informational texts online. In order for students to be fully literate, they must be able to read, write, and communicate in both print and digital environments (IRA, 2009). The Common Core includes standards related to drawing information from both print and digital sources, as well as presenting information through diverse media. Therefore, when teaching students how to gain knowledge from informational texts, we should provide them with opportunities to read both print and digital texts, as well as opportunities to communicate their understanding of these texts in many ways, including orally, through writing, and through multimedia components. The purpose of this chapter is to explain how to help students express their understanding of informational texts through multiple modes, using a strategy I call Multimodal Explanatory Composition.

When engaging in Multimodal Explanatory Composition, students use multiple modes of response—such as a combination of audio, images, drawings, writing, and color—to demonstrate their understanding of a text and other related elements. Demonstrating understanding through these multiple modes is not only consistent with the CCSS but is also consistent with the way we read or gain new information in the 21st century (Leu et al., 2004). In 2003, Gunther Kress pointed out a shift in communication that is still occurring. He argued that the printed word is no longer the dominant mode of communication or text in our society and that multiple modes—including image, sound, movement, color, and text—are now used to communicate ideas. Text is no longer fixed and limited to printed words but is dynamic and consists of all of the aforementioned modes of communication. Furthermore, these modes are typically not used in isolation but are most frequently used together to create more powerful and complete messages. Because of this shift in how we both consume and produce information, it is imperative that we teach students how to both read and write multimodal texts (Hassett & Curwood, 2009). Multimodal Explanatory Composition, a strategy that should follow the reading of an informational text as a way of demonstrating understanding, provides one method for teaching students to produce multimodal texts.

How Do I Do It?

The teacher first identifies the primary instructional goal and standard related to reading informational text. This is an important step to ensure that the Multimodal Explanatory Composition that students create is closely tied to the standard being addressed. The instructional goal or standard should be revisited throughout the activity to ensure that the student work produced is closely tied to the goal.

Then, the teacher identifies the modes of composition that would likely support the goal. For example, if the primary standard being addressed is "Determine two or more main ideas of a text and explain how they are supported by key details" (RI.5.2; NGA & CCSSO, 2010), the teacher may decide that in addition to producing regular text, it will be helpful for the students to illustrate their understanding of the complex science text they read with images and to use audio recording to explain their thinking.

Next, the teacher identifies the digital tool that will best support the instructional goal and will allow for the modes of composition determined to support the instruction in the previous step.

The teacher then provides his or her regular instruction related to the reading standard and explains the activity. However, before allowing students to begin their response, the teacher should explain the type of response expected from students, describe the digital tool or tools that will be used, and provide clear expectations for the task.

At that point, students can begin composing their multimodal explanation to illustrate their understanding of the informational text by first determining their key points. Students should consider what modes of expression they could use to best explain their understanding of the informational text they have read. Although the teacher has already determined what features the students need access to (such as image and audio tools), he or she should encourage the students to consider any type of mode or feature that could support their response. For example, students may determine that in addition to using images and audio, they will draw a diagram to support their ideas or will distinguish their ideas through the use of color.

Finally, students create a plan for presenting their ideas, giving special consideration to how they will combine modes in a way that will best convey their message. After this process, students are ready to begin their composition.

To illustrate Multimodal Explanatory Composition, the remainder of this chapter provides a classroom example using a presentation app called Explain Everything. Through this demonstration I will illustrate how to simultaneously address several Common Core standards related to informational texts. Explain Everything allows the user to combine images, drawings, shapes, writing, multiple colors, and an open layout to create slides that can be enhanced with an audio recording and produced as a movie. All of the features are contained within the app so that the user does not have to exit the app to find images or access the recording feature. The example illustrates how to address the following standards in the Reading, Writing, and Speaking and Listening strands (NGA & CCSSO, 2010). I have selected fifth-grade standards. However, this strategy and use of this app could be modified to suit any grade level.

- **RI.5.2:** Determine two or more main ideas of a text and explain how they are supported by key details; summarize the text.

- **RI.5.4:** Determine the meaning of general academic and domain-specific words and phrases in a text relevant to a *grade 5 topic or subject area.*

- **RI.5.7:** Draw on information from multiple print or digital sources, demonstrating the ability to locate an answer to a question quickly or to solve a problem efficiently.

- **RI.5.9:** Integrate information from several texts on the same topic in order to write or speak about the subject knowledgeably.

- **W.5.6a:** With some guidance and support from adults, use technology, including the Internet, to produce and publish writing as well as to interact and collaborate with others.

- **SL.5.5:** Include multimedia components (e.g., graphics, sound) and visual displays in presentations when appropriate to enhance the development of main ideas or themes. (NGA & CCSSO, 2010)

Classroom Example

This activity takes place in conjunction with students reading an informational text. In this illustration, students have previously read an informational text about New York City. The students' first task is to determine the main ideas of the text and support those ideas with details from the text (RI.5.2; NGA & CCSSO, 2010). Once they've determined a main idea, they illustrate the main idea on the first slide of their Explain Everything presentation. In this example, the student determines that the main idea was that New York City is very crowded. Students can use any of the tools available to explain their thinking. The student types the main idea (figure 10.1), illustrates with a copyright-free photo obtained through Creative Commons, and then records herself further explaining her thinking.

Source: Licensed under Creative Commons Attribution 2.0. ⓘ *http://creativecommons.org/licenses/by/2.0*

Figure 10.1: Student explanation of main idea.

Next, students add details from the text that support the main idea (RI.5.2; NGA & CCSSO, 2010). In this case, the student chooses to create another slide with the details, but she could have added the details to the same slide. The student again chooses to include writing and copyright-free images on the slide, but she also provides an explanation of each image in an accompanying audio recording. (See figure 10.2.)

Source: Licensed under Creative Commons Attribution 2.0. ⓘ *http://creativecommons.org/licenses/by/2.0*

Figure 10.2: Details to accompany the main idea.

Then students demonstrate their understanding of several words and concepts from the text by grouping the words into examples and nonexamples as related to New York City (RI.5.4; NGA & CCSSO, 2010). In this example (figure 10.3), the student decides to use text to group the words and provide distinction between the concepts.

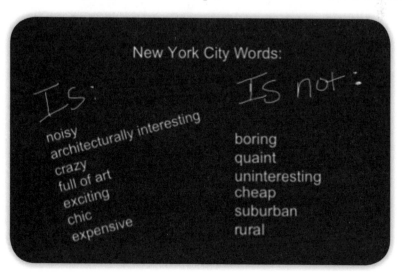

Figure 10.3: Example and non-example groupings of vocabulary related to a concept.

He then explains his thinking about the two categories in an accompanying audio recording.

Finally, students further examine the topic. By searching online for information they will need to know if they were going to visit New York City, they demonstrate their ability to draw on information from multiple digital sources to answer a question (RI.5.7; NGA & CCSSO, 2010). Students are instructed to find three pieces of information that would be important to know and are guided on possible search terms to use. Figure 10.4 illustrates information that this student finds and the websites where he finds the information. The student elaborates on each of the pieces of information in his accompanying audio recording.

Figure 10.4: Additional information about New York City found through an online search.

With the Explain Everything app, all of the slides and their accompanying audio recordings are compiled into a video as the final product. In this example, the students upload the video to a class YouTube account directly from the app to publish their work. In doing so, students demonstrate their ability to use the Internet to publish their writing (W.5.6; NGA & CCSSO, 2010). The Explain Everything app also allows videos to be saved to the camera roll or exported to Evernote, Dropbox, or Google Drive. View the final video for this example on YouTube (Hutchison, 2013).

Your Turn

By using the Multimodal Explanatory Composition strategy, teachers can provide students with an engaging way to interact with informational text, address multiple Common Core standards simultaneously, and use digital technology to support students' abilities to produce multimodal texts. When using the strategy, it is important that teachers maintain focus on their instructional goals. It can be easy for the technology to become the focus and overwhelm the instructional goal if instruction is not carefully planned. Alternatively, it may be easy for teachers to see all of the possible constraints of digital tools, causing them to avoid integrating technology into their instruction at all; but careful planning can overcome each of these possible constraints. To guide and structure your planning, you may wish to use a tool such as the Technology Integration Planning Cycle for Literacy and Language Arts to help plan your instruction and overcome possible barriers (Hutchison & Woodward, 2014). Visit http://tipcycle.wix.com/tech-integration for more information about this cycle. This cycle helps teachers select appropriate digital tools based on their instructional goals and provides a strategy for considering how to address multiple Common Core standards simultaneously with digital technology.

Finally, before using the Multimodal Explanatory Composition strategy, you should carefully consider how it fits into your larger classroom goals and your plan for introducing new digital resources and skills to your students. Considering students' previous experiences with both informational text and digital tools will help inform the instructional approach and will likely result in engaged students and greater success.

Use the Multimodal Explanatory Composition strategy to help your students see how much more powerful their ideas can be when they use multiple modes of communication. By producing such texts, students will also likely become better readers of these types of texts, which they will find often online. Although you may encounter challenges when integrating digital technology into your classroom, you are providing students with the opportunity to develop the skills necessary to be literate in the 21st century. Therefore, it is important to find ways to overcome such challenges so that your students can have the opportunities they need in order to become fully literate.

Jill Castek, PhD, is a research assistant professor at Portland State University with the Literacy, Language, and Technology Research Group. Prior to joining the faculty at Portland State, she was a post-doc with the Learning Design Group at the Lawrence Hall of Science, University of California, Berkeley, where she explored the use of digital tools to encourage science and literacy learning. Jill earned a doctorate from the University of Connecticut where she was a fellow in the New Literacies Research Lab.

Megan Goss is a senior curriculum developer with the Learning Design Group, at the Lawrence Hall of Science, University of California, Berkeley. She designs instructional sequences for the Learning Design Group's integrated science and literacy curriculum. In addition, she leads several teams of designers, participates in research endeavors through the university, and presents at conferences. A former elementary teacher, Megan provides professional development opportunities for teachers nationwide.

CHAPTER 11

Annotation Apps: Supporting Middle School Students' Interpretation of Science Texts

By Jill Castek and Megan Goss

Reading science texts can be quite difficult for adolescents. Not only is the content often unfamiliar and conceptually challenging, but the texts themselves contain features such as visual representations that are essential to gaining a rich understanding of the text. Many students aren't sufficiently prepared to interpret these features (Carnegie Council for Advancing Adolescent Literacy, 2010). Studies of adolescent readers suggest that comprehension difficulties arise because of students' lack of familiarity with the content as well as their lack of familiarity with the unique textual attributes that reading in a given discipline requires (Shanahan & Shanahan, 2008). In addition, many adolescents lack the strategies necessary for monitoring their comprehension. When they encounter difficult, disciplinary-specific texts, they aren't prepared to read them closely and often do not attend to their own understanding as they read (Lee & Spratley, 2010).

One way to address the difficulties students encounter when reading disciplinary texts, such as science texts, is to teach them strategies that enhance their comprehension along with techniques for enacting specific ways of thinking. Apps, specialized programs used on mobile devices, can allow students to annotate, or mark up, texts digitally. They also offer a highly interactive digital environment for addressing many of the concerns both researchers and teachers raise about close reading. The use of annotation apps in science, for example, has been shown to enhance students' abilities to identify the most essential information within a text (Sherer et al., 2009).

The purpose of this chapter is to introduce approaches for using digital annotation apps to support close reading of science or other disciplinary texts. Some comprehension monitoring affordances that digital annotation apps support include the ability to:

- Pose questions about the text and share those questions with other students

- Annotate visual representations and summarize their meaning

- Make connections to ideas in the text

- Summarize important ideas

The use of apps has rapidly increased in schools; their use is changing the ways students experience and think about texts. For example, collaborative-learning features in annotation tools such as Diigo are unique because they allow students to view, read, and respond to one another's annotations. Diigo's collaborative features foster an environment in which students can share their thinking to enhance content understanding (Castek, Beach, Cotanch, & Scott, 2014). Such apps also serve to promote disciplinary literacy strategies and ways of interpreting science texts that are unique to that discipline (Beach & O'Brien, 2015; Castek & Beach, 2013). For instance, the DocAS app provides students with features that allow them to add annotations to pdf texts that can be customized for font, size, and text color preferences. Use of these features supports active and engaged reading. Students can employ the Diigo and DocAS apps when reading science texts to help them target specific information and summarize key claims or findings related to their prior knowledge (Herman, Gomez, Gomez, Williams, & Perkins, 2008; Herman & Wardrip, 2012).

Students read more actively when they employ digital annotation apps to pose questions and make connections. They also gain insight by reading their classmates' annotations, which leads to enriched interpretations of ideas (Castek et al., 2014; Coiro, Castek, & Guzniczak, 2011). In a study of sixth graders, students built on each other's questions with their own digital annotations (Castek et al., 2014). Findings show that examining each other's annotations fostered collaborative inquiry. Specifically, students used annotations to pose further questions, integrate their experience and prior knowledge with ideas from the text, and react to each other's ideas. The collaboration strategies students engaged in focused their attention on key ideas within the text. Responding to peers and responding to the text itself, a form of text analysis, were the most common strategies students engaged in within their annotations.

How Do I Do It?

Our experience working in science classrooms has shown us that reading texts is often the least compelling activity a teacher can present, especially when contrasted with the excitement, discussion, and critical thinking that traditional inquiry activities can offer. However, reading can be used to promote inquiry, and the use of apps in reading instruction opens the door for the deeper thinking and social interaction associated with inquiry-based activities. Students who are introduced to annotating texts with apps learn to ask questions of the text, create connections to classroom activities, and summarize important ideas, right on the text itself. In addition, they can highlight important ideas, such as evidence and claims in a written argument, in order to share these with peers.

Apps allow students to have a conversation with the text that is made visible through the creation of annotations. Some apps, such as Diigo, even allow students to share their questions in a public forum, where the class can work together to answer the questions posed and come to a deeper level of understanding of the text through this collaborative work.

The first step in establishing reading as a form of inquiry is to provide students with a rationale that promotes this stance. One way to encourage this mindset is through teacher modeling using a think-aloud technique. When implementing this technique, read a section of text aloud and stop often to show students your annotations and explain your metacognitive processes. This modeling demonstrates that the primary role of text in science is to provide information that should be questioned, critiqued, and actively engaged with during reading. Through years of schooling, students are often trained to see text as the ultimate source of information—as something that can't and shouldn't be questioned. As a result, many students comb through text for the so-called right answers. Repositioning text as an essential part of the inquiry process encourages students to question, wonder, and engage with text in a very different way.

Using the text to ask questions is a great strategy to make reading a form of inquiry. Posing questions allows students to situate themselves in an inquiry frame of mind as they read. It also provides a way for them to monitor their own comprehension throughout the reading process. Students can use apps to create these questions, and can then share questions with other students in the classroom. This approach offers the additional benefit of everyone being engaged in discussing main ideas.

When encouraged, students we have worked with have shown an amazing ability to own the creation of meaningful annotations during reading, and thus their personal learning. The example in figure 11.1 (page 104) shows a student who has learned to use strategies such as posing questions and making connections as a method for processing her own experience as she reads. She has taken this job seriously; her thoughtful responses to the text are clearly laid out and captured with her many annotations. Additionally, because you can see her thought processes so well, the teacher has a window into her student's thinking during reading, which is simply not available with traditional reading methods. It is important to note that this student actually takes the time to read and annotate the visual representations that accompany the text, which is imperative when reading science texts.

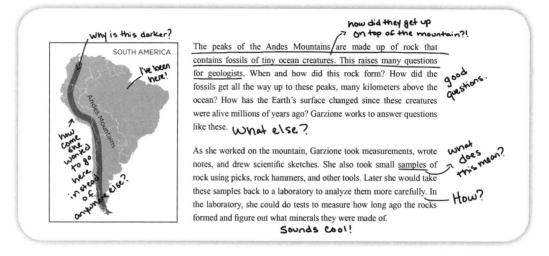

Figure 11.1: A student's annotated science article.

Figure 11.2 shows another student who employed a different set of strategies when reading; he highlighted and made annotated comments digitally using DocAS. Both hand-written and digital annotation methods work to help students engage more deeply with the texts they are reading, however, digital provides more customizable options for color, font, and text size.

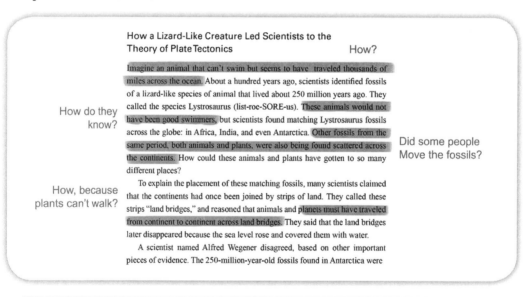

Figure 11.2: A student's digitally annotated article using DocAS.

Teachers can use annotations to examine students' thinking and monitor their misconceptions. They can also provide feedback to guide students' thinking and make note of content that may need to be revisited. Thus the process of annotation can be a useful formative assessment tool.

Classroom Example

Seventh graders in Melanie Swandby's science class took part in a unit on wind energy produced by wind turbines. To explore the pros and cons of wind turbines, students read articles written by the teacher that included a pro article arguing that wind power has a number of positive benefits and a con article arguing that wind power is not cost effective and has negative effects (Swandby, n.d.).

Students received instruction and modeling on how to use annotations to formulate interpretations from these pro and con articles. As students read the two articles, they used the DocAS app to pose questions and make connections across texts and annotations. Students then used the notebook feature within the app to synthesize thinking and formulate written arguments for or against the use of wind power (drawing evidence from the articles they read). At that point, Melanie directed students to skim back through the articles to identify key points to support the pro or con position they felt was best supported by the evidence they collected.

The class then engaged in a whole-group discussion prompted by projecting their annotation questions in response to the wind-power articles, both pro and con. Students also responded to each other's annotations before generating their final written summary in the form of an argument made up of a claim and multiple pieces of evidence. Figures 11.3 shows one student's argument, which he drafts as a result of annotating both texts.

The wind turbines should be repaired because it is a waste of the beautiful landscape

In the early 1980s residents learned of a new wind farm project to be built in their town. They knew there were risks, but believed that the reduction in their use of traditional energy sources, and the positive impact on the environment, would be more beneficial than the scenery that they called home. Ms. Stockton thought that because of the size of the farm, the benefits of the wind turbines would reach people all over California.

Unfortunately, what she and the residents of Tehachapi Pass were left with was miles of unattractive turbines and enough energy for only about 350,000 people each year. That's only about 1% of the population of California!

To look even closer at the wind farm would show that there are many turbines are unmoving and broken. Many have been that way for decades. Because there is no law that broken turbines have to be torn down or repaired, the private companies that own and operate them find it easier to simply build new ones, taking up even more land space and inconveniencing more residents.

There are plans to expand the wind farm near Bakersfield and residents of Tehachapi Pass are left to wonder if their town will be taken over by the ominous blades and resulting noise.

The wind turbines should've never been built there because it makes the beautiful landscape unattractive and it only powers 1% of the California population which is about 35,000 people

Figure 11.3: A student's draft argument that considers both sides of the issue.   Continued on next page →

The electricity we use daily in our homes comes mostly from burning coal. The energy we use for powering cars comes from burning oil. Both of these resources are limited, cause pollution, and can have a negative impact on the environment. It is important that we invest in finding alternative sources of energy because CO_2 emissions are rising and contributing to climate change. Does all the electricity I use in my house work by burning coal?

Wind power is one alternative source of energy that has many clear advantages. Wind power is virtually free. After a wind turbine is built, there is little to no cost to produce wind power. It is possible for individuals to install wind generators at home to produce electricity, and over time, this investment in clean energy would certainly pay off for individuals and for the environment. Many states currently offer money back to those who install wind generators in their homes. Once the turbines are installed and working, homeowners would not have to pay taxes for this energy source, nor would they have to pay an expensive monthly charge to a utility company. Is it possible to power everything in your house on wind energy?

That's a good idea to install wind generators in your home

How much would it cost to install wind generators in your home?

Wind power is free?!

Argument:
Everything has something bad about it, wind energy is renewable but sometimes it's a waste of energy. In my opinion it's a bad thing because if one of the wind turbines is broken there is no law for that company to fix them. Yes some people might say it's renewable and it causes no pollution, wind energy has some things that are good about it but overall it's a waste of space and money to build. Wind . . .

As students' misconceptions and struggles are revealed through their annotations, peer discussion can help them work through some of these sticking points. As discussed previously, through the use of annotation apps, students can work in partners to annotate the text and respond to their peers' questions. Engaging in a second reading of the text encourages refinement of their thinking and clarification of ideas.

A classroom blog is another way to share thinking in an immediate, public way. Students can use the discussion forum on the blog to pose their own questions or respond to questions about the text or the significant content discussed in the text. Often, with many voices weighing in, a problematic misconception can be dealt with in an engaging and time-efficient way.

In the blog entries shown in figure 11.4, students are struggling with the idea that fossil remains of similar lizards are found on two distinct, separate continents. Instead of attributing this to the fact that the continents were once connected, students insist that the lizards swam between the continents. Eventually, as the blog conversation persists, students refer back to the text to clarify their thinking. During the discussion, quotes from the text began to emerge in the blog entries as evidence supporting their claim. One student provides textual evidence that it is continents moving rather than lizards swimming that accounts for the similar fossils. This turns out to be an

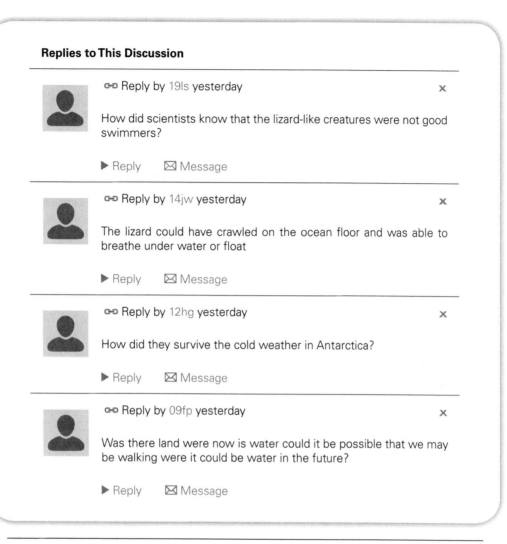

Figure 11.4: Students' blog discussion about their annotations.

impactful learning opportunity in this classroom that may never have been reached if students hadn't been offered the time and public space in which to work out their ideas.

A conversation such as this would have been hard to have without technology. The blog allows multiple voices and points of view to emerge almost simultaneously. This makes the problem feel relevant, exciting, and urgent. If students are engaged in dissecting the text in a more traditional way, such as by raising their hands and offering ideas one by one, it is likely that getting to the answer will take so long that many students will disengage before it occurs. In addition, it is unlikely that misconceptions will have been as easily raised and worked through, since students are often reluctant to share them with their peers. An anonymous blog allows students to take risks with their thinking and to feel more comfortable voicing potential solutions.

Having an archive of students' thinking helps the teacher pinpoint concepts that need work and devote an extended discussion time to them. The result is responses that are more thoughtful and are drawn from information found in the text.

Your Turn

Discussions that take place during inquiry expose students to different claims and supporting evidence. In these collaborative contexts, students can employ digital annotation tools to highlight and summarize specific sections of a text and then share ideas with their peers. Here's how to get started.

Introduce active reading guidelines to your students.

- Think carefully about what you read. Pay attention to your own understanding.

- Ask questions and make connections as you read. Remember— no question is too simple!

- Examine all diagrams, photographs, and illustrations carefully. Consider how they go with the text.

- Discuss what you read with others to build ideas together.

Sign up for a Diigo Educator account, and become familiar with the DocAS app.

- Go to the Diigo Educator Accounts site (Diigo Help, n.d.) and the DocAS iTunes preview (Nine Square, 2014) to download and explore these apps.

- Post articles, or links to online content, on your classroom website for students to access.

- Model the annotation strategy thinking aloud while actively annotating the text. This process may include questioning, clarifying, and making connections.

- Prepare a list of categories students can refer to as they read (such as questions, connections, points that need clarification) to summarize the annotation strategy.

- Invite students to annotate using the active reading guidelines previously introduced.

- Review students' annotations to assess their engagement with texts. Look for evidence of the annotations you introduced.

Providing students opportunities to engage in these processes with a range of different texts will encourage their strategic use of digital annotations for understanding science concepts.

Conclusion

Annotating during reading is a powerful way for students to monitor their own comprehension and engage with the complex content found in many science and other disciplinary texts. Employing the use of apps for annotation engages students productively with technology and provides a shared context for productive discussion. As students make annotations, they can creatively and flexibly present their thinking (using specific highlighting colors, fonts, text sizes, and annotation positioning). Annotation apps such as Diigo and DocAS provide a useful way for students to both keep a record of their thoughts and share them with others. Implementing the use of these digital tools gives students a motivating and memorable way to think and reflect as they read.

 **W. Ian O'Byrne** is an assistant professor of educational technologies at the University of New Haven. Ian is the coordinator of the Instructional Technology and Digital Media Literacy program at the University of New Haven. He is currently a member of the American Educational Research Association, the International Reading Association, Literacy Research Association, and the National Council of Teachers of English. He also serves on the Policy and Legislative Committee and is the Area 10 cochair and e-editor for the Literacy Research Association. He also serves on the Literacy, eLearning, Communication, and Culture Committee for the International Reading Association. He is the current department editor for "Multiliteracies: Production and Consumption" for the *Journal of Adult and Adolescent Literacy*. His research examines the literacy practices of individuals as they read, write, and communicate in online spaces. To learn more about Ian's work, visit http://wiobyrne.com or follow @wiobyrne on Twitter.

 **J. Gregory McVerry, PhD,** is an assistant professor of education at Southern Connecticut State University. He received a doctorate in educational psychology from the University of Connecticut as a Neag Fellow serving in the New Literacies Research Lab. Greg teaches and researches at the intersection of literacy and technology. He is the current e-editor for the Literacy Research Association and is a member of the Technology, Communication, and Literacy Committee. Greg is also a member of the media and digital literacies collaborative of the National Council of Teachers of English. In addition, he is the new literacies section editor for the *Connecticut Reading Association Journal*. He has published and presented dozens of articles and papers in national and international journals. Greg is involved in many schoolwide initiatives to improve literacy outcomes using technology.

CHAPTER 12

Online Research and Media Skills: An Instructional Model for Online Informational Texts

By W. Ian O'Byrne and J. Gregory McVerry

Given the increasing importance of online informational text in schools and society, educators must develop instructional models finely tuned to build the knowledge, skills, and dispositions students need as they read online from diverse cultures outside the classroom walls. The Internet era is totally different from the way most teachers were educated. It will define and redefine what literacy is and how individuals learn. We're all well aware that outside of school, students regularly read and write using online tools. Schools, unfortunately, sometimes view this as a distraction rather than an opportunity to educate students in a medium they are accustomed to working within. Through the use of online informational texts in teaching and learning activities, teachers can help students recognize text structures and features and use them to effectively communicate to multiple audiences in school and in personal communications. To that end, this chapter details an instructional model designed to support students as they search and sift through online informational text.

Guided by the RAND Reading Study Group's report (2002) we know that reading comprehension is an active, constructive, meaning-making process in which the reader, the text, and the activity play central roles. Reading informational texts often proves to be a bit more challenging for students (Duke & Pearson, 2002), as these texts serve the purpose of communicating information about the natural or social world (Duke & Purcell-Gates, 2003; Weaver & Kintsch, 1991). Additionally, informational texts include complex concepts, specialized vocabulary, and unfamiliar structures that significantly impact a reader's ability to locate, understand, and use the information contained therein (Cox, Shanahan, & Tinzmann, 1991; Kintsch, 1992; Weaver & Kintsch, 1991).

The intersection of these two areas proves problematic for teachers and students using online informational texts for two reasons. First, students are often allowed to collaboratively search, synthesize, and comprehend online texts with peers while working online (Coiro, 2003; Wade & Moje, 2001). Little work has been conducted in this area to identify best practices for scaffolding this metacognitive process (Coiro, 2003; Kanuka & Anderson, 1998). Second, use of online informational texts requires teachers to permit students to make liberal use of information that hasn't been vetted and may sometimes be unreliable (Metzger, 2007). Thus, there is a degree of risk and trust between the teacher and the students to stay focused and to productively accomplish the steps necessary to understand and comprehend online content.

We developed and tested the Online Research and Media Skills (ORMS) model to address these concerns and support educators and students as they authentically and effectively use online informational texts. The purpose of the ORMS model is to prepare students for a digital and global economy while also reinforcing reading, writing, speaking, listening, and viewing of content area knowledge. There are three cornerstones in the ORMS model that support lifelong reflective learning in conjunction with the authentic, productive, and ethical use of applications required in today's global economy.

1. **Online collaborative inquiry:** The collaboration and co-construction of a body of information by a group of local or global connected learners as they search, sift, and synthesize online informational texts

2. **Online reading comprehension:** The skills, strategies, practices, and dispositions students need to locate, evaluate, and synthesize information during problem-based inquiry tasks (Leu, O'Byrne, Zawilinski, McVerry, & Everett-Cacopardo, 2009)

3. **Online content construction:** The process by which students construct, redesign, or re-invent online texts by actively encoding and decoding meaning through the use of digital texts and tools (O'Byrne, 2013)

These three cornerstones identify important aspects of literacy-based instruction and connect to the Mozilla Web Literacy Map, which defines *web literacy* as the skills and competencies necessary to effectively read, write, and participate on the web (Mozilla Webmaker, n.d.). The Mozilla Web Literacy Map identifies three strands (exploring, building, and connecting) required to be web literate now and in the future (McVerry, Belshaw, & O'Byrne, in press). Online collaborative inquiry is most closely aligned with the connecting strand of the Web Literacy Map. Online reading comprehension is most closely aligned with the exploring strand of the Web Literacy Map. Online content construction is most closely aligned with the building strand of the Web Literacy Map.

To help you better understand the intricacies of the three cornerstones, we developed an open, online educational resource (see Denlinger, n.d.). Feel free to follow along with the modules of the open resource, or complete aspects of the resource for digital badges. The online resource will help you make sense of the theory and practices associated with this model.

How Do I Do It?

To begin using the ORMS model, we first need to expand the definition of *text* to include visual, digital, and other multimodal formats (Alvermann, 2002; Cazden et al., 1996; Rose & Meyer, 2002). This larger perspective of the learning experience requires a continual examination of the knowledge, skills, and dispositions that impact these formats as they work together. This broader view of text also requires us to be comfortable as we make liberal use of unvetted information encountered online. In addition, it's important to recognize the difficulty of trying to stay focused and accomplish the steps necessary to understand and comprehend online informational content.

We advise that educators using the ORMS model focus on integrating one cornerstone into a given unit or theme at a time. We believe the work identified by the cornerstones, and in relation the strands of the Web Literacy Map, are appropriate in all grade levels and all content areas. The decision to integrate the ORMS model into your classroom does not need to be a school- or districtwide mandate, although it would be easier to support individual classroom teachers if that were the case. It is advised that educators and building or district administrators conduct a crosswalk of the ORMS cornerstones and curricular maps or plans to identify opportunities to authentically embed the skills and practices into instruction. Finally, it is advised that educators and schools review the building and district acceptable use policies to ensure that they protect students and teachers as they engage in these learning activities.

Classroom Example

Here, we briefly share three examples of units that integrate each of the cornerstones of the ORMS model. These examples focus on school environments from elementary to high school. Note that the ORMS model has also been used in higher education as well. The units for secondary school populations must be designed for interdisciplinary work between the English classroom and the content area classrooms.

Online Collaborative Inquiry

Josué Calderon works with students to locate, analyze, and think critically about online and print-based informational texts in a high school U.S. history class. Specifically Josué develops a unit that focused on the freedoms identified in the Bill of Rights as students read *1984* by George Orwell. The curriculum for Josué's class relies heavily on the evaluation of primary and secondary source documents in students' research. In groups, the students read print-based sources and sources from the Internet and library databases. Within their groups, the students collaboratively edit a Wikispaces site developed for this project by the teacher. Student groups are encouraged to include images and videos on the wiki pages to support comprehension of the written text. In journal entries made in their spiral-bound notebooks, students reflected offline on how different forms of text (images, audio clips, and video) further enhanced their work process and product.

Online Reading Comprehension

Second-grade teacher Lilith Vasakolan frequently uses chapter books, picture books, and online informational texts with students to build background knowledge about science area content. In one specific unit, she wants to have students collectively read materials on animals that live in various regions of the planet. Specifically, Lilith shares with students a collection of materials about animals that live underwater. Together they read about sharks, whales, or octopuses. During the unit, Lilith also reviews grade-appropriate websites, which she then pulls up on the interactive whiteboard. Together the class works to notice and name elements of the chapter books, picture books, and webpages that helped them learn about their topic. Lilith invites students up to the interactive whiteboard to allow them to indicate what they learned and provide a think-aloud lesson for the students to learn from one another. She video records the screen and audio dialogue of students from these interactions and uses this information to assess student learning and inform future instruction.

Online Content Construction

Two middle school teachers, Christina Threet and Ezekiel Elliott, work collaboratively with each other to support students across classes on their team. This process is even more complex as they expand their view of informational text to include multimodal formats (such as images, audio, and videos). Christina helps students in her reading class develop their own blogs, allowing them to document their learning process across all of their classes. In his mathematics class, Ezekiel encourages students to post to their blogs about their work process and possible challenges they encountered as they worked with mathematical concepts. Over time, Christina and Ezekiel encourage students to include student-constructed diagrams, graphics, audio, and video in their blog posts. Ultimately, student-work process descriptions became part of the informational texts the teachers use in teaching content and concepts to future students.

Your Turn

Once you have a better understanding of the ORMS model, find a way to embed the skills and practices into your curriculum. Begin by selecting a theme or unit that you love to teach during the year. Consider natural opportunities within your curriculum to embed elements of the ORMS model into your current instructional plans. We believe it is much easier to focus on one cornerstone at a time in a lesson or unit plan than trying to cover all three.

Once you have reviewed the elements of the ORMS model, select the cornerstone best suited to enhance your specific student learning objectives. Which one makes the most sense in relation to how you want your students to work with online informational text? Do you want them to think critically? Do you want them to work collaboratively as they research and synthesize this information into one source? Do you want them to blog reflectively and develop a multimodal composition?

Embed the ORMS cornerstone into this unit or theme and develop materials. We suggest that you develop all of the graphic organizers and scaffolding materials that you would traditionally use in a lesson with students. We also urge you to develop a digital learning hub to share these materials with your students. The *digital learning hub* is loosely defined as a classroom or teacher website used to share or connect with students.

After you have developed the instructional materials and loaded them online, teach the unit. Test the unit or theme with your students to see how the inclusion of the ORMS model and associated digital texts affects teaching, learning, and your planned student learning objectives. While teaching the unit or lesson, pay attention to questions or challenges students have with the content or digital texts and tools that you use in instruction. Integrate elements of a reflective practice (Dewey, 1933; Schön, 1987) in your review, as well as reflection on instruction and materials used. One of the simplest ways to reflect on instruction and the use of the ORMS model is through the use of the three questions identified in the reflective model Gary Rolfe, Dawn Freshwater, and Melanie Jasper (2001) developed: (1) what, (2) so what, and (3) now what. After teaching your unit or lesson plan, ask yourself the following questions, or modify your own.

1. *What* was I trying to achieve?

2. *So what* could or should I do to improve on my use of these digital texts and tools?

3. *Now what* do I need to do in order to improve my teaching and inclusion of this ORMS cornerstone?

Use this feedback to revise and refine future use of the ORMS model in your classroom. Use the ORMS open, online resource (Denlinger, n.d.) to get more ideas for implementing this in the classroom, and share your own ideas with others.

Conclusion

Comprehension of informational texts is often challenging for students. In general, educators do not offer young students enough practice in learning how to read informational texts in school (Duke, 2000; Duke, Bennett-Armistead, & Roberts, 2003), despite the many calls to provide elementary students with more instructional experiences with informational texts (see Chall, Jacobs, & Baldwin, 1990; Duke, 2000; Gregg & Sekeres, 2006; Smolkin & Donovan, 2001) and the available research-based instructional strategies (see Biancarosa & Snow, 2006; Davis, Spraker, & Jushman, 2005). This lack of experience often results in students being unable to fully and deeply comprehend the informational texts that have become so prevalent on the Internet (Biancarosa & Snow, 2006; Duke, 2000, 2004; Leach, Scarborough, & Rescorla, 2003). Instructional models like the ORMS model provide opportunities for educators and students to expand their view of text, while also negotiating online and offline informational texts in the classroom.

PART V | Comprehension of Literary Texts

Narrative or literary texts are a staple of many literacy classrooms. Many educators have relied on Louise Rosenblatt's transactional theory to best understand how readers make meaning from the texts they encounter. Based on John Dewey's theory of experience as transaction, Rosenblatt (1995) proposes that readers have different ways of entering a text based on personal experiences. Instead of reacting or even interacting with texts, readers *transact* or engage in a continual to-and-fro process while experiencing the text. Rosenblatt (1995) contends that "the teacher's job is to foster fruitful interactions or, more precisely, transactions between individual readers and individual literary texts" (p. 26). As teachers guide students through the transactional process of meaning-making, it is important to consider the instructional approaches we might employ during instruction.

One way to aid students in their comprehension of literary text is through strategy instruction. According to Diane Lapp, Douglas Fisher, and Kelly Johnson (2010), in order to comprehend a story, students must be able to "infer, co-construct, and analyze what the author intended" (p. 423). True comprehension requires students to independently apply specific approaches when reading and to know when certain approaches will work best. Teachers can model specific strategies or can conference with students to better understand the challenges each student faces during reading. One-on-one conferences can serve as a way for teachers to share strategies that address an individual student's needs. It is critical that students understand the purpose of the strategy and that the teacher models how to apply and adapt the strategy to meet students' needs as readers.

Literary classrooms often rely on discussions as another way to guide students through a text; however, they are often led by teachers and dominated by a few students (Smagorinsky, 2008). While it is important for students to have opportunities to talk about their reading, there are many possibilities for organizing classroom discussions beyond the teacher-led, whole-class model. One often-made recommendation is to give students opportunities to engage in conversations with their peers. This allows more students to participate in both structured and unstructured literary discussions.

Whether through specific tools for strategy use or as a way to facilitate discussions, technology can expand opportunities and possibilities for students to transact with literature. In part V, the authors explore how readers use technology to read, study, and engage with literature. Lotta Larson and Bernadette Dwyer provide an exploration of online literature circles with online literature response options. J. Gregory McVerry and W. Ian O'Byrne explore how digital tools allow students to annotate literature and make meaning from the text. Finally Blaine E. Smith and Nicole Barrick Renner explore how students can use experiences with hypertexts to engage in literary analysis. Readers have many possibilities to access meaning in literary texts. The chapters in this part demonstrate how technology can expand those possibilities.

Lotta Larson, PhD, is an associate professor at Kansas State University in Manhattan, Kansas, where she teaches courses in literacy and technology. Her research examines the use of technology, including ebooks and digital reading devices, to support literacy learning in K–12 classrooms. Lotta is a former elementary teacher who enjoys working with teachers and students as they implement technology and explore new ways to enjoy both digital and print texts.

Bernadette Dwyer, PhD, is a lecturer in literacy studies in the Education Department of St. Patrick's College, Dublin City University, where she teaches at undergraduate and postgraduate levels. Prior to joining the faculty, she was a classroom teacher and reading specialist, with extensive experience at all elementary school levels, including high-poverty school districts. Her research focuses on the development of online reading comprehension and digital tools to support language, literacy, and learning across the content areas.

CHAPTER 13

Digging Deeper With Reader Response: Using Digital Tools to Support Comprehension of Literary Texts in Online Learning Environments

By Lotta Larson and Bernadette Dwyer

We live in an information age where interactions in digital reading and writing environments infuse our daily lives. In a traditional literacy classroom, students read print texts, respond to their readings in written response journals (whose only audience may well be the classroom teacher), and exchange ideas in traditional face-to-face literature discussions. However, in the new literacies classroom, effective learning is increasingly dependent on social and collaborative learning strategies, which can potentially reach far beyond the classroom walls as students assume diverse responsibilities as consumers and producers of information and content (Dwyer, 2010, 2013; Larson, 2009). Digital interactions can potentially redefine the nature of literacy and what constitutes being literate in an ever-changing world (Leu, Kinzer, Coiro, Castek, & Henry, 2013). In addition, digital reading environments transform the relationship between reader, text, activity, and sociocultural context (McEneaney, 2006; Snow, 2002). Digital texts provide "scaffolded digital reading environments" (Dalton & Proctor, 2008, p. 303), where the reader can access a multitude of multimodal supports (such as note-taking tools, customizable settings, and access to a digital dictionary) at the click of a button. Hence, digital texts, or ebooks, often blur the lines between reader and writer, as the reader can annotate, modify, and respond to the text in new and creative ways (Dwyer & Larson, 2014).

As new literacies constantly evolve and consequently require new skills, strategies, and dispositions, teachers are challenged to transform reading and writing instruction (IRA, 2009). As students collaborate with peers through online literature discussions in a global learning space, they may co-construct meaning and response through discussion and negotiation and from multiple and diverse perspectives while concurrently building agency and identity (Alvermann et al., 2012) in a participatory culture (Jenkins, 2006). Furthermore, classroom studies posit that the affordances ebooks provide may promote literacy skills, student motivation, and reading comprehension when implemented effectively (Hutchison, Beschorner, & Schmidt-Crawford, 2012; Larson, 2010).

How Do I Do It?

While reading ebooks, students create meaning by responding to and analyzing the literature. In most ebooks, students can personalize the reading experience by using a plethora of tools and features. For example, they can adjust the font size, activate audio narration, or look up unfamiliar words in a digital dictionary. Furthermore, in response to the literature, students can highlight passages, insert annotative comments, and add digital thinkmarks directly on the ebook page (Dwyer & Larson, 2014). Similar to adding sticky notes to a print text, the insertion of digital thinkmarks allows students to capture and archive fleeting thoughts and responses to text as they are reading (figure 13.1).

The medium's ability to allow responses *throughout* the reading experience, rather than merely at its conclusion, supports comprehension while providing an ongoing account of students' thoughts, questions, or concerns (Hancock, 2004). While annotations in a print-based text are, of course, possible, most teachers balk at the idea of students writing in the margins of traditional books. Digital thinkmarks, on the other hand, can easily be erased. Furthermore, these digital notes can be shared electronically with other readers. Because ebooks and digital reading devices (Kindles, Nooks, iPads, and so on) vary, it is important to explore the availability and suitability of specific tools and features.

Students' personal responses on these ebook platforms can then serve as springboards for literature circles, grand conversations, or collaborative response in online literature discussions (figure 13.2, page 124). The Internet offers diverse opportunities for such collaborative meaning-making and response, including asynchronous message boards, blogs, collaborative writing platforms, and multimodal posters.

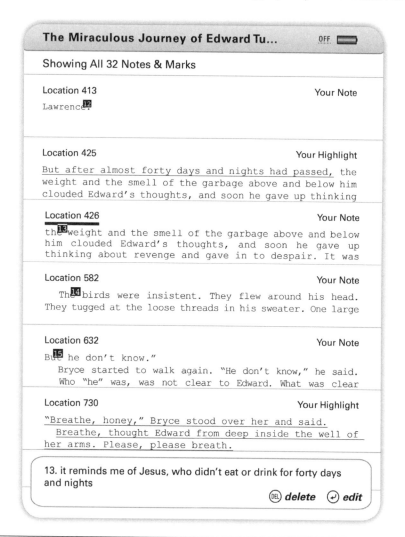

Figure 13.1: Sample digital thinkmarks.

Asynchronous Message Boards

Message boards, or discussion boards, allow students to engage in text-based conversation organized into topic-based discussion threads. Message boards are usually asynchronous, allowing students the flexibility to post comments in their own time and space. This format provides students equitable opportunities to share their previously inserted digital thinkmarks, voice opinions about the text, and engage in collaborative reader response. Students who are shy, struggling as readers, or linguistically diverse may hesitate to share ideas in a traditional, face-to-face literature circle. The asynchronous format, however, provides all students with ample thinking time before formulating and posting responses (Larson, 2009). Many school districts provide accessible message boards for classroom use. Readily available alternatives include Blackboard (www.blackboard.com) and Moodle (https://moodle.org).

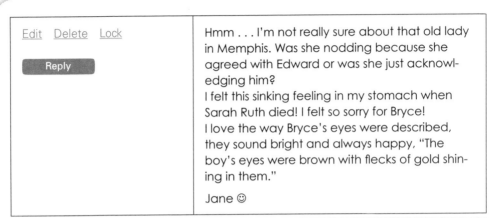

Edit Delete Lock

Reply

Hmm . . . I'm not really sure about that old lady in Memphis. Was she nodding because she agreed with Edward or was she just acknowledging him?

I felt this sinking feeling in my stomach when Sarah Ruth died! I felt so sorry for Bryce!

I love the way Bryce's eyes were described, they sound bright and always happy, "The boy's eyes were brown with flecks of gold shining in them."

Jane ☺

Hanna Kindle (hannakindle)	RE: Chapters 16–20
Posted: 27/04/12 07:50 Edit Delete Lock Reply	Hello Jane! Hanna here! I also loved the way Bryce's eyes were described. Xoxoxo ☺

Katie Kindle (katiekindle)	RE: Chapters 16–20
Posted: 27/04/12 07:50 Edit Delete Lock Reply	I felt really sad when Sarah Ruth died. I think Edward did too. I think that this was the most loving family that Edward has been in so far. I was really happy when Edward arrived in the family because I think that Sarah Ruth really needed something that cheered her up and took her mind off of how sick she was. I do think that the woman in Memphis was Pellegrina because of the description they used in the book, which was . . . "An old woman leaning on a cane stepped up close to them. She stared at Edward with deep, dark eyes." I have a really strong feeling that this was Pellegrina. The chapters were described really well, and I think that the author put loads of thought into the chapters. I love the way they described Bryce's eyes . . . "brown with flecks of gold shining in them." I don't think Edward found the dancing too enjoyable, but I think he was happy once he was with Bryce. The father was hugely irresponsible, but he could have experience. The book doesn't mention anything about the Mother, so something could have happened to her! We can't judge a book by its cover! ☺

Figure 13.2: Digital reader responses for sixth-grade students on an asynchronous message board.

Blogs

Blogs (short for *web logs*) can be personal, single-author webpages or interactive forums, allowing teachers and students to begin conversations or add to content already published on the blog (Richardson, 2010). For example, in response to literature, students may share their thoughts about the book, illustrations or pictures depicting scenes from the story, or links to related websites. Educators should carefully consider how the blog is published and shared (for instance, public, private, or password protected). Common blogs teachers and students use include Edublogs (http://edublogs.org), Kidblog (http://kidblog.org/home), and Weebly for Education (http://education.weebly.com). See figure 13.3 for an example.

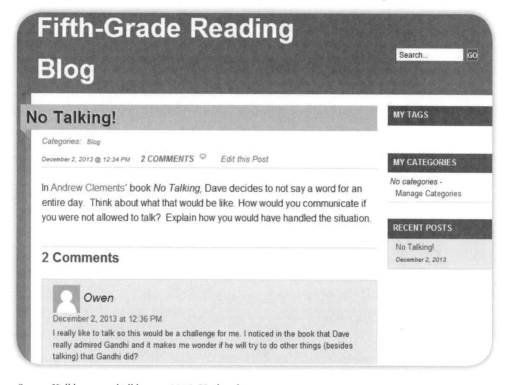

Source: Kidblog, www.kidblog.org, 2015. Used with permission.

Figure 13.3: Fifth-grade reading blog using Kidblog.

Collaborative Writing Platforms

Collaborative writing platforms are web-based word processors that allow students to weave their individual compositions into co-authored texts. In response to literature, students may bring their digital thinkmarks or excerpts from their message board conversations to collaboratively compose a book review. PrimaryPad (http://primarypad .com) is a site specifically designed for schools. (See figure 13.4, page 126.) This user-friendly tool encourages students and teachers to work together in real time.

Source: PrimaryPad, 2015. Used with permission.

Figure 13.4: Student annotation conversation.

MixedInk (www.mixedink.com) also provides ways for students to write together, edit peers' work, and merge individual thoughts and ideas into one document.

Web-Based Multimodal Posters

As an alternative to traditional literature response projects, students can create web-based multimodal posters with embedded images, audio, video, music, and links to other websites. While particular tools and features vary, many platforms offer specific information or features for educators, including ways to manage class sets of posters and opportunities for students to interact and collaborate. User-friendly options include Glogster (http://edu.glogster.com), Biteslide (www.biteslide.com), NewHive (http://newhive.com), and Smore (www.smore.com) (figure 13.5).

While all of the tools described here provide opportunities for online collaboration and communication, it is important for teachers to familiarize themselves with multiple tools before selecting one that best supports learning goals and unique needs of individual students (Harrison, Dwyer, & Castek, 2014).

Book Discussion

THE MIRACULOUS JOURNEY OF EDWARD TULANE

PLOT SUMMARY

The Miraculous Journey of Edward Tulane by Kate DiCamillo (2006) portrays the account of Edward Tulane, a haughty porcelain rabbit who loves only himself until he is separated from Abilene, the little girl who loves and adores him, and encounters new places, new adventures and many new owners until he finds the true meaning of friendship and love.

OUR THOUGHTS ABOUT THE BOOK!

- It was a wonderful book!
- The author pulled me in to the story right away.
- I like how Edward and Abilene were united in the end.
- I felt sad about the children who lost their mother and had a mean father.

WEB RESOURCES THAT RELATE TO THE BOOK

- Author website http://www.katedicamillo.com/
- Book trailer video https://www.youtube.com/watch?v=tOJYmO2vZy4
- Wikipedia about Edward Tulane
  http://en.wikipedia.org/wiki/The_Miraculous_Journey_of_Edward_Tulane

Figure 13.5: Sample Smore-like flyer.

Classroom Example

In a rural school in the Midwest, students in Betty Johnson's sixth-grade classroom read a selection of award-winning novels on Kindle ereaders. While reading, each student inserts digital thinkmarks filled with questions, ideas, and personal responses to the plot. Every few days, the students meet in classroom-based literature circles to share their digital thinkmarks, engage in critical thinking, and collaboratively respond to their readings. Betty's students also log on to an online message board to further shape and enhance their understanding as they construct meaning with other readers in an online global literature circle.

Sixth-grade students in Bridget Ryan's class in Dublin, Ireland, also engage in classroom-based literature circles and join Betty's students in the online message board conversation, as they, too, are reading the same novels on Kindles. Both Betty and Bridget carefully modeled how to spark rich conversations by constructing open-ended discussion prompts that relate to the literature. A careful review of the asynchronous message board transcripts suggests that the sixth graders make sense of the texts through a multimodal dialogue during which peer collaboration engenders both reflective and generative processes and deepens responses to texts. Students craft responses that suggest immersion in, involvement with, and interpretation of texts, while concurrently building a sense of agency, identity, community, and affinity within a participatory culture. (See Dwyer & Larson, 2014, for a more comprehensive description of the study).

Your Turn

Before engaging students in ebook reading and collaborative online literature response options, carefully consider the technology available, as well as the instructional goals and objectives. There are many different ways to read and access ebooks. A range of technology platforms, tools, and devices are available, from computer-based apps to ebook reading devices; some ebooks can be downloaded to a device while others must be read online. The specific tools and features also vary depending on the device used and the book itself. Again, you can guide your students in various forms of response by familiarizing yourself with the affordances of the ebooks and devices available to you.

You must also decide the best option for you, your students, and your learning objectives. For example, multimodal posters allow students to creatively incorporate music, art, and video in their responses; blogs offer opportunities for feedback from an extended audience; and asynchronous message boards allow students to respond at their own pace and in their own time.

In addition, determine the size and membership of each collaborative group. In this chapter, we showcased a global online literature circle in which students from the United States and Ireland came together to share their thoughts about what they were reading. While the books remained the focus, the sixth graders engaged in constructing a community culture, identity, and space and discussed their similarities and differences in terms of culture, religion, language, and school experiences.

Readily available Internet sites such as ePals (www.epals.com) or GlobalSchoolNet (www.globalschoolnet.org) offer students unlimited opportunities for collaboration as they communicate with other students from around the world, with published authors, subject-area experts, or special interest groups (such as members of community-based civics or service organizations, retired teachers associations, or candidates enrolled in university teacher education programs). Carefully explain and model expectations for collaborative response. Students may need to practice how to write effective discussion prompts (see the ReadWriteThink lesson plan *Thoughtful Threads: Sparking Rich Online Discussions* for suggestions [Larson, n.d.]), and insightful replies. Furthermore, decide on the frequency and length of posts, along with specific criteria for content, conventions, and presentation to help students understand, and achieve, high-quality work.

Conclusion

The Common Core State Standards for English language arts (NGA & CCSSO, 2010) suggest that even young students should be ready to read for deep meaning and that interpretation of literary texts involves more than an understanding of basic plot structures (Calkins, Ehrenworth, & Lehman, 2012). Combining ebook reading with individual interpretation and analysis of the text, along with collaborative and thoughtful response in online learning environments, offers promising opportunities for supporting and deepening students' individual meaning-making while appreciating and learning from multiple perspectives of peers.

J. Gregory McVerry, PhD, is an assistant professor of education at Southern Connecticut State University. He received a doctorate in educational psychology from the University of Connecticut as a Neag Fellow serving in the New Literacies Research Lab. Greg teaches and researches at the intersection of literacy and technology. He is the current e-editor for the Literacy Research Association and is a member of the Technology, Communication, and Literacy Committee. Greg is also a member of the media and digital literacies collaborative of the National Council of Teachers of English. In addition, he is the new literacies section editor for the *Connecticut Reading Association Journal*. He has published and presented dozens of articles and papers in national and international journals. Greg is involved in many schoolwide initiatives to improve literacy outcomes using technology.

W. Ian O'Byrne is an assistant professor of educational technologies at the University of New Haven. Ian is the coordinator of the Instructional Technology and Digital Media Literacy program at the University of New Haven. He is currently a member of the American Educational Research Association, the International Reading Association, Literacy Research Association, and the National Council of Teachers of English. He also serves on the Policy and Legislative Committee and is the Area 10 cochair and e-editor for the Literacy Research Association. He also serves on the Literacy, eLearning, Communication, and Culture Committee for the International Reading Association. He is the current department editor for "Multiliteracies: Production and Consumption" for the *Journal of Adult and Adolescent Literacy*. His research examines the literacy practices of individuals as they read, write, and communicate in online spaces. To learn more about Ian's work, visit http://wiobyrne.com or follow @wiobyrne on Twitter.

CHAPTER 14

Coding and Connecting Complex Literature

By J. Gregory McVerry and W. Ian O'Byrne

Fallacies spread like wildfire. These misconceptions, such as the role of literature in the Common Core State Standards, roar through popular culture, littering the landscape with charred half-truths. The CCSS, while calling for a greater balance of informational text, in no way ban or limit the role of literature in the English language arts classroom. In fact, by casting a greater role on disciplinary literacies (Shanahan & Shanahan, 2008) the CCSS may actually liberate ELA teachers from the shackles of colleagues claiming all writing and reading instruction belongs in the ELA classroom.

The CCSS call for an increase in the complexity of literary texts read in the classroom. In fact, the anchor standards focus on the ideas of using evidence to validate inferences, analyze themes and characters, compare modalities, and evaluate an author's choice of words and text structure. This approach doesn't require shifts in instruction but rather recognition of better practices. In order to comprehend complex literature, students must focus on text-based talk and text-based analysis (Fisher, Frey, & Lapp, 2012). They must also extend meaning by transforming or creating their own literary responses (Smagorinsky, 2008). It is through responses during and after reading that students will truly comprehend complex literary texts.

Current trends in education, such as close reading, place meaning within texts rather than in the connections readers make to the text. In fact, David Coleman, architect of the CCSS English language arts standards, defined *close reading* as paying attention to "what lies within the four corners of the text." This has led to a critical view of literature responses that emphasize background knowledge, personal experiences, and biases. Instead, the textbook publisher guidelines, designed for Common Core alignment, stress responses that place all meaning within the text (Pearson, 2013).

However, other researchers place meaning outside the text (Beach, 2012). Scholars may define *comprehension* as a transaction with the reader (Rosenblatt, 1985). They may place meaning within society at large (Bakhtin, 1981). In general, these perspectives view meaning-making and literacy as a socially constructed act. Literature responses, it is argued, while grounded in the text, cannot be separated from our lives.

In today's networked world of digital tools, teachers need not choose one specific philosophy (Labbo & Reinking, 1999). Instead they should remix the ideas of others. Yes, interpretations of texts are unlimited, but authors do use text structure and word choices to constrain meaning the reader will make (Kress & van Leeuwen, 2001). Paying attention to text matters. At the same time, texts exist within larger and competing social narratives (Kirkland, 2013). Thus, recognizing context also matters.

Given the influence of digital text and tools, it is hard to argue that meaning, in regard to complex literature, could be found solely in the text or even as a transaction between the reader, the text, and the activity. Instead, meaning-making is distributed across multiple networks and texts. Students, when reading complex literature, may download the book to an ereader, watch *Thug Notes* summaries on YouTube (Wisecrack, n.d.), post fan fiction to writing communities, and read literature response blogs. This multimodal metamorphosis allows teachers to use digital texts and tools to teach students how to code texts through annotation and connect with other readers through discussions.

Purposeful Analysis of Text

Text annotation is as old as text itself, yet too many students highlight or color words without analytical reasoning. We need to encourage readers to engage in purposeful coding of texts, which involves creating an evolving mark-up system to support understanding. The act of annotation through purposeful coding requires active and analytical reading. Thus, there is no text annotation without purpose. Annotating without purpose is highlighting.

Class and small-group discussions also help students recognize key ideas and details, determine craft and structure, and analyze the ideas in a text. Teachers can use digital text and tools to encourage specific talking strategies (Resnick, Salmon, Zeitz, Wathen, & Holowchak, 1993) that support comprehension of complex literature.

Another common misconception surrounding literature is that the CCSS do not call for specific literature and point to appendix B as a recommended list. Yet if teachers read the anchor standards for literature more closely, they will see specific calls to read such texts as Shakespeare and early American literature. There are several ways that technology can help teachers access such texts. For example, if educators visit Project Gutenberg (www.gutenberg.org), they will find everything from Shakespeare's plays to Mark Twain's American classics. More importantly, these tales are available as pdfs, epub files, and html files. This flexibility allows teachers to build in opportunities for both purposeful coding and discourse involving complex literature.

How Do I Do It?

Many digital texts and tools marry text-based analysis or text-based talk. Teachers can use social annotation sites to support reading of complex literature. There are options that will match the needs of any district. For a web-based platform, educators can use Lit Genius (lit.genius.com). This website allows you to annotate texts in public or privately as a class. Students can add images, videos, and texts to their annotations. They can then discuss the annotations of the texts left by peers. Students are awarded IQ points as they interact.

If your students use iPads, there is an iOS app Subtext. As a reading application, Subtext allows students to annotate and discuss texts while teachers quickly track progress. Teachers can assign books to students or to groups. Teachers can also build in questions and activities. Finally you track progress by being able to quickly sort and search student annotations and discussions.

On Chrome-based computers, or on the Chrome browser, you can use Hypothesis (https://hypothes.is). A Firefox extension is coming soon. This tool allows you to click on an extension and annotate any web-based file. Hypothesis is a non-profit organization committed to open web standards.

Classroom Example

During the winter of 2014, students from across the globe took part in the #Walkmyworld project. The ten-week "class" had students share images to document their world. They then read and responded to the poetry of Robert Hass. Finally they wrote poetry about their worlds. As part of the project, participants (which included students from kindergarten to graduate school) annotated Hass's work on Lit Genius (http://genius.com/2808124/Robert-hass-the-seventh-night). These annotations included the line-by-line analysis called for in the instructional shifts of the Common Core. Yet they also included maps and videos that could help build background knowledge. The annotations were then commented on as students discussed the text.

Your Turn

While all the options discussed share many affordances, I turn now to Subtext to illustrate both the power and ease of social annotation. When you install Subtext, you have to sign in using a Google or Edmodo account. From there add a new book, download the user guide, or create a class of students. Creating a class of students results in a private group and allows a teacher to track progress. While Subtext has the capability to organize their premium content by grade-level bands using the ATOS readability scale, we will focus on complex literature.

The first step is to save an epub file in the open domain and then read the file using Subtext. On your computer or tablet, go to Project Gutenberg. Next, search for a text that would fit the anchor standards, such as *The Adventures of Huckleberry Finn.* Then save the file to Google Drive or Dropbox. Once you are on a device that has the Subtext app available, open Google Drive or Dropbox, and choose the file to open in Subtext. Once you open a book in Subtext, it will change the pedagogical practices of reading in your classroom forever. Students can select any text, and the app will give them the option to highlight, discuss, google, or copy the text.

Highlighting allows the reader to tag a text. The reader can make strategic decisions about the key details or author's craft. For example, say a classroom was working on characterization. Students could read parts of the story that allow them to make inferences about Huck. They could then highlight the passages and add a summary of why that selection reveals elements of Huck's character. The highlight will appear in the chosen color, and a paper clip will be next to the text. Students can also choose to share and discuss their highlights. This approach transforms digital texts and tools into an efficient method for tracking growth of understanding. Imagine giving students a piece to annotate at different points in the year. If you examine the tags students assign to highlights and the section of texts they choose to annotate, you will gain insight into the skills the Common Core State Standards require.

Subtext also embeds text-based discussion directly into the books students read. The discussion features are very rich. The discussion is directly connected to an element within the text. As a reader or teacher, you can decide who can see the comment, mark the "spoiler alert" button, and decide who can reply.

Embedding assessments and text-dependent questions is a very powerful tool; disembodied literary analyses are unnecessary. No good reader says, "That was a great book, so now I should sit down and answer some multiple-choice questions." Disconnecting our assessments from the texts has always made little sense. It isn't a discipline-specific practice readers in the field use. A literary critic would not write a book review without turning the pages of the book. Being able to include our checks for understandings within the text helps model good practice.

Connecting your students is the final element that makes social annotation tools such as Subtext a powerful tool to support the reading of complex literature. Books, articles, and discussions can then be shared within and across groups of students. Teachers can assign texts to the entire class or to literature circle groups. Educators can also create groups for a specific unit. If you are doing a genre study, different groups could be made for different titles. Or perhaps your district has a common reading across grade levels. Imagine the power of a school- or districtwide discussion.

Conclusion

Teachers do not have to tremble at the thought of tackling the increased complexity in literature the Common Core State Standards require. In fact, using open educational resources and powerful apps such as Subtext, teachers can increase the efficacy and efficiency of their better pedagogical practices. We know that text-based analysis and discussions increase students' abilities to make meaning with complex literature. Utilizing digital texts and tools allows educators to bring these practices together in a way that supports learners in a digital environment.

 **Blaine E. Smith, PhD,** is an assistant professor in the Department of Teaching and Learning at the University of Miami. Her research focuses on the digital literacy practices of urban youth in and out of schools, with special attention to their multimodal composing processes, perspectives, and products. Her work also focuses on teachers' technology and literacy integration and the development of innovative multimodal methods of analysis. Blaine received her doctorate in the Language, Literacy, and Culture program from the Peabody College of Education and Human Development at Vanderbilt University. To learn more about Blaine's work, visit http://literacybeat.com or follow @blaineesmith on Twitter.

 **Nicole Barrick Renner** is a research associate at the Stanford Center for Assessment, Learning, and Equity (SCALE), where she specializes in student performance assessment in English language arts. Prior to joining SCALE, she taught high school English at East Nashville Magnet School in Tennessee. Nicole holds an MEd in learning and instruction (secondary English education) from Vanderbilt University's Peabody College of Education and Human Development. Her research interests include multimodal composition, performance assessment, and talk-based pedagogy as tools for student engagement and deeper learning. To learn more about Nicole's work, follow @RennerEnglish on Twitter.

CHAPTER 15

Linking Through Literature: Exploring Complex Texts Through Hypertext Literary Analysis

By Blaine E. Smith and Nicole Barrick Renner

Consuming and creating multimodal texts in digital environments involves new and different ways of thinking (Dalton & Proctor, 2008; Mayer, 2008). Carmen Luke (2003) explains that "hypertext environments demand horizontal or lateral cognitive mobility" across disciplines, genres, modalities, and cultural zones (p. 401). Furthermore, multimodal meaning-making requires an understanding of how modes interweave and interact to communicate a unique message (Jewitt, 2009). Even though these sophisticated orchestrations of modes typically occur in out-of-school contexts for youth (Ito et al., 2010; Smith, 2014)—ranging from original artistic creations to remixes of online content—literacy teachers can leverage the complex thinking multimodal projects demand by applying them to the comprehension and analysis of literature (Hundley & Holbrook, 2013; Jocius, 2013; Smith, 2013).

The hypertext literary analysis is designed for students to examine the multiple layers of meaning in a complex passage through a meaningful application of technology in the spirit of the Common Core State Standards. Within PowerPoint, students isolate and explicate key words and phrases by hyperlinking them to written explanations and related media. Multiple modes are also employed—including text, music, images, animation, and videos—to help students dig deep into the textual features, intertextual connections, and personal responses that produce meaning in fiction and poetry. For example, in a hypertext literary analysis of Lucille Clifton's poem "Homage to My Hips," the creator hyperlinks a PowerPoint slide that contains the original poem to other slides that include Clifton's biographical information, intertextual and pop culture connections, a YouTube video of Clifton reciting the poem, an analysis of literary devices, and a personal response. Images, color, videos, and music are also used purposefully to organize, supplement, and extend the written analysis. Visit www.literacybeat.com for an example.

This type of nonlinear and multimodal analysis requires students to develop skills central to Common Core ELA anchor standards, including reading and comprehending a complex literary text, interpreting words and phrases with connotative and figurative meanings, and examining themes, structures, and points of view (CCRA.R.1–6; NGA & CCSSO, 2010). The limited space of individual PowerPoint slides demands thoughtful and "effective selection, organization, and analysis of content" (CCRA.W.2; NGA & CCSSO, 2010), while the spatial quality of linking encourages organization based on relationships among ideas rather than the templates or formulas that we often see underlying student writing. This strategy also promotes many Common Core ELA writing goals around organization and revision, and it directly scaffolds the standards that ask students to "make strategic use of digital media and visual displays of data to express information and enhance understanding of presentations" (CCRA.SL.5; NGA & CCSSO, 2010). Importantly, the design features of this project are not "icing on the cake"; they are baked right in and are integral for the analysis. Students must think of their audience and develop an interactive digital product an outside user can navigate smoothly and, more importantly, *learn* from. These are the kinds of real-world demands that inspired the CCSS and the design of the hypertext literary analysis.

How Do I Do It?

The advantage of using a common program like PowerPoint is that it is readily accessible and relatively familiar; however, with a little instruction and exploration, students can create products that are not at all recognizable as traditional linear slideshows. With its hyperlinking feature, tools for basic image manipulation, transitions, animations, and the capacity to embed sound and video, PowerPoint allows students to generate engaging, multilayered, interactive products.

Preparing for the Hypertext Literary Analysis

A hypertext literary analysis can be as simple or as complex as you want it to be. It can also be used to explore a wide variety of text types and textual features, but the key components remain the same. The first step is to choose a complex text or passage to analyze, such as a poem or an excerpt from fiction. Whether the text is predetermined or students are given a choice in their selection, it must be a manageable length to fit onto one or two PowerPoint slides. The skill of selecting a rich excerpt for explication can be embedded into the project. Next, the teacher must identify a set of textual features to examine. These might encompass the full gamut of literary devices, or the task could focus on a carefully selected set of features such as connotation, tone, or figurative language. If studying the elements of fiction, students could link and explain clues to character development or apply reading strategies like making predictions and asking questions. Any features that a student might annotate or analyze in a text are fair game. Graphic organizers, dialectical journals, or other planning tools can be used to scaffold and organize the textual analysis before students begin composing (visit **go.solution-tree.com/technology** for instructional tools).

Creating the Hypertext Literary Analysis in PowerPoint

This strategy uses PowerPoint to create a multimodal hypertext with interconnected slides. The composing process begins by inserting the text to be analyzed on a blank PowerPoint slide, which functions as the anchor of the hypertext. Next, students create a deck of blank slides that can easily be linked from the analyzed text. Use the Insert menu and designate the desired destination of the word or sections of text to hyperlink it to other slides. Most links will lead to other slides within the document, but hyperlinks can also be used to connect to other documents or to websites. It is imperative to consider the reader's experience when creating the hypertext literary analysis, including anticipating the journey he or she will take through the slides. The hypertext should offer multiple pathways through the content and not contain any dead ends where the reader is stuck, so including navigational hyperlinks—such as *home*, *back*, and *next*—and testing out links by using the preview function in PowerPoint are key.

Once a clear structure has been established, it's time to begin incorporating multiple modes for analysis. Analysis slides will, of course, include written explanations of the textual features being explicated, but this strategy also asks students to use media to deepen and support their analysis. PowerPoint allows users to embed images, audio, and video and offers tools for editing and layering these media. Students can manipulate their chosen media to reflect themes in the text or to illustrate their personal response. Even more basic tools like background color and style, font color and style, and slide layout can be employed intentionally to support analysis or to organize information.

Classroom Example

Urban twelfth-grade students in an Advanced Placement literature and composition class created hypertext literary analyses for *The Things They Carried* (O'Brien, 1990), a work of fiction focusing on a platoon of soldiers during the Vietnam War. While creating their analyses, students participated in a scaffolded Digital Writer's Workshop (Dalton, 2012/2013; Dalton & Smith, 2012), designed with the goal of supporting students in seeing themselves as *designers* (The New London Group, 1996) and understanding how to use multiple modes for expression and communication. The workshop approach also developed a supportive class community in which students shared their work regularly and relied on one another as resources. Students worked in pairs and selected specific passages from a chapter of their choosing, which they had read closely. They then hyperlinked the passage to examine literary elements such as metaphors, irony, and theme. Students also hyperlinked intertextual connections, including other literary works, films, and popular culture references, as well as key words and phrases, questions, and personal reactions.

As a result, students created complex and thoughtful hypertext literary analyses that incorporated multiple modes and media to explore themes and personal responses to the novel. In their reflections and interviews, students often described combining complementary modes to connect to the underlying emotion or theme of their analysis (Unsworth, 2006). For example, Monica hyperlinked her analyzed passage to a PowerPoint slide that she saw connecting with a main theme: that while death, pain, and loss are universal, humans use stories to create meaning and even beauty from those experiences. Her visual collage mixed plot-specific images that represented the focal character's premature death at age nine with abstract images, including a tattered teddy bear placed on a grave and a dandelion with some seeds flying away in the breeze, which she felt represented "a loss of innocence." Reinforcing this thematic connection between loss and beauty, she also included the song "If I Die Young" by The Band Perry to "strike the heartstrings" of her audience. Through a sophisticated layering of modes, she represented plot events, tone, intertextual connections, and a prominent theme of the novel. This thoughtful mélange of image and sound supported and deepened her written analysis, which she placed on connecting slides.

Students also worked with various modes to develop a multisensory experience indicative of the novel's context or story. This effect was achieved through the incorporation of sights and sounds that transported an audience into O'Brien's narrative world. For example, Evelyn included an analysis of the phrase "just listen," which she argued was central to the theme of her chosen passage, and layered a background image of a "calm, spooky, and dark" landscape that related to what characters see in her chapter. Then, she added two songs pre-set to play simultaneously to create an audio mash-up effect that mimicked "the weird mixture of music" that characters heard. In an interview, Evelyn explained her goal for the slide:

> The text is like really really vivid. It makes you feel stuff, so I wanted the audience to feel the same thing. I chose the picture because they [patrol officers in the novel] went up to the mountains and it was spooky so it's like dark and tinted . . . there are also weird echo sounds. It's really, really spooky, so that's what I was trying to get across . . . it's authentic.

Through the purposeful use of multiple modes, Evelyn sought to create an authentic experience for her audience by recreating the diegetic senses that characters experienced.

Along with fostering an in-depth and multimodal understanding of a complex passage, the hypertext literary analysis was engaging for students and opened up space for creative freedom and personal expression. Evelyn described the assignment as "the most creative" project she had "ever done in [her] life" and confessed that working with multiple modes involved "way more brain power" than writing a traditional essay. The hypertext literary analysis allowed some students to communicate in ways not afforded with a written essay. Another student explained that integrating images and sound into his analysis allowed him to "put exactly how [he] was feeling about the passage into words." (For a more comprehensive description of the study, see Smith, 2013).

Your Turn

You can scaffold the hypertext literary analysis process in a variety of ways and to varying degrees. In the previous example, students were given compositional freedom; however, students can also be given PowerPoint templates in which to build content. While every classroom context is different, there are important considerations that apply to any classroom. Here are a few lessons learned from our experience that may ease the process of implementing the strategy.

Provide Models and Demonstrate the Process

When asking students to develop a product using unfamiliar technology, it is wise to attempt the project yourself first. PowerPoint may not seem unfamiliar, but its design and hyperlinking features are actually quite extensive and go beyond what most people use for a traditional presentation. (Visit **go.solution-tree.com /technology** for a video tutorial on hyperlinking in PowerPoint). Creating your own hypertext literary analysis has two important instructional advantages. First, it familiarizes you with the technology and allows you to discover potential stumbling blocks. Second, if you do not have previous student work to use as exemplars, it can provide a model for students, who may have difficulty conceptualizing the finished product. It often works well to leave your example incomplete so that you can actively model aspects of the process in class and incorporate student suggestions and feedback. This helps students understand not only the process but also the technical and creative considerations a designer could make (Dalton, 2012/2013).

Provide Explicit Technical Minilessons

Depending on your students' comfort level with the required technology tools for this project, it may be necessary to design and implement separate minilessons that focus solely on the technical skills needed to successfully complete the project. While it is important to allow students compositional freedom as they complete their own hypertext document, structured technical minilessons or activities can familiarize students with the tools and help you assess where further support will be required. An initial lesson should take place before students launch their own creative process, but plan to implement frequent as-needed minilessons throughout the workshop process to avoid overwhelming students and having to repeat instruction.

Leverage Students' Technical Expertise

While it is important to be deeply familiar with the technology yourself, allowing students to occasionally take the expert role is not only a lifesaver when your technical expertise reaches its limits, but it also develops a collaborative workshop environment where students can leverage their outside interests and skills in the classroom. Use surveys or other means to learn about students' interests and plan ahead for a few students to lead minilessons, or help students get comfortable standing up for impromptu sharing sessions about techniques they either already know or just discovered through experimentation.

Prepare for Roadblocks

It is extremely important to plan for technological roadblocks of all kinds. Model resourcefulness for your students by treating roadblocks as learning moments, but prepare to minimize them by considering a few logistical questions. Where will you point students to find public domain images, music clips, and sound effects? Can you provide override access for potentially blocked sites such as Google Images and YouTube? If not, can you provide a set of preapproved media resources? To avoid lost work, prearrange cloud storage or access to flash drives and require students to save frequently and in multiple locations.

Ask Students to Reflect on Their Process and Final Product

Along with providing opportunities for students to informally and formally share their work, it is essential to have them submit reflections with their final hypertext literary analysis. In these assignments, students can address specific questions aimed at uncovering their process, design decisions, and connections to the text. Not only are these reflections an important part of the learning and composing process (Graham & Perin, 2007), but they can better illuminate student thinking, purposeful rhetorical decisions, and complex use of modes. By enacting this modally rich process of analysis, composition, and reflection, students can develop not only their discrete reading skills as envisioned by the Common Core but also their identities as readers and designers who engage meaningfully with literary texts.

PART VI | Reading Across Disciplines

Disciplinary literacy refers to the application of specific literacy practices in the texts of particular fields or disciplines (Fang & Schleppegrell, 2010; Moje, 2008; Shanahan & Shanahan, 2008). According to Elizabeth Birr Moje (2008), disciplinary literacy requires the interplay of three competencies. First, students must learn the discourses and practices particular to the field. Second, students must have opportunities to enact the identity of disciplinary experts. Finally, students must acquire the knowledge necessary to engage in disciplinary learning.

Instructional approaches for disciplinary literacy assist students in gaining specialized knowledge in order to understand how to read, write, and think in subject-specific ways. Additionally, students learn the particular nuances of literacy practices associated with the discipline. This allows students to be close readers of complex content area texts as they learn the particular genres, conventions, and terminology the discipline values.

The Common Core State Standards have called for content area teachers to teach reading practices integral to their field. The CCSS in History/Social Studies, Science, and Technical Subjects are based on the idea that content area teachers will use their expertise to teach, guide, and engage students in reading, writing, speaking, and thinking relevant to their particular field (NGA & CCSSO, 2010). The Next Generation Science Standards and the College, Career, and Civic Life Framework for Social Studies State Standards echo this call.

The chapters in part VI provide specific insights into how technology can guide teachers' disciplinary literacy instruction in content area classrooms. Michael L.

Manderino, Corrine M. Wickens, and Elsa Andreasen Glover share how classroom blogs can be a powerful platform for students to engage in inquiry-based learning in content area classrooms. Zhihui Fang, Lauren Eutsler, Suzanne Coatoam Chapman, and Yang Qi explore the use of ereaders as a learning tool, through apps for annotating texts and learning academic language, in content area classrooms. Finally, Phillip Wilder and Danielle Herro explore disciplinary inquiries by investigating how teachers use digital resources to engage students in close reading of text. These chapters demonstrate that technology can offer effective ways not only to address standards and employ best practices, but can also be used to promote students' deep reading and understanding across the disciplines.

Michael L. Manderino is an assistant professor of literacy education at Northern Illinois University. His research investigates the intersection of disciplinary literacy and digital literacies at the secondary level, including how students process multimedia texts in discipline-specific contexts. He is a former high school social studies teacher of fourteen years. To learn more about Michael's work, follow @mmanderino on Twitter.

Corrine M. Wickens is an associate professor in the Department of Literacy Education at Northern Illinois University and a former secondary English language arts teacher. She teaches undergraduate and graduate courses in secondary content area literacy instruction. Her research interests examine the intersections of sexuality and schooling, adolescent literacy, and young adult literature. To learn more about Corrine's work, follow @cwickens1 on Twitter.

Elsa Andreasen Glover is a Nationally Board Certified seventh-grade English language arts and social studies teacher at Kaneland Harter Middle School in Sugar Grove, Illinois. She has taught middle school for the past sixteen years and is a technology coach. To learn more about Elsa's work, follow @elsainga on Twitter.

CHAPTER 16

Classroom Blogging to Develop Disciplinary Literacy

By Michael L. Manderino, Corrine M. Wickens, and Elsa Andreasen Glover

By focusing on the construction of content knowledge, classroom blogging affords students multiple opportunities to engage within specific disciplines through (1) inquiry, (2) collaborative dialogue, (3) active meaning-making with a range of multimodal resources, and (4) evidence-based argumentation. These key principles are informed by shifts toward calls for disciplinary literacy instruction.

Disciplinary literacy has been suggested as a more effective approach for supporting students' reading and writing of complex disciplinary texts in contrast to traditional, generic content area reading strategies (Buehl, 2011; Moje, 2008; Shanahan & Shanahan, 2012). Content literacy instruction treats reading comprehension as a generalized set of skills that does not necessarily take into account the particular literacy practices unique to each discipline (Moje, 2008; Shanahan & Shanahan, 2008, 2012). In contrast, "disciplinary literacy involves the use of reading, reasoning, investigating, speaking, and writing required to learn and form complex content knowledge appropriate to a particular discipline" (McConachie & Petrosky, 2010, p. 16). Thus, content instruction in a discipline should model and support students' use of disciplinary reading, reasoning, inquiry, speaking, and writing. This chapter discusses how to use classroom blogging as a support for disciplinary learning and literacy.

How Do I Do It?

When classroom blogs have authentic purposes and authentic audiences, they can be a powerful platform for developing writing skills within disciplines. Elsa Andreasen Glover maintains a classroom blog on Kidblog (www.kidblog.org) and publishes posts regularly for her middle school students or seventh-grade students to respond to in order to expand classroom discussion and encourage further thought. Students can respond to their teacher, blog with each other, or blog with individuals outside their own classroom if desired—as long as those individuals have been given access to the blog. Thus, the blog serves as a secure virtual community that can encourage academic discussions with multiple audiences. In regard to disciplinary literacy, blogging can also serve as a powerful tool to apprentice students' reading, writing, thinking, and talking in the disciplines.

Creation of an Inquiry Stance

First and foremost, inquiry is at the heart of disciplinary practice (Buehl, 2011; Langer, 2011; Manderino & Wickens, 2014). The quest to address and find answers to problems drives the knowledge that is produced, communicated, and critiqued in the disciplines (Shanahan, 2009). Figuring out the essential questions to ask helps provide a significant organizing framework for instruction (Wiggins & McTighe, 2005).

To effectively incorporate disciplinary literacy in the classroom, teachers need to model an inquiry-oriented stance that is reflective, thoughtful, and questioning. Why is this character acting this way? How might we corroborate this evidence? What other evidence might we use? Through a classroom blog, teachers can demonstrate an inquiry stance through the framing of the questions students will respond to in their blog.

Writing Tasks That Elicit Dialogue and Revision

Classroom blogging as a disciplinary activity expands on long-standing writing-to-learn principles, namely that the writing focuses on content, is metacognitive, and reinforces comprehension (Monte-Sano & De La Paz, 2012). Moreover, effective classroom blogs should be interactive and dialogic. Students write for an authentic audience and interact around given questions and tasks. This interaction can prompt students to write more, to engage in introductory disciplinary reasoning skills, to think more critically, and to refine their ideas through subsequent revisions.

By replying to their own posts as well as others' posts, students can see their thinking evolve. Thus, the dialogue and interaction, the nature of the prompts, and the physical layout of the blog encouraged Elsa's students to write more and to think more critically.

Evidence-Based Argumentation

To foster writing for argumentation, tasks should be framed in a way that encourages students to use text-based evidence in their responses. One strength of a blog is how teachers and students can incorporate a variety of disciplinary texts (such as primary sources, scientific diagrams, video clips, and text quotes) to encourage students to synthesize texts, refer responses to a shared text, and use specific evidence to support their claims. Given the Common Core State Standards' emphasis on reading and synthesizing across multiple texts, this takes on increased significance.

Multimodalities in Classroom Blogs

Blogs, like traditional discussion boards or even traditional print texts, can be straightforward texts—linear and one dimensional. However, a narrow use of traditional texts and writing tasks can diminish part of the power of blogs in the current digital era, which allow the teacher and students to add hyperlinks, images, and videos that supplement the learning tasks.

Images are just one example of multimodal texts than can support disciplinary writing. Other potential resources could include student-selected or student-generated images, video, and music that connect to the text, the task, and to students' own lives in important ways.

Classroom Example

Elsa Andreasen Glover has used blogging to facilitate disciplinary literacy instruction in her English language arts classes and her social studies classes. In her initial post during the unit on the labor movement, Elsa modeled inquiry stance by posing questions that did not have clear answers.

> Hello Fellow Historians:
>
> This week we've been learning about John D. Rockefeller and Andrew Carnegie and the Robber Barons. I think it's amazing that they both started life rather humbly and through their own grit and determination became two of the most wealthy men in our country. After earning all that wealth, both Carnegie and Rockefeller realized they had to pay back society—so they funded a lot of philanthropy. Although this philanthropy still impacts us today, Carnegie and Rockefeller were not always the most honest or fair businessmen. How do you view your entrepreneur? Is he a Robber Baron or a Captain of Industry? In your paragraph be sure to provide details and support to prove your opinion.

Her questions opened up spaces for students to construct their own arguments about Rockefeller and Carnegie. They also indicated that she does not have the final and single right answer, which is important for students to understand as they begin to craft their own arguments about historical events in general and subsequent historical interpretations.

While the interaction in Elsa's classes provided much of the impetus for students' revisions, Elsa also explicitly framed the revision process within the task itself. For example, later in the unit on the labor movement, Elsa noted in her introduction to the task, "We have to remember to think about unions, strikes, working conditions, and the workers' need for a paying job." However, students had trouble with some of the abstractions of the movement, so she added an addendum, in which students had to reply to their own first comment and discuss how two events or actions led to a given outcome. She then provided a sentence starter: "The Triangle Shirtwaist Factory Fire helped the labor movement get better working conditions because [enter your outcomes here]."

One student, Meg, initially posted this response:

> The labor movement did not make a big difference on workers, owners and managers. After the labor movement, there was a lot more laws for safety and working conditions. The owners/managers didn't even bother following those laws. They still locked doors, didn't pay workers enough, and had bad working conditions. Some of those working conditions were having no bathrooms, dangerous equipment, and long working hours.

In her follow-up response, she deepened her understanding:

> The Homestead Strike did not help the labor movement have higher wages because there were strikebreakers hired in substitute of the striking workers. The main outcome of that labor movement was that it made the union have a lot less power, which made people not want to be part of it anymore. The haymarket did not help the labor movement either.

Using a blog allowed Meg's thinking to evolve on the topic in ways that written papers may not.

As the semester progressed, Elsa also used the blog to investigate World War I from an American perspective. To guide student responses, Elsa also used primary source material from the Sedition Act passed by Congress as an anchor text. Her framing of the task began with the Sedition Act and was followed by a series of guiding questions, which then required students to support their answers with specific textual evidence:

> The Sedition Act says, "Whoever, when the United States is at war, shall willfully utter, print, write or publish any disloyal, profane, scurrilous, or abusive language about the form of government of the United States or

the Constitution of the United States, or the military or naval forces of the United States, or the flag of the United States, or the uniform of the Army or Navy of the United States into contempt, scorn, contumely, or disrepute, or shall willfully utter, print, write, or publish any language intended to incite, provoke, or encourage resistance to the United States . . . shall be punished by a fine of not more than $10,000 or the imprisonment for not more than twenty years, or both."

In class, we began to talk about why this law was put into place. But now's your chance to really think about it. What is the purpose of this law? Do you think that a simple "I am not sure that this war is right" statement should land someone in prison? What sorts of disloyal language should not be acceptable during wartime? Why?

Following is an excerpted example from Alan in response to the questions Elsa posed.

The Sedition Act was a violation of our freedom of speech right and nativists knew that they could use this as a weapon against immigrants. Our freedom of speech allows us to say what we want and express our feelings. By passing the Sedition Act, they take away that freedom. Immigrants were already in danger because of nativists and this law gave nativists a new weapon.

Alan demonstrated content area reasoning in his blog post by using the anchor text as well as his knowledge of the First Amendment to respond to the original teacher-initiated questions. When designing blog topics, it may be profitable to include more than one resource for students to incorporate into their response.

To achieve a multimodal approach, Elsa often incorporated images as part of the writing prompts themselves, using the power of the images to help contextualize or frame the task itself in social studies. In the unit on World War I, Elsa incorporated a political cartoon called *Chain of Friendship* to prompt students' thinking about the causes of the war and the importance of alliances at the time. The cartoon required the students to make inferences about the source and connect the text they had read with the political cartoon.

As these examples demonstrate, classroom blogging supported Elsa's students' historical inquiry with primary and secondary sources. Elsa modeled through her prompts that the study of history can be contested and requires interpretation. She also integrated primary sources like the Sedition Act and secondary sources like the political cartoon *Chain of Friendship*. The blog served as a platform to support disciplinary literacy in history by moving away from traditional textbook instruction and toward historical inquiry using historical sources to construct historical arguments.

Your Turn

When designing a curriculum that incorporates a classroom blog, make sure you intentionally design your units around identified disciplinary goals and objectives. Classroom blogging should support these goals. There are several options for free classroom blogs. Kidblog (www.kidblog.org) is easy to set up and manage. You create individual accounts for the students, approve what posts become public, and can manage the entire site from your account. Other sites like Blogger (www .blogger.com) provide a wider audience for students but offer less teacher control. As demonstrated in the previous examples, the tool should not drive the instruction but facilitate it.

Next, develop inquiry questions that create a meaningful purpose for blogging. Students tend to write more when they understand the purpose behind the task. Be sure to encourage initial interactions on the blog with "get to know you" prompts or writing tasks that begin with personal experiences. Asking questions about music or students' favorite movies is an easy introductory activity into blogging. You also want to construct blog tasks that encourage collaborative dialogue. Create opportunities for peer responses or an audience outside of your immediate classroom.

In addition, classroom blogs should engender active meaning-making with a range of multimodal resources. Develop opportunities for students to construct their own evidence-based arguments through their blogs. A student's blog can be a powerful space to interrogate new ideas, demonstrate expertise on a particular topic, or challenge existing interpretations about a topic. Your use of a classroom blog should encourage students' intellectual discourse with their peers, yourself, and others. Ultimately, classroom blogs should be generative by building on previous tasks. We encourage the integration of classroom blogging that is recurring and consistent to support students' writing as a means to learn disciplinary content over time.

Conclusion

Researchers note ways blogging can provide students with opportunities to write for expanded audiences (Colwell, 2012; Wolsey & Grisham, 2007). In Elsa's classroom, blogging also allowed her middle school students to more substantively read, write, and reason with disciplinary texts. Blogging can be an activity that facilitates active inquiry by making student thinking visible and dialogic. Thus, blogging has the potential to move students beyond simple regurgitation of content to active meaning-making and interpretation of content.

Zhihui Fang, PhD, is professor and head of Language Arts, Reading and Children's Literature (LARC) in the School of Teaching and Learning at the University of Florida. Zhihui has authored numerous publications on language and literacy education and has received funding for his research and outreach efforts from federal and state departments of education, private foundations, and professional organizations. His research since the early 2000s focuses on the language demands of disciplinary reading and writing. He is particularly interested in exploring the use of evidence-based language and literacy practices to support teaching and learning in academic disciplines. Visit http://education.ufl.edu/larc to learn more about Zhihui's work.

Lauren Eutsler is a doctoral student at the University of Florida and has been an elementary teacher for seven years teaching all subjects in grades K–6. Currently, she is teaching a variety of courses to preservice teachers. She is the technology chair for Kappa Delta Pi, an international honor society for education. Her interests and research focus on reading in the content areas with an emphasis on the use of technology to help K–12 students become successful learners.

Suzanne Coatoam Chapman is a visiting lecturer and doctoral candidate in the School of Teaching and Learning at the University of Florida. She earned her master's and specialist degrees from the University of Florida. Suzanne returned to the university with experience teaching at the elementary and middle school levels. Suzanne also worked as a reading coach for six years. Suzanne's research focus is on the development of disciplinary literacy through a focus on the cognitive, social, and semiotic practices of disciplinary experts.

Yang Qi is a doctoral candidate in the School of Teaching and Learning at the University of Florida. She received her bachelor of arts in English language and literature from Zhejiang University in China and her master of education in Teaching English to Speakers of Other Languages from the State University of New York at Buffalo. As a graduate assistant at the University of Florida, she taught English for Speakers of Other Languages methods and content area literacy courses to preservice teachers. Her research interests include scientific writing in secondary schools, how writing is taught to accommodate all students, especially English learners, and how to coach English learners to become effective writers.

CHAPTER 17

Using eReaders to Enhance Literacy Instruction in the Content Areas

By Zhihui Fang, Lauren Eutsler, Suzanne Coatoam Chapman, and Yang Qi

Reports suggest that a staggering number of students in grades 4–12 lack both motivation and proficiency to read texts across academic content areas (see Biancarosa & Snow, 2006). This lack is especially troubling given the recommendation by the National Governors Association Center for Best Practices and the Council of Chief State School Officers that students "must read widely and deeply" from "high quality, increasingly challenging literary and informational texts" to be college and career ready (NGA & CCSSO, 2010). To ameliorate this situation, literacy educators have explored new ways of promoting learning and literacy development. One productive line of inquiry is the use of new technologies—such as iPads, iPods, ereaders, laptops, desktops, websites, applications, Promethean boards, SMART Boards, and assistive technology devices—to engage and enhance student learning and literacy development in the content areas. For example, Jill Castek and Richard Beach (2013) describe how to use apps to "help students access information, interpret and share information, and create multimedia products" in science and literacy learning (p. 554). Other uses of the 21st century technologies for literacy learning have also been described (see Barone & Wright, 2008; Beach, 2012; Beach & O'Brien, 2013; Hull & Stornaiuolo, 2010; Karchmer et al., 2005; Larson, 2010; Putman & Kingsley, 2009). Taken together, this body of work suggests that the affordances of technology can be exploited in innovative ways to support students' content learning and literacy development.

In this chapter, we focus on the use of ereaders as a learning tool to motivate and engage students, support content learning, and promote literacy development across content areas. An ereader is a portable electronic device with WiFi access that allows people to read and interact with digital texts either locally on the device or over a network. With its portability, convenient storage, wireless access, multimodal features (such as video, audio, and hyperlinks), and interactive tools (such as inserting and deleting texts, highlighting and underlining passages, inserting notes and recording audio comments, and manipulating text size and screen layout), the ereader allows students to engage with text in more interactive and enjoyable ways. A variety of ereaders are available, including the Amazon Kindle, iPad, Sony Reader, and Barnes & Noble Nook, as well as other lesser-known devices such as the Cybook, Kobo Glo, iRex iLiad, and ECTACO jetBook.

Research involving ereaders, albeit still in its infancy, has shown promising results, suggesting that the digital tool can be an effective means to foster students' literacy development. For example, Amy Hutchison, Beth Beschorner, and Denise Schmidt-Crawford (2012) find that using iPads in a fourth-grade classroom helps the teacher not only teach print-based basic literacy skills (such as sequencing, cause and effect, retelling, and visualization) but also introduces new literacy skills associated with the 21st century's technologies (such as navigating the different features of a digital text, recognizing how the size and placement of the boxes on the screen help convey meaning, and communicating digitally with other readers). Lane Clarke and Kevin Besnoy (2010) investigate the use of a digital device with access to electronic texts in two eighth-grade social studies classrooms, reporting that the tool enables students to interact with text in more engaging and enjoyable ways than does the textbook and helps them with such reading skills as "chunking the text, focusing on the text, and pacing their reading" (p. 51). Similarly, Twyla Miranda, Dara Williams-Rossi, Kary Johnson, and Nancy McKenzie (2011) report that reluctant middle school readers who read high-interest chapter books and stories on the Amazon Kindle for fifteen to twenty-five minutes during their remedial reading class period express high levels of satisfaction with their ereaders, are motivated to read, and demonstrate engagement with text reading.

As one of the most innovative media for delivering text, ereaders are gaining popularity in K–12 education. With the advent of new devices, such as tablets and "ultrabook" notebook computers, ereaders are increasingly used to supplement or even supplant traditional print-based textbooks in school (Beach & O'Brien, 2012). For example, Florida school districts are required to "spend 50% of their annual instructional materials budget to purchase digital content" in the 2015–2016 school year (Florida State Board of Education, 2012, p. 12). Given the rising popularity of ereaders as a learning tool in school, it is important that teachers learn how to effectively integrate the tool into their daily classroom instruction.

How Do I Do It?

Teachers who are new to the ereader can observe the following steps to ensure its effective implementation in classroom instruction. Because there are multiple makes and models of the ereader, the first step is to decide which is most appropriate for instructional needs. Typically, the educational resource application or interface will determine which device should be used, such as the iPad or other ereaders with Internet capabilities. A needs analysis discussion with a member of the manufacturer's sales team can accomplish this. Sometimes, a bulk discount can be negotiated if the entire school is involved. Once the ereaders arrive, teachers should become familiar with the applications available and the benefits of the WiFi network. They should also learn how to use the device to help build students' content knowledge, increase motivation, access a variety of resources, and engage in deep reading of texts across content areas.

One type of app that is of particular value to content area reading instruction is the pdf annotator. The app allows students to take notes, highlight, and reference any reading converted into a pdf document. It also has a designated tab for document notes, which allows for quick review or summarization of learning. The app lets teachers view and assess students' reading responses; it also lets students revisit what they have read and annotated in preparation for class discussion. Aside from reading text on a pdf, students can also conduct web searches to locate and read or view additional resources. In addition, teachers can provide guiding questions to help students think critically about their readings and searches and become strategic when citing evidence from the readings to support their interpretation or argument during subsequent group discussions or writing. Teachers can also facilitate group discussion using jigsaw (Aronson, Blaney, Stephan, Sikes, & Snapp, 1978), reciprocal teaching (Palincsar & Brown, 1986), or other activities (see, for example, Fang, 2013/2014).

Classroom Example

Tom Whitaker, an eighth-grade history teacher, uses the ereader for an introductory unit on the Holocaust. The students in Tom's class vary in their reading proficiency and background knowledge on the topic. Tom knows introducing texts that are more accessible to them in the beginning of the unit can increase student motivation and knowledge. These simpler texts provide students with the foundational understanding they will later need to create connections and learn new information from richer, more complex texts.

History includes a variety of perspectives and experiences because "no single story can capture all that is true about a historical event" (Wineburg, Martin, & Monte-Sano, 2011, p. 89). Cognizant of this, Tom selects texts from two different sources in this introductory lesson. The students use iPads to open an app called StoryPod JHC (Jewish Holocaust Centre, 2013). This interactive app provides students with an opportunity to hear from ten Holocaust survivors. As students interact with the app, they can see pictures, writings, and video interviews with the survivors. Clicking on picture frames, pamphlets, and similar items found in the story of each survivor gives students the opportunity to develop rich background knowledge about the events of the Holocaust from those who lived it. This exploratory activity also spurs students' interest, motivating them to engage with the remaining content of the unit.

On the following day, Tom presents students with more voices from the Holocaust. Students use their iPads to visit the interactive website Coming of Age Now (www.comingofagenow.org). This website provides students with firsthand testimonials of thirteen survivors of the Holocaust. Each of the survivors' experiences is chronicled through a brief five-chapter text. Interspersed in the chapters are video testimonials from the survivor, links to definitions of technical terms, and links to related artifacts referred to in the chapters.

Tom introduces students to the texts in the website through the use of the Jigsaw strategy. The students are each assigned a survivor to become an expert on. Those assigned to the same survivor form expert groups where they pore over the information Tom has provided. Using the ereader, students read through their assigned chapters, view the testimonials, review new terminology, and identify relevant artifacts. During this time, students also take notes on the important elements of the text. Once this activity is complete, students return to their expert groups and report their findings to students who were assigned other survivors. After sharing, Tom engages the whole class in a discussion of the similarities among the survivors' stories and the feelings students experienced as they read through the documents.

Through class discussion, the students have gained a basic understanding of some of the events and stories of the Holocaust. Tom decides that the students are now ready to tackle more challenging texts. So, on the following day, he presents students with excerpts from Michael Berenbaum's (2005) *The World Must Know*. This book provides the reader with the history of the Holocaust as detailed through the United States Holocaust Memorial Museum. Tom has already downloaded the excerpts in a pdf format (available at www.2shared.com) on all of the students' ereaders. He knows that this complex text contains many language features—such as generic nouns, technical vocabulary, long noun phrases, nominalizations, metaphorical realizations of causality, conflation of time and cause, and sandwich texture (Fang, 2012)—that may prove challenging for his students. He encourages students to search for meanings of unfamiliar words using the built-in dictionary on the ereader. He also models how to paraphrase the dense and abstract language into wording that is more familiar (for more on this, see Fang, 2008). Once he feels the students are comfortable with paraphrasing, he asks them to work in groups to paraphrase and summarize sections of the text as they read to demonstrate their own understanding.

Once in the document, students can click on the annotate function to include their own paraphrasing. They can also use this function to record questions they have about the text or to highlight unfamiliar vocabulary. (See figure 17.1.) As Tom assists and monitors the groups, he is able to quickly review what students have annotated on their ereaders. This quick and informal assessment provides Tom with the information he needs to determine if students are successfully interpreting the meaning of the text and what additional help they may need. It is also possible for the students to save their work for Tom to revisit at another time.

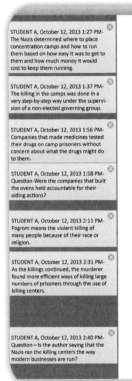

STUDENT A, October 12, 2013 1:27 PM-
The Nazis determined where to place concentration camps and how to run them based on how easy it was to get to them and how much money it would cost to keep them running.

STUDENT A, October 12, 2013 1:37 PM-
The killing in the camps was done in a very step-by-step way under the supervision of a non-elected governing group.

STUDENT A, October 12, 2013 1:56 PM-
Companies that made medicines tested their drugs on camp prisoners without concern about what the drugs might do to them.

STUDENT A, October 12, 2013 1:58 PM-
Question-Were the companies that built the ovens held accountable for their aiding actions?

STUDENT A, October 12, 2013 2:11 PM-
Pogrom means the violent killing of many people because of their race or religion.

STUDENT A, October 12, 2013 2:31 PM-
As the killings continued, the murderer found more efficient ways of killing large numbers of prisoners through the use of killing centers.

STUDENT A, October 12, 2013 2:40 PM-
Question—Is the author saying that the Nazis ran the killing centers the way modern businesses are run?

The location and operation of the camps were based on calculations of accessibility and cost-effectiven[]the hallmarks of modern business and administrative practice. The killing was done coolly and systematically under the supervision of bureaucr[]German corporations profited handsomely from the industry of death. Pharmaceutical firms tested drugs on camp inmates without any regard for toxic side effec[]ompanies bid for contracts to build ovens and supply the gas used for exterminatio[] German engineers working for Topf and Songs supplied one camp alone with forty-six ovens capable of burning 500 bodies an hour.

From the crude violence of the November pogro[]1938, the murder process escalated to ever more sophisticated levels of bureaucratic manageme[]Murder by mass shooting carried out by the mobile killing units, which was seen as having a dangerously unsettling effect on the penetrators, gave way to killing centers where a small staff could efficiently murder thousands of people daily without coming directly in contact with the victims. The kind of ingenuity and control of inventory and cost that is prized in modern industrial practice wa[]tionally brought to bear on the process of deconstruction. (Berenbaum, 2005, pp. 103–104)

Source: Berenbaum, 2005, pp. 103–104.

Figure 17.1: Sample student annotations.

Once students have completed reading with annotation, Tom has them participate in reciprocal teaching with a conceptually rich and challenging section of the text. This activity provides students the opportunity to continue to monitor their understanding of the document through structured discussion. Students are assigned different roles, such as asking questions, clarifying understanding, summarizing information, or making predictions. As students act out their roles, they have the opportunity to verbalize their paraphrasing and find answers to previously unanswered questions in the readings.

To wrap up the unit, Tom has each student write an essay explaining why it is important to study and learn from the Holocaust and what he or she can do to combat prejudice, discrimination, and violence in current times. The essay is evaluated on the accuracy of its content; the degree to which interpretation and argument are supported with evidence from multiple primary and secondary sources; evidence of contextualizing, questioning, and corroborating and synthesizing sources; and use of language to facilitate presentation of information, development of argument, infusion of perspective, and structuring of text. Students are encouraged to use other apps—such as Popplet, iBrainstorm, MindMeister, or SimpleMind—to help them plan their essay. Finally, students present their essays in class using PowerPoint or Prezi.

Your Turn

Although the classroom example provides an explanation of how the ereader can improve literacy instruction in a history classroom, it is important to note that you can utilize the ereader in any other content area in much the same way. The first step is to familiarize yourself with the many functions of and available apps for the ereader. With WiFi capabilities, the ereader provides teachers a multitude of resources for building students' motivation, content knowledge, and literacy skills. However, not every website or app will be appropriate for the objectives of each lesson. As you search for apps or websites on your instructional topic, it is important that you take the time to preview and interact with any of the resources you plan to share with your students. For example, if you are a high school English language arts teacher searching for an app on F. Scott Fitzgerald's *The Great Gatsby*, you may come across free apps for study guides, trivia challenges, and interactive games. However, only a few of these apps actually provide background and educational content regarding the literature. You should take the time to interact with a number of different apps or websites on your topic before selecting one that best meets your needs.

Once you've chosen an app or website to aid background-knowledge development, you should demonstrate for students how to effectively use the technology to gather information. This scaffolding will save time and alleviate student confusion. Similarly, when introducing the ereader as a tool for annotation, you should explicitly teach students how to ask questions or paraphrase prior to introducing the technology. Once students are comfortable questioning and paraphrasing text, you can guide them on how to paraphrase with the annotation function of the ereader.

Conclusion

Content area learning inevitably involves text reading. New technologies such as ereaders enable students to access a wide range of relevant texts, make text reading a more interactive and enjoyable experience, promote the development of both traditional and new literacy skills, and support content learning in transformative ways. Schools that implemented ereaders report marked increase in their students' learning gains. For example, Clearwater High School in Florida adopted ereaders in 2010 and saw its students' Florida Comprehensive Assessment Test reading scores "jumped 18 percent the first year of Kindle use and 14 percent the second year" (Paquette, 2013). To ensure smooth integration of new technologies such as ereaders into the school curriculum, efforts must be taken to address pressing issues of teacher beliefs and knowledge (fear of new technologies or limited technological and pedagogical knowledge), resources (lack of planning time and technical support), and assessment (testing traditional literacy skills and content knowledge without attention to new literacies) (Hew & Brush, 2007). Only then can the potentials of new technologies for supporting content learning and promoting literacy development be fully realized.

 **Phillip Wilder** is an assistant professor of literacy in the Eugene T. Moore School of Education at Clemson University, where his primary research investigates how instructional coaching supports both responsive teaching practices and the disciplinary literacies of adolescents. To learn more about Phillip's work, follow @phillipmwilder on Twitter.

 **Danielle Herro** is an assistant professor of digital media and learning in the Eugene T. Moore School of Education at Clemson University. She teaches courses centered on integrating social media, games, and emerging technologies in classrooms. Dani is a recipient of the Edmund W. Gordon MacArthur Foundation/ETS Fellowship for 21st Century Learning and Assessment. Her research interests include examining game play and game design, app development, and digital media in teaching and learning environments. To learn more about Dani's work, follow @daniherro on Twitter.

CHAPTER 18

Supporting Inquiry With Digital Texts in School Disciplines

By Phillip Wilder and Danielle Herro

Marcus, Sarah, and Thomas sit together in Jason Pankins's eighth-grade U.S. history class viewing a four-minute YouTube video titled "Historic Pullman Community" (City of Chicago TV, 2011) on one of the class iPads. While Marcus and Sarah hear about the rise of George Pullman's railroad car business and his vision of a community for his workers, Thomas jots down group ideas and rearranges text on their three-slide PowerPoint summary. In this class, interpreting and defending history has become the norm, and on this day, these three students—asked to describe the 1880s Pullman Factory Community to their peers—begin their historical inquiry by building an initial understanding of the origins of Pullman's empire. In subsequent days, the students will analyze online primary and secondary sources to explore an inquiry question debated among historians: should George Pullman be remembered as a friend or foe of Chicago workers? With the National Governors Association Center for Best Practices and the Council of Chief State School Officers promoting close reading of rigorous texts in elementary through secondary classrooms, building inquiry around texts becomes just as important as the close reading of disciplinary texts (NGA & CCSSO, 2010). In this chapter, we explore building inquiry in adolescent classrooms. The approaches advocated in this chapter, however, can be adapted for nearly all grade levels and classrooms.

New forms of communication suggest that technological progress and globalization will fashion distinctly different literacies—predominately accessed on mobile devices (Madden, Lenhart, Duggan, Cortesi, & Gasser, 2013; Rideout, 2011). Adolescent ownership of tablets mirrors the same rate as adults in the United States, with one in four teens owning a tablet (Madden et al., 2013). In addition, mobile-device access and use among adolescents has steadily increased at a rate greater than 50 percent per year since 2011 (Madden et al., 2013). At a slower yet notable pace, K–12 schools are following suit, even though Project Tomorrow (2011) notes a "huge increase in interest across the education sector in mobile learning" (p. 4), citing educators' beliefs in the potential for increased and untethered access to research, writing, analysis, and resource sharing. Yet, while many teachers now consider combining print-based and digital-literacy practices a priority, they continue to struggle—naming inadequate technical, logistical, and professional development support as obstacles to full integration (Hutchison & Reinking, 2011).

At the same time, it is widely recognized among educational researchers and practitioners that competence with texts involves much more than print-based interaction and comprehension. Colin Lankshear and Michele Knobel (2011) write at length about thinking of literacy as a social phenomenon shaped by electronic or digital means, including combinations of text, audio, video, and animation. Gunther Kress (2003) suggests the dominance of images and the computer or tablet screen over traditional print-based writing and reading challenges traditional classroom literacy instruction. According to Kress, "books simply cannot provide the same level of multimodal production and interpretation of sound, image, and print through music, graphics and interactive text, as technology" (as cited in Fahser-Herro & Steinkuehler, 2009/2010, p. 56). Digital resources provide a means of building background knowledge, creating inquiry with disciplinary topics, and scaffolding student thinking with digital texts. This chapter presents a strategy for using digital resources to build a rich context for the close reading of disciplinary texts.

How Do I Do It?

We often neglect to do our own up-front thinking about texts prior to designing literacy instruction for our adolescent readers. Up-front thinking involves teacher analysis of digital resources to identify how the resources support inquiry within disciplines, the ways discipline experts might use and critique the resource, and the possible difficulties our students could encounter.

Begin by identifying questions valued in your discipline as you use and evaluate possible digital tools to support student inquiry. In U.S. history, Marcus, Sarah, and Thomas analyzed primary sources in order to decide how the Chicago Historical Society should display and present Chicago railroad tycoon George Pullman's relationship to his workers. In science, they could be asked to examine existing claims about the quality of water in schools, collect evidence through their own water tests, and then use collaborative writing to reason and justify recommendations to school officials. In language arts, they could be asked to closely observe, interpret, critique, and then possibly mirror how writer Jacqueline Woodson develops tone when contributing to an online journal for young authors.

As you evaluate digital resources such as apps, clips on YouTube, and web tools, consider how adolescents use these resources and interact with the unique demands of digital resources (McEneaney, 2006; Reinking, 1992). For instance, you might ask: "How might viewing a specific YouTube clip on George Pullman be challenging for my students?" "What does making sense of a selected ebook passage on dimensions of water quality require of my students?" "What could be challenging for my students when reading one of Jacqueline Woodson's blog entries?" Adolescents need an authentic reason to read. Assignments should be rooted in your discipline's goals for reading, and the unique challenges of reading digital texts should shape them.

Next, with a question and digital resources in mind, explore the topic with students. Students need time to build prior knowledge about the inquiry topic, just as Marcus, Sarah, and Thomas need time to build prior knowledge about George Pullman prior to analyzing his role in causing the Pullman Strike. For example, a webquest with preselected digital resources on the rise of organized labor in the United States, an app demonstrating the water cycle, or a National Public Radio interview with Jacqueline Woodson about her writing craft can provide students with the initial forays into the chosen topic. Assigning groups of students to research an initial aspect of the topic, synthesize their current understanding, and share out information with other peer groups can prepare students with the foundational knowledge needed to closely read subsequent digital texts.

Finally, scaffold close readings of digital texts to produce discipline-specific arguments. Once you've identified potential digital texts for extended analysis, share a performance task that provides students an opportunity to demonstrate, display, or discuss their answer to the inquiry. Model expert thinking with digital texts, and provide students with digital spaces (such as blogs, graphic organizers, or Google Drive) to record evidence. Differentiate student reading of digital resources by altering the content (genre, complexity), process (individual, paired, or group reading), and product (essay, report, presentation) of the reading experience.

Classroom Example

Marcus, Sarah, and Thomas reconvene in Jason's U.S. history class. Each student receives an email reminding them to check the calendar app (iCal) for presentation dates for the inquiry project on organized labor. A document of unit information and instructions is attached to forward to their parents. Their group will design a presentation display on George Pullman for the Chicago Historical Society and then defend their rationale while explaining how the reading of digital resources impacted the argument.

Jason begins class by showing a short YouTube video in which historians debate the priorities of George Pullman and whether Pullman should be remembered as a greedy business tycoon insensitive to the economic needs of his workers or a railroad pioneer who rose to success due to personal ambition. When the video concludes, each student posts an initial response to the inquiry question on the class blog. Minutes later, Jason instructs students to find their Dropbox folder and open the first of four primary source documents related to George Pullman and his workers' 1894 strike. During previous units of study, Jason has introduced students to four types of historical reading skills: (1) sourcing, (2) corroborating, (3) contextualizing, and (4) close reading (Wineburg, 2001). According to Samuel Wineburg (2001), historians "source" by "reading the source of the document before reading the actual text" (p. 510). To model sourcing, Jason stands by his SMART Board and displays "Typescript of Interview With George Pullman From the *New York Press*, December 1, 1897" and discusses how the identity and motivation of the *New York Press* journalist might have influenced what students could find in this particular primary source document. Over time, Jason intends to improve how his students independently "sourced" historical texts, so his modeling reflects his awareness of a gap in their reading habits as novice historians in his class.

Throughout the remainder of class, Marcus, Sarah, and Thomas use the highlight, sticky note, text bookmark, and dictionary functions in the pdf as they read, organize, make choices, pose questions, and discuss each of the primary sources. When his peers cannot remember the chronological order of events, Marcus opens up the timeline on the class blog to figure out whether another source, an article titled "George Pullman's Letter to President Grover Cleveland," was written before or after the Pullman Strike. They record evidence from each source under "Friend" or "Foe" in the graphic organizer provided in the class Dropbox folder.

Jason requires students to source, corroborate, contextualize, and closely read as expert historians. Using multiple digital resources to construct and defend historical narratives concerning George Pullman, students closely read with a clear inquiry purpose and an authentic task in mind. The inquiry culminates with peer reviews of the Chicago Historical Society presentation display proposals and a whole-class debriefing of the credibility of individual sources and how the digital nature of the sources influenced students.

Your Turn

Content area knowledge and inquiry must be prioritized when digital resources are used as a medium for adolescent thinking. Mobile devices can support inquiry and provide the collaborative scaffolds necessary for critiquing and challenging content area texts. In order to design this learning, consider each stage of this strategy and plan with the end in mind.

When conducting initial thinking with digital resources, identify inquiry questions valued in the discipline. How can you connect inquiry questions to content area standards? Are questions framed in interesting ways for adolescents? Are the questions allowing multiple points of view and varied directions for adolescent arguments? What are the literacy demands of selected digital resources? What is the quality of the content? Which skills are demanded of users? Will individual students, groups of students, or the entire class use digital resources?

After students are introduced to the inquiry and begin exploring the topic, provide students with guiding questions to consider. What is interesting about this topic? What is new information to you? What does not make sense? Building cognitive dissonance and building prior knowledge of the topic should be the foremost goals of this stage. After students have explored the topic, provide students with a performance task. Carefully design this performance task based on the needs of your specific students. What will students produce in order to show their understanding of the topic and their proposed solution or argument? Will the performance task assess both conceptual knowledge and literacy within the discipline? How can you demonstrate or share a sample performance task while naming the criteria needed to evaluate the quality of the performance task?

Finally, when scaffolding the close reading of digital texts, differentiate the content and process of disciplinary reading. How can the interests, abilities, and knowledge of students influence which digital resources they use to build their argument? What options can you provide? What graphic organizers or digital tools could help students record information and collect evidence?

Before modeling content area thinking with digital resources, consider student needs. What additional digital sources do students need to read? How could student discussion or writing be used to help students think? What digital tools could help students collect information and organize knowledge? Also consider how to display or share student work. How could digital media support student presentation of knowledge with and to peers? In what ways could student knowledge be produced, published, or made public to groups in the community? Finally, how could you include students in the assessment of their own disciplinary knowledge?

Conclusion

Like Marcus, Sarah, and Thomas, students need classrooms where close reading is more than a cold-reading Common Core State Standards activity to be implemented. Instead, if students are to develop the habits of thinking with rigorous texts—as espoused in the CCSS—teachers must design opportunities for students to use disciplinary texts as windows into disciplinary inquiry. Identify inquiry questions valued in a discipline while evaluating the thinking demands of various digital resources. Explore multiple perspectives prior to thinking in depth with select digital resources. Additionally, scaffolding the content, process, and product helps students learn the depths of content area, rigorous texts.

PART VII | Motivation for Reading

Motivation and engagement are critical for developing students as lifelong readers. *Motivation* refers to the "desire, reason, or predisposition to become involved in a task or activity, [and] *engagement* refers to the degree to which a student processes text deeply through the use of active strategies and thought processes and prior knowledge" (Kamil et al., 2008, p. 26). Motivation and engagement are incredibly important for reading instruction and students' literacy achievement (Gambrell, 2011a; Kamil et al., 2008). If students are motivated to read, they will read more, and more reading leads to higher levels of reading achievement. However, research notes that students' motivation to read declines as they move from elementary school through middle and high school (Kamil et al., 2008). As researchers and educators work to better understand this phenomenon, they have identified specific factors associated with motivation and engagement.

First, educators can connect reading to students' life experiences to spark students' intellectual curiosity. Gay Ivey and Peter Johnston (2011) note that when students are reading texts relevant to their lives, they have a personal connection with reading. Second, students need opportunities to discuss their ideas with peers (Ivey & Johnston, 2011; Lapp & Fisher, 2009). Diane Lapp and Douglas Fisher (2009) note that when students engage in conversations about their reading, they are not only interacting with their peers, but they are also transacting with the text on a deeper level. Finally, students need to have choice in the materials they read (Ivey & Broaddus, 2001). The ability to self-select what one reads has been repeatedly linked to higher motivation as students are more likely to become personally invested in their reading (Ivey & Broaddus, 2001).

The chapters in part VII explore how technology used during reading instruction can motivate and engage students. Kristen Srsen and William Kist share how students' reading motivation increases when engaged in filmmaking, creating videos of canonical works of literature. Elizabeth A. Edmondson's chapter explores how using technology, such as ereaders, bridges students' out-of-school reading experiences to their school reading experiences. Similarly, Salika A. Lawrence, Carrie E. Hong, Marie Donnantuono, and Geraldine Mongillo share how the iPad apps VocabularySpellingCity and One Minute Reader can engage and motivate young readers.

 **Kristen Srsen** teaches English and theater and directs theater productions at Bay High School in Ohio. She received her master's from New York University and is currently working on her PhD in curriculum and instruction at Kent State University.

 **William Kist** teaches undergraduate and graduate courses in adolescent literacy at Kent State University. He has three books and over fifty articles and book chapters to his credit. To learn more about Bill's work, visit www.williamkist.com or follow @williamkist on Twitter.

CHAPTER 19

"I Wanted to Film, So I Read the Book": Filmmaking in the English Classroom

By Kristen Srsen and William Kist

"Ms. Srsen," the student said, "I want you to know that this is the first book I've read in high school. I wanted to make a film, so I read the whole book last night."

After years of struggling to motivate students to read classic novels in English classes, Kris decided to try a new teaching strategy that involved film. At the high school level, reading is taught primarily within the English classroom. In the tradition of English education, one of the main reading skills taught is the ability to read canonical texts as a literary critic would. It is a common experience for high school English teachers to have difficulty motivating students to read the canonical works and to have them respond to these reading experiences with meaningful literary criticism. For the past several years, Kris had noticed that, when her students watched films about classic novels, they quickly, easily, and willingly would expand on the story elements—characterization, plot points, inferences, and even mood and tone; however, when she would ask for the same information about the novel during in-class discussions, they did not express the same interest. Thus, since their motivation to read and discuss the novel seemed lackluster, and their interest in "reading" the film was so captivating, she decided to have her students create their own films of the canonical texts she was reading.

Film and its digital incarnation (video) have been used as motivational tools in classrooms for decades, with film exhibition often used as a reward for good behavior or achievement (Kist, 2008). Guides have been written for how to integrate the viewing of films (film literacy) into the English language arts classroom in more meaningful ways (Costanzo, 2004; Golden, 2001). However, the onset of consumer video cameras and videocassette recorders in the 1980s and 1990s, followed by the development of desktop video applications and streaming video capabilities in the 2000s, has made the process of filmmaking more accessible for teachers and students alike. Researchers have described the motivational power and transformative nature of the learning experience when students are given the opportunity to make their own films or, in this case, videos (Bucolo, 2011; Gainer, 2008; Hall & Stahl, 2012; Spires, Hervey, Morris, & Stelpflug, 2012). Ultimately, Kris was motivated to attempt this film project on her own because it provided a space for her to tie canonical literature into the curriculum through an alternative medium that fostered student creativity and individualization. Kris designed the project so that her students could personalize the classic novel through several means.

From the beginning of the project, Kris asks each group to choose the genre or style of film to illustrate the novel, chapter, poem, or short story. Some groups choose to film literal interpretations of the plot and dialogue of their chapters, while others modify them to mimic television shows like *Dr. Phil*, *Judge Judy*, *America's Next Top Model*, *Jersey Shore*, or even *The Real World*. Because video interpretations of the novels require extensive analysis of the text from each group member, every student is motivated to read, evaluate, and analyze the literature to make connections between the literature and his or her chosen genre. Of course, teaching close reading is one of the major goals of the Common Core State Standards (NGA & CCSSO, 2010).

Before the filming begins, students also learn different elements of film literacy—camera angles, dialogue, sound effects, costuming—that every director and author must consider before creating a story. (This could be accomplished by teaching mini-lessons, so the students are aware of how these techniques help build characterization and story elements.) Before filming, each group also determines how they will use these techniques to illustrate the necessary story elements—point of view, characterization, symbolism, themes—in their film interpretations. For example, the students are required to use different camera angles to create specific points of view. They also use music and sound effects to create specific moods and tones. Most importantly, the students incorporate their knowledge of certain literary criticism perspectives—feminism, historical criticism, psychoanalytic criticism, Marxism—and apply that school of thought to their interpretations of characterization, dialogue, and settings. Essentially, the film project allows students to use film techniques to foster a deeper understanding of print texts and vice versa, all while immersed in certain key critical theories used in literary criticism.

How Do I Do It?

Kris describes the process: To begin creating movies from canonical literature, I first thoroughly ground the students in various literary criticism theories. Teachers can incorporate the different styles of literary criticism in different ways. For instance, during the school year, teachers can discuss one new style of literary criticism for each novel unit (up to five) and then have students choose one of those styles for the film unit. Or, the teacher can spend one school week to discuss five different types of criticism—one per day—before the filming begins. For each day, the teacher can provide students with an overview of one style of criticism—feminism, Marxism, and so on—and have the students analyze and find elements in a poem or short story that highlight the different elements of the criticism discussed that day. Once the students have a firm grasp on a few different types of literary criticism, they can then independently analyze a new piece of literature for the film unit.

I then explain the assignment—each group is required to choose or highlight symbolism, themes, characterization, dialogue, setting, critical theorists, character psychoanalysis, and naturalism elements from the canonical text in the video or film. How they choose to highlight these elements in their films is up to them. The rubric I developed (figure 19.1) has elements of both film literacy and literary criticism.

After almost an entire semester of studying different methods to analyze literature, it's time for you to use your creativity to create a movie and a presentation!

You can use several different methods—camera angles, music, sound effects, pictures, interviewing, acting—to highlight the criticism and details from your chapter. (Also, even though you will present this information in a movie, I will still ask you additional questions about your symbols, criticism, and so on at the conclusion of your film presentation.)

Date Final Project Due in the Public File: _____

Presentation Date: _____

1. **Book Materials in Your Movie (40 points)**

   Criticism (10 points): Utilize any information we have learned in class and find one or two articles to get all of your information.

   - You need to find quotations from one literary critic and/or a new piece of criticism that supports your chapter analysis or presentation.

Figure 19.1: Sample film rubric.

Continued on next page →

- Complete a review of each piece of literary criticism you use. Include at least five ideas in your movie.

- Provide me with a copy of your criticism and research the day before you present.

Symbols (5 points): Cover at least three symbols—characters, settings, or objects—in your chapter. What do these symbols reveal about a character, conflict, or theme?

Naturalism (5 points): Highlight at least three qualities of Naturalism; list specific pages where these qualities are highlighted.

American dream (5 points): Highlight the characters' dreams: their fulfillment, failure, or both. (At least 3 characters)

Psychoanalysis (5 points): Analyze each character psychoanalytically. (At least 3 characters)

Theme (10 points): What is the major theme or topic discussed in your chapter? Where are some situations or quotations that depict that topic? (Pick one theme topic from your chapter. Then, find three quotations about that theme topic and write a theme statement about that topic.)

2. **Movie Presentation (40 points)**

Script guidelines (5 points): Briefly review the plot points of your chapter. Then, create a movie script to follow the chapter.

Storyboard (5 points): Create a minimum of five slides (listing setting, characters, dialogue, or sound, as necessary).

- The first slide should be the title page with members' names, chapter, genre, movie title, and due date.

- The second through fourth slides should be plot points.

- The last slide should list credits for actors, titles, sources (music, sound effects, pictures), and so on.

Creativity and plot outline (30 points): *Following are some suggestions—*

- Talk show, dating show, interview. Have an interviewer (Oprah, Stephen Colbert, Ellen, a literary critic) ask interviewees (*Of Mice and Men* characters) questions while incorporating the symbols, criticism, and so on in their answers.

- Reality show. Create your own reality show or make a parody of a reality show (*America's Next Top Model*, *Real Housewives*, and so on). Have the characters recreate their lives or use interviews, like a reality television spoof.

- MTV concept. Make a parody of an MTV show (*The Real World*, *MTV's MADE*, *America's Best Dance Crew*, *MTV Cribs*, and so on) with your characters, and so on from *Of Mice and Men* (OMM).

- Game show. Spoof television shows like *Family Feud*, *Survivor*, or *Jeopardy!*.You could have questions on each slide, and the class or your filmed characters can guess the answers for each question.

- Mockumentary. Recreate the scene from your chapter and spoof the film requirements in it.

- Yearbook. Take photos of important plot points and have voice-overs explaining how they tie into the film requirements.
- Wax museum. Film the characters, and tell details about them.
- *Cops* concept or court scene. Put a character on trial.

3. **Presentation Skills and Movie Delivery (20 points)**

   Paralanguage (5 points)

   Knowledge of book (5 points)

   Focus, participation, and organization (5 points)

   Creativity (5 points)

If you don't finish something, it will be a "0" for the missing material.

Total Points: _____ / 100 points

Names: _____   Chapter: _____

1. **Book Materials in Your Movie**
    • Criticism _____ / 10 points
    • Symbols _____ / 5 points
    • Naturalism _____ / 5 points
    • American dream _____ / 5 points
    • Psychoanalysis _____ / 5 points
    • Theme _____ / 10 points
	/ 40 points

2. **Movie Presentation**
    • Script guidelines _____ / 5 points
    • Storyboard _____ / 5 points
       • First slide: Title page with members' names, chapter, film genre, film title, and due date
       • Second slide: Movie title and so on
       • Last slide: Credits listing actors, titles, and so on
    • Creativity and plot outline
       • Sound effects or music _____ / 5 points
       • Dialogue _____ / 5 points
       • Camera angles _____ / 5 points
       • Characterization _____ / 5 points
       • Plot points _____ / 5 points
       • Props or costumes _____ / 5 points
	/ 40 points

Continued on next page →

3. **Presentation Skills and Movie Delivery**	/ 20 points
• Paralanguage (volume, diction, enthusiasm, and so on) _____ / 5 points • Knowledge of book (delivery) _____ / 5 points • Focus, participation, and organization _____ / 5 points • Creativity _____ / 5 points	
Total:	/ 100 points

Any inappropriate content in this presentation—vulgarity, nudity, swearing, slurs, or inappropriate acting choices—will result in an automatic failure for every individual in the group. If you have questions, ask first!

While your film might be a parody, you need to ensure that you pick your subjects carefully. Don't cross the line!

Once I provide the rubric, students begin to determine which story elements—specific dialogue, images, and plot points—they will cover from their chapter in their film. Then, they must determine how they will interpret—either literally or satirically—their chapter in the film. Finally, they must determine what specific type of criticism they will highlight in their film.

Students can begin the brainstorming process once they know their groups, chapter, and rubric requirements. By organizing their ideas on a film overview worksheet (figure 19.2), the students will know what genre (style of film), props (objects), mood (music and sound effects), and action (plot points) they need to cover in their film. For homework, students are encouraged to visit websites like SoundBible (www.soundbible.com) and Stonewashed (www.stonewashed.net) or their iTunes libraries to begin finding and downloading sound effects or music that they might want in their films. Beginning with the film overview worksheet helps students organize their film details—how to use camera angles to highlight point of view; how to use music to create mood; how to use props to highlight symbolism—while simultaneously helping the teacher cover the objectives necessary for the specific unit of study.

After the students finish brainstorming on their film overview worksheets, they are given a blank storyboard template so they can begin organizing their central plotlines. Storyboard templates can be found online, and teachers should encourage students to try different templates to find the one that best suits them. (For sample storyboards, search "storyboard template" on either www.utdallas.edu or www.bbc.com). For each picture within the storyboard, students are required to

Film Requirements and Overview

Title of the Film: _____   Book Chapter: _____

Group Members:

Criticism and Theory

What criticism or theory are you covering in your film?

What elements, characteristics, or theorists are you highlighting in your film (list at least three qualities)?

Setting

Where are you filming?

How does this location support the story elements and criticism?

Provide direct quotations and dialogue.

List criticism and outside-source quotations.

Characters

What characters are in the scenes? Who is playing each character?

Figure 19.2: Sample film overview worksheet.

Continued on next page →

What costumes and props will you use to distinguish between the different characters?

How do you use each character's movement, voice, and so on to meet the criticism and film style?

Action

What are the plot points?

Mood

What mood do you want to create?

What songs and sound effects will you use to help create the mood?

Camera Angles and Movement

What camera angles will you use?

How and why do these camera angles help create a specific point of view?

How will this help support the style of criticism you are using?

action (what aspect of the plot they are covering), and (5) sound (what effects they will add during editing). Once I determine the locations my students want to film, I secure permission for those locations—auditorium, lunch room, classrooms, gym—on the selected days. If they film outside of school, the students need to make sure that they finish all of the filming before the class begins editing the films.

Once the completed storyboards are reviewed and approved, the students start filming. The completed footage is uploaded to Dropbox, and then the editing begins—students edit their videos using programs like iMovie or Windows Movie Maker. I've noticed that many students do the editing entirely on their smartphones. Cute CUT, iMovie, and Videoshop are among the apps frequently used. These programs and apps allow the students to add subtitles, music overlays, sound effects, video transitions, and video effects to enhance the overall quality of the work. Once the videos are complete, the students will present their videos in class, so the students can reflect on not only the literature elements and types of criticism but also on their experiences during the assignment. Each student is responsible for evaluating each group's movie and providing feedback about it on a review sheet.

Using filmmaking to teach literary criticism can also lead to other uses of film and video in the English classroom. For example, the students could create literal interpretations of short stories or in-depth adaptations of narrative poems. When the students make literal, abstract, or satirical adaptations of canonical texts, it provides students with the opportunity to use their artistic talents to "own" a classic tale within an authentic and highly motivating experience. Students who are given the space to *choose* how they can interpret the classic novel are more eager to want to read, understand, and interpret the work. In this project, the students are encouraged to put their own artistic interpretations in the writing, filming, and editing. No one is telling them that their creativity is wrong; they are free to play with the literature and criticism to make it their own. For my students, finding ways to make connections between a classic author and their own voices is thrilling; they want their peers and their teachers to see how they made connections to criticism artistically and theatrically. The student becomes the center of the novel interpretation, not the teacher, and this spurs the students on to create and lead in the literacy process.

Classroom Example

During the study of the novel *Of Mice and Men*, students interpret the classic text in several different ways. Most choose to parallel or parody their chapter in videos using popular television shows as inspiration. For example, one group chooses to describe the settings in the book, much as the rooms are described in *MTV Cribs*, with a particular focus on the disparity between the rich and the poor. Other groups choose to use the reality show *The Real World* for their interpretations, opening their films with snapshots of each character in a specific pose, just like the show. In addition to creating parodies of MTV shows, some groups choose to mimic courtroom shows such as *Judge Judy*. In these videos, the students provide a psychoanalytic interpretation of each character during the questioning of each character in the courtroom. Each group finds a way to incorporate creativity with their critical theory analysis of choice regardless of the style of video they choose.

The students also use different film affordances to highlight critical elements as well. Each group is required to use music as one technique to establish a set mood or tone for its film. For films based on chapter 6 in *Of Mice and Men*, one group chooses Boston Pops Orchestra's performance of Carl Orff's "O Fortuna" to show the drama surrounding Lennie's death, while another group plays Sarah McLachlan's performance of "Angel" to show the sadness of his death. In addition to music, some students modify the dialogue from the novel to match the genre or style of their films, using rap, slang, or even iambic pentameter. Through their group collaboration, they work together to make connections between the author's intent for the novel and their film interpretations of that novel. Because this project gives students the space to own the reading and make it their own via film, they not only take the time to read the classic literature, but enjoy the reading and the filmmaking as well.

Your Turn

Creating films from classic texts generally takes fifteen days of class. To incorporate this activity into the course of study, you must first choose the classic text you would like your students to read. Teachers can choose several different types of texts, including a book the students read for a summer reading assignment, a play, or a canonical text. (If the teacher chooses something the students read over the summer, the students will have a stronger grasp on the plot, when they revisit the text for homework or in-class readings.)

Day 1

Once the text is chosen and read, the students divide into groups, and the teacher or students designate the chapter and type of criticism each group must incorporate into each film. A teacher might choose to print specific literary criticism pieces for the students, or the teacher can direct students to a particular website, like Gale Literature Resource Center, so the students can find types of literary criticism themselves.

For homework that night, the teacher should have the students reread their specific chapters so they can mark important dialogue, symbols, and events. Then, the students should summarize the literary criticism or analysis. (The teacher can either provide a summary of the criticism being studied or have the students research it themselves.)

Days 2–3

The next day, the students will begin brainstorming their films. In their groups, the students complete the film review worksheet (one forty-five-minute class) and storyboard (one forty-five-minute class). Be sure to check that each element of the rubric is highlighted in the storyboard before each group begins filming.

Days 4–6

Once the worksheet and storyboard have been completed, the students can begin filming (about four forty-five-minute classes) at school in locations that you and the administration deem appropriate. Because of the nature of the film project, you may also want to send out an email to the staff to keep them informed about the project.

Days 7–13

Once the students have filmed their entire chapters, have the students upload their films to Dropbox before school the next day. Then, the students will need approximately six forty-five-minute classes to edit their films. Before they begin editing in their groups, teachers should take one class period to review the major editing steps: how to add sound, upload videos, add transitions and effects, and overlay titles. While they edit, continue to assess whether the students have incorporated the required story elements and criticism in their film adaptations.

Days 14–15

After the editing is finished, the students present their videos in class. After each video presentation, each student will individually write a review of each group's film. The teacher will question the group about any unclear plot points, criticism elements, or text interpretations. Once the presentations are finished, allow the entire class time to reflect on their experiences—what they would have done differently, what they enjoyed most, what they learned about criticism or themselves, what struggles they encountered, and so on. Through this connection of film and literature, the students should be more motivated to not only do the reading but also analyze and interpret the literature to relate to their own lives as well.

Although incorporating film units into the classroom might seem daunting at first, any teacher, at any grade level, can utilize this strategy to increase reading motivation. Elementary teachers can take stories from the curriculum—fables, nursery rhymes, or chapter books—and film the students acting out the scenes by themselves, with puppets, or with frozen images. Once the film-stories are complete, the class can "reread" the films when they watch them as a class. (If the students recreate frozen-filmed images, the teacher or students could always add subtitles or read the story aloud at the same time.) Middle school teachers also can use this project to teach different types of literature. For example, the middle school students can record or film chapters or poems from their class textbooks or novels. The teacher might have the whole class (in small groups) film the same story, poem, or chapter, but change the dialogue or lines to meet a different genre or time period being studied. They can then showcase their recordings or films to the class.

In short, whether you choose to start with smaller literary works—a nursery rhyme, fable, or book chapter—or with something more extensive—an epic poem or piece of canonical literature—the options are endless. Providing students with the opportunities to take what they are reading and interpret those stories in different ways allows the teacher to see what aspects of the stories the students understood and what aspects they need more instruction on. Students, teachers, and parents are looking for alternative strategies to encourage literacy development in and outside of the classroom. In an age when students are plugged in to their cell phones, televisions, and computers, finding a way to tie paper-based texts to screen-based texts is often challenging.

Conclusion

The film project described in this chapter allows students to take novels and give new life to them through film and music. Providing them with a school-based activity to showcase these films—which students might see as predominantly housed outside of school—not only motivates them to read assigned texts but helps them discover a little bit about their own identities as well. This assignment allows for a free space to read, explore, and create.

As one of Kris's students explains, "Ms. Srsen . . . you know why I want to do this? It's because I'm free to say what I want to say. I don't have to worry about punctuation or writing; I can just read and act. We all can. And, you know what I've realized? It's not half bad. Oh . . . and our video's going to be pretty awesome."

Now, what teacher wouldn't get excited about that?

 **Elizabeth A. Edmondson** has taught high school English for ten years, served as chair of the English Department, and was named director of the middle school at Gilmour Academy in Gates Mills, Ohio. She is pursuing a doctorate in curriculum and instruction with an emphasis in literacy at Kent State University in Kent, Ohio. To learn more about Elizabeth's work, follow @EdmondsonEDU on Twitter.

CHAPTER 20

eBooks and eReaders: Removing Obstacles, Improving Motivation

By Elizabeth A. Edmondson

Ray Bradbury once said,

> I still love books. Nothing a computer can do can compare to a book. You can't really put a book on the Internet. . . . [People] want to read books. Books smell good. They look good. You can press it to your bosom. You can carry it in your pocket. (as cited in Moore, 2000)

I love books, too. And I love Ray Bradbury—so much so that I have dedicated entire months of my curriculum to teaching *Fahrenheit 451* to reluctant freshmen, hoping to convince them that they should also love Ray Bradbury. So it is with a heavy heart that I must disagree with him on this one.

You see, over my last ten years as a teacher, I've noticed that fewer students linger in the smell of a new novel or get excited about a freshly cracked book spine. As a matter of fact, research tells us that fewer students are identifying themselves as capable readers at all (Alvermann, 2001). Our students' lives happen in both the physical world and in cyberspace. They are digital natives, fluent in the language of technology, computers, the Internet, and video games (Prensky, 2001). They do not share the previous generation's commitment to and affinity for paper, and unfortunately, they associate this traditional model with literacy learning and fail to recognize their digital, socially networked, out-of-school literacy activities as powerful learning tools (Pitcher et al., 2007). They don't pass notes in my class; they text when they think

I'm not looking. They don't draw on my desks when they're bored; they Snapchat. They get excited when someone brings the newest Apple product to class, and contrary to Mr. Bradbury's thoughts, they *do* like their books on the Internet, on their Kindles, and on their iPhones. While Bradbury insists that people want traditional, physical books, I contend that there is a burgeoning population of those who don't.

These digital native adolescents' perceptions of themselves as readers affect their motivation to engage in literacy activities (Alvermann, 2001). As technology is further entrenched in the lives of teens, there is a growing need for educators to "address the discrepancy between the types of literacy experiences students encounter at school and those they practice in their daily lives outside the school environment" (Larson, 2010, p. 16). The closer that literacy activities and tasks match the values, needs, and goals of students, the more likely students will be motivated to engage, expend effort, and sustain interest in them (Pitcher et al., 2007). Del Siegle (2012) reports that "digital natives expect more from their reading experience, and the apps and e-books being developed are changing the way young people interact with the printed word" (p. 140). Educators must look for ways to motivate students in the English and literacy classroom by validating student preferences, redefining literacy practices, and narrowing the gap between students' out-of-school literacy practices and in-class reading and writing activities.

The use of ebooks and ereaders in the classroom is one such way to honor outside literacy practices in the classroom and motivate students to engage in literacy learning. The novelty of a new technology gadget plays a significant role in student motivation, and ereaders have enormous potential to entice reluctant readers (Miranda, Johnson, & Rossi-Williams, 2012). Up 5 percent since 2012, 28 percent of Americans report that they have read an ebook in the last year; however, only 4 percent report reading ebooks exclusively, suggesting that paper texts remain the backbone of American literacy practices (Zickuhr & Rainie, 2014). This increasing trend toward digital texts is consistent with growing numbers of ereaders, such as Amazon's Kindle, Barnes & Noble's Nook, or even Apple's iPad, in homes across the country. Siegle (2012) asserts that

> e-books have changed the publishing world and the way students interact with the written word. . . . Educators and parents who embrace this revolution in reading and writing gain an additional tool to promote literacy skills and help prepare their students to be literate in the 21st century. (p. 143)

This chapter explores my use of ereaders and ebooks in my tenth-grade English classroom and the consequent improvement in student motivation.

How Do I Do It?

My journey using ebooks in the classroom began when a student declined a paper copy of Mark Twain's *The Adventures of Huckleberry Finn* that I offered him.

"I'll just read it online," he told me, "I don't want to carry that thing around in my book bag."

Convinced that he'd change his mind in the next few days, I acquiesced; yet, he never asked for that hard copy. After hearing from a number of students who were completing their homework assignments by reading the books online, I followed their lead and sought out ways to support their preferences.

Step 1: Design a Plan for Your Classroom, Seek Administrative Support, and Purchase Devices

My students' newfound intrinsic motivation to read online inspired me to write a proposal to purchase six ereaders. After days of researching, I ultimately decided Nooks were best for my classroom. iPads were too expensive for this experiment, and Kindles didn't offer the face-to-face technical support that I wanted. If something went wrong with a device, I wanted to be able to take my device to an actual *person* and have them help me. Nooks were a good choice for me, but another device might be a better fit for your classroom and your students.

My proposal detailed my observations of student interest in the classroom and current research on the connection between technology and student motivation. It also included a cost breakdown of each device and a stipend for purchasing ebooks. My principal was receptive to my idea, especially because I had taken the initiative on my own.

Step 2: Select Student Participants and Send Permission Letters to Their Parents

After purchasing my devices, I brought them into my classroom and told my students that I was looking for volunteers to try them. Despite their previous enthusiasm for all things electronic, very few students jumped at the opportunity. I later found this was due to the fact that they were scared to borrow something so expensive from me; they were scared that they would break it. I reassured my students that if the Nook broke, they did not need to pay for the repairs. I sent home a letter to the parents of my six volunteers seeking permission for their child to use an ereader in place of a traditional textbook at no additional cost to them. The parents of all six gave their consent.

Step 3: Set Up the Devices, Schedule an Orientation Meeting, and Hand Them Over to the Students

I used a label maker to label each Nook with a number. Then, I preloaded the books we would be studying onto the devices for the students: *Hamlet*, *The Adventures of Huckleberry Finn*, and *Lord of the Flies*. Most works of classic literature are public domain; thus, I was able to download the books for free. I also had a small sum of money to purchase additional independent-reading books for my students.

There was an instant buzz surrounding the ereaders. I planned an afterschool orientation to show them how to charge the Nook, turn it on and off, download a title, navigate the book, highlight, and add comments; however, I quickly discovered that there was no need to train students on the new technology. My digital native students taught themselves how to advance the pages and highlight and define unfamiliar terms in about ten minutes.

Step 4: Follow Up Periodically

Since this was my first time with the ereaders, I let the same six students keep the Nooks for the entire year. In later years, I rotated them around with each book, giving more students the opportunity to use the technology. You'll have to decide which model will work best for your classroom.

Not only were students intrigued with the possibility of having access to a new "toy" in class, but once the lessons started, they were intrinsically motivated to go above and beyond the requirements of the lessons. The Nook, or any ereader for that matter, offers an ease of experience not available with a traditional paper book. In my ten years of teaching I've come to realize, the fewer obstacles in the way of homework, the more likely it is to be completed. At the end of the year, three of the six students using the Nooks went out and purchased their own for future use.

Classroom Example

From my observations of students working with ebooks and ereaders in the classroom, I saw three major themes emerge in their work. The first is *ease of access*. As long as there is a device, there is the book and the ability to do one's homework. Students had the option of reading the book on their Nooks, which really just serve as a substitution for a paper book. However, they also had the ability to read the book on their smartphones via the Nook app. One particularly forgetful student regularly left his Nook in his bed, but he was still able to participate in the class discussions and activities because he could access the text through his iPhone. This idea caught on like wildfire, and I heard of students reading on their phones while waiting for buses or on their computers via the Barnes & Noble website while bored in other classes.

For the students who didn't have the Nooks, I emailed links to the online versions of the books and also posted the links on my class webpage so they too could have easy access. If there is a device and a will, there is a way.

The second reason is *ease of personalization*. It might seem trivial, but teachers would be neglectful to dismiss the importance of a book's physical aesthetic to students. Who wants to read a book that is falling apart, has yellowing pages and tiny print, or that just plain smells weird? The Nooks motivated students with the possibility of personalization. They made it possible to personalize the reading experience for each student by giving them the opportunity to adjust the style of font as well as the size of it. They could also change the background color, making it higher or lower contrast and brighter or dimmer to meet their lighting needs. Furthermore, students could highlight and add personal comments to the text, all of which are visible to them on the Nook's text, the Nook app, or the online version. No longer are students required to read with a pen in hand. While certainly not a necessity to the act of reading, ereaders provide an added convenience, which can motivate students to complete their assignments carefully and thoughtfully.

The third reason is *ease of access to resources*. Perhaps most notable is that the Nooks motivated my students to be active, engaged readers. They were the types of readers I had always wished and encouraged them to be. Thanks to the dictionary feature, they frequently looked up vocabulary encountered in the readings. My students reported that this was the most helpful function of the Nook. Since the device was connected to WiFi, they often supplemented their assigned reading with Wikipedia articles that defined, clarified, and expanded the ideas they encountered in the stories. Also, the Nook's search function allowed students to easily find quotes to contribute to class discussions and support their arguments. Rather than flip through hundreds of pages of text, all a student needed to do was remember a few key words and they could locate the quotes they were searching for. Before the ereaders, only the most dedicated readers would engage in this type of active reading, but the Nooks afforded students easy access to resources, which motivated them to go beyond the assignment and to fully embrace the reading.

I discovered that my students with the Nooks were not only completing the assigned reading but were prone to reading ahead. Most of them indicated that reading didn't "bother [them] as much" because they could not physically see how many more pages awaited. With a book, the reader can easily see how many pages are left in the assignment, and perhaps more intimidating, the rest of the book; this isn't the case with an ebook. While ebooks do offer page numbers and percentages at the bottom for students to monitor their progress through the text, these indicators seemed to have significantly less effect on my students' morale than did an inch of paper in their hands.

Your Turn

Adolescents are intrinsically motivated to read and participate in literacy activities when their voices are heard and their interests validated (Lapp & Fisher, 2009). Start by paying attention to what captures your students' attention—especially if it is something nonacademic—and work from there. The more continuity they see between their personal interests and the curriculum, the more motivated they will be.

While technology and dollar signs seem to go hand in hand, it is important to note for interested teachers that incorporating digital versions of texts can be done very inexpensively and to varying degrees. This is not an all-or-nothing endeavor. Offering students alternatives to paper books, whether as a link to a pdf or on an ereader, decreases some of the obstacles to reading and therefore increases student motivation.

Not every teacher will have funding for a class set of Nooks or Kindles, but don't let that be a deterrent, as many works of classic literature are in the public domain and are available for free online. Project Gutenberg (www.gutenberg.org) alone offers more than forty-two thousand free titles. Google Books (http://books.google .com) and Internet Archive (www.archive.org) are also good sources for free ebooks. With such vast ebook libraries available, teachers have more freedom and flexibility in the texts they teach and their ability to differentiate according to student ability and interest. While reading these texts online does not require the purchase of any special hardware, it does require an Internet connection for access (Siegle, 2012).

Encourage students with smartphones to download helpful apps. Amazon's Kindle and Barnes & Noble's Nook both have apps so that readers can access their books on a great number of devices other than basic ereaders. Thanks to the Cloud, bookmarks and personal notations will transfer from device to device if students are using more than one to complete their reading. And while they are downloading apps, have them download a dictionary app for quick and easy access while they are reading paper books or completing other assignments.

For schools with rich technology environments, 1:1 computer programs, or formalized bring-your-own-device programs, identify a single edition of an ebook as your class text and forget the paper copy altogether. This will save your school from investing in and maintaining classroom sets of books.

One thing that has become clear to me on this journey: books may not fit nicely in your pocket, but an iPhone does. Try it out!

 **Salika A. Lawrence, PhD,** is an associate professor of literacy at St. John's University. Salika is coordinator of the literacy PhD program. She is a former middle and high school teacher with the New York City Department of Education. Her research interests include literacy instruction, adolescent literacy, and teacher education and professional development. Publications include the edited book *Critical Practice in P–12 Education: Transformative Teaching and Learning* as well as articles that appear in such journals as *The Journal of Literacy and Technology* and *Teacher Education and Practice*.

 **Carrie E. Hong, PhD,** is an associate professor of literacy at William Paterson University of New Jersey. Her research interests include reading, writing, and balanced literacy; literacy teacher education; and teacher preparation for teaching students from diverse linguistic and cultural backgrounds. Publications appeared in *Teacher Education Yearbook XXI, Teaching and Learning With the Net Generation*, and *The Journal of Inquiry and Action in Education*.

 **Marie Donnantuono** is coordinator of the Woodrow Wilson New Jersey Teaching Fellowship at William Paterson University of New Jersey and an instructor of literacy. She received National Board Certification as a teacher and is a certified educational media specialist. Her research interests include instructional strategies for readers using informational text, best practices for creating balanced literacy environments, and in-service programs for educators in professional development schools. Her publications have appeared in *University and School Connections: Research Studies in Professional Development Schools*.

 **Geraldine Mongillo, PhD,** is the chair of the Department of Educational Leadership and Professional Studies at William Paterson University of New Jersey and a professor of literacy. Research interests include intervention strategies for struggling readers, preparation of reading specialists, and the professional development of in-service teachers. Publications have appeared in *Teacher Education Yearbook XXI* and the *Journal of College Reading and Learning*. Visit www.wpunj.edu/coe/departments/elps to learn more about Geraldine's work.

CHAPTER 21

Using Literacy iPad Apps for Reading Motivation

By Salika A. Lawrence, Carrie E. Hong, Marie Donnantuono,
and Geraldine Mongillo

We know that cognitive factors such as the use of metacognitive reading strate-gies, knowledge of language, and good reading skills are a necessary foundation for determining the proficiency of good readers, but they may not be enough to support students' reading, especially as students move through grade levels (Lau, 2009; Melekoglu, 2011). The intrinsic aspect of reading—the desire to read for enjoyment—is often influenced by extrinsic factors such as choice, goals, incentives, and access to a wide array of reading materials including different genres (Gambrell, 2011b; Pecjak & Kosir, 2008). Students who are intrinsically motivated to read see value in the activity or are interested in the material, especially when they can choose what they read and learn (Gambrell, 2011b). The motivation to read supports read-ing instruction because motivated students display self-efficacy when they believe they "can be successful at reading . . . and [are willing] to take on difficult reading material" (Becker, McElvany, & Kortenbruck, 2010; Pecjak & Kosir, 2008, p. 148), including grade-level texts and nonfiction, informational texts.

Digital tools can foster the motivation for students to read and engage because these tools give them access to interesting texts, resources, and stimulating tasks (Guthrie & Alao, 1997; Guthrie et al., 2006). First, technology is particularly use-ful for providing access to a wide range of high-interest, authentic nonfiction and informational texts. Digital tools can heighten students' motivation to read by introducing them to new material, genres, and writing styles and by offering them a way to do immediate research on topics that interest them. Second, technology facilitates the opportunity to differentiate reading to meet the needs of individual students—students can self-monitor and interact with texts adapted for their reading interest and levels. Essentially, students can become motivated learners under differentiation, because a teacher can tailor learning to better address their individual needs and learning styles (Tomlinson, 1999). Through differentiated reading, students show greater interest in material because they have more ownership in their learning and are more likely to engage in discussions (Barone & Wright, 2008), and they can demonstrate what they know in different ways (Tomlinson, 1999). With technological tools, students can self-select authentic reading material based on individual interest, a defining characteristic of intrinsic motivation that helps students perform better in educational contexts (Patall, 2013).

As the Common Core State Standards call for technology to be incorporated seamlessly into instruction, classroom teachers must take on the responsibility and meet the expectations for technology integration (NGA & CCSSO, 2010; International Society for Technology in Education, 2007, 2008). Still, little guidance has been provided for teachers to select and effectively incorporate technology into their classrooms. Technology is constantly changing; therefore, teachers need strategies for selecting, evaluating, and incorporating technology into their reading instruction.

Teachers can use technology to move beyond basic literacy instruction (Gee, 2008) and differentiate for individualized learning to help students develop into independent learners (Barone & Wright, 2008). A growing number of teachers are exploring the possibilities of using tablets such as the iPad in their classrooms (Wainwright, 2013). Using the iPad is convenient for classroom instruction because apps associated with this tool can be used to differentiate for reading instruction with leveled independent reading, personalized vocabulary, practice activities that reinforce skills, or assessments for ongoing progress monitoring. The iPad "has most of the capabilities of a desktop or laptop computer, but with additional unique affordances, such as a multitouch screen and a seemingly endless variety of applications" (Hutchison et al., 2012, p. 15). Teachers can use the apps available through the iPad as individualized learning tools to organize a student's personal library with leveled, self-selected reading material, to arrange instructional resources and differentiated assessments (Tomlinson, 1999), and to evaluate students' literacy performance. Additionally, iPads provide teachers with the potential to integrate technology during direct instruction or guided practice by modeling or scaffolding literacy strategies.

Most effective literacy apps are games with self-monitoring capabilities. These games appeal to students because the apps are interactive, and students can choose from many options; they also motivate students by challenging and pushing them to the next level in a user-friendly way. Thus these features work as extrinsic motivators that enhance student learning independently through immediate feedback and progress monitoring. The self-monitoring aspects of the apps foster extrinsic motivation by providing students with review or further feedback, giving many options to choose, and providing clear and visual directions. Apps with a self-monitoring feature draw students' attention to self-assessment and urge students to set goals.

Two literacy apps discussed in this chapter, VocabularySpellingCity and One Minute Reader, can be used together to engage and motivate students in the reading process. They are most appropriate for students from kindergarten through grade 8. These apps are particularly helpful in improving students' fluency—the ability to read quickly with accuracy and expression (Caldwell & Leslie, 2005; Nettles, 2006)—and comprehension of nonfiction texts. Additionally, the apps give students access to the texts for repeated reading, which is an effective strategy for improving sight word vocabulary, reading rate, fluency, and comprehension (Caldwell & Leslie, 2005). Using these apps can extrinsically motivate students by giving them real-time feedback of their reading performance so they can self-monitor their progress, for example, during repeated reading.

VocabularySpellingCity is a free app with learning games that facilitate opportunities for students to build sight word recognition of a teacher-created list of vocabulary words and to construct their own vocabulary word list. Users can also pay a membership fee and gain access to more resources, such as additional games and the ability for students to complete and submit assignments through the app.

One Minute Reader is a reading app consisting of nonfiction stories with embedded audio files and vocabulary definitions. At the end of each story, readers are assessed with four comprehension questions, one of which focuses on vocabulary. Oral-reading fluency is also assessed, and students can track their reading progress.

How Do I Do It?

On the iPad, students complete a pretest with the One Minute Reader app. The pretest is a cold, oral reading of a nonfiction passage, which the student self-selects from the app. The student answers four multiple-choice questions at the end of the passage. After completing the pretest, the student creates a list of unknown words or words pronounced incorrectly. Then the student will use the designated literacy-based apps on the iPad for independent practice and differentiated instruction to improve his or her reading fluency and sight word vocabulary. Following is a list of literacy-based apps:

- Sight word development
  - One Minute Reader (fluency, vocabulary, comprehension)
  - Sight Word Bingo (spelling)
- Phonemic awareness and phonics
  - Licking Letters (spelling)
  - Starfall Learn to Read (phonics)
- Vocabulary and spelling
  - SpellingCity (vocabulary, spelling)
  - Wordle (vocabulary, spelling)
- Online books
  - Doodle Buddy (visualization)
  - Reading A–Z (online leveled books library)

A student can use the VocabularySpellingCity app, for instance, to complete sight word drills and vocabulary activities using the list of selected unknown words from the pretest. The student then rereads the pretest story from One Minute Reader several times to improve sight word recognition and fluency. The student also has the option to read along with an audio recording, which can serve as a model for fluent reading. Following this practice, the student takes a posttest, using the same story, to see if there is improvement on the four multiple-choice comprehension questions as well as his oral-reading rate.

Classroom Example

Diane Brandon, a tutor in a university-based reading clinic that serves students one on one from local schools, is a certified English language arts teacher enrolled in a graduate reading specialist certification program. Diane uses the iPad to augment her instruction of her tutee, Carlos, in the areas of vocabulary, comprehension, and fluency. Carlos is a fifth-grade bilingual student in an urban school. He has an interest in reading, but lacks the motivation and desire to engage in reading. His greatest reading difficulty is comprehension. However, he also shows weaknesses with fluency, vocabulary, and spelling, which contribute to his comprehension difficulties.

Diane instructs Carlos to read a text from One Minute Reader to practice his vocabulary, comprehension, and fluency. He selects and reads the passage, "Dark Climb." The app's level 5 (equivalent to the fifth-grade reading level) text is a short informational passage, which has multiple-choice questions based on literal or inferential comprehension at the end. Carlos first reads the text aloud. As he reads, he has difficulty with several of the vocabulary words, such as *particularly, disease, consequently*, and *excelled*. Next, Carlos listens to the story, and then he reads it silently. His results show that he reads silently at a faster rate than he reads orally. He answers four out of four multiple-choice questions correctly. Diane observes that he looks back to the text to help him answer the questions. He also asks Diane for help whenever he needs clarification. Using the vocabulary words he has difficulty with, Carlos completes the crossword puzzle, a game in the One Minute Reader app, as an additional activity. Carlos's effort and interest increase over time. Diane finds that he shows more enthusiasm in expressing oral and written responses to texts he reads. One Minute Reader serves as a model for fluent reading and helps Carlos read better with expression.

For additional spelling practice, Diane gives Carlos a spelling test using a word list at his grade level. He listens to each word being pronounced and used in a sentence. Then he attempts to spell each word, but incorrectly spells such words as *their, friend, thought, doesn't, carry*, and *believe*. Diane instructs Carlos to read the words out loud to her. Then she tells him to select one activity from the VocabularySpellingCity app she has downloaded onto the iPad. The app includes eight different games: Spelling TestMe, HangMouse, TeachMe, Sentence Unscramble, Word Unscramble, Missing Letter, Alphabetize, and Audio Word Match.

At first, Carlos chooses to play HangMouse to practice his spelling words. Diane loads a list of words from the spelling test into the app and then briefly explains the directions of the game. Then Carlos fills in the blank. Next, Carlos chooses the activity Missing Letter, in which he finds the missing letter for each of the spelling words on his list. During the next tutoring sessions, Carlos plays three other activities—Alphabetize, Audio Word Match, and Word Unscramble—before taking a spelling posttest. Given a choice of different games, he is motivated to keep practicing his spelling words.

Over time, Diane withdraws her assistance while Carlos works independently. In the subsequent tutoring session, he plays the spelling game twice. Then on the posttest, he spells eleven out of twelve words correctly, making 41.6 percent growth from the pretest.

Your Turn

After assessing students to determine their spelling or vocabulary needs, use the assessment data to select apps that will allow students to practice their spelling and vocabulary and improve their comprehension. For example, visit www.apple.com /itunes and download iTunes. Once installed on your computer, open iTunes, and click on the App Store tab on the top of the screen. Then to browse for apps, type *literacy phonics*, *literacy spelling*, or *literacy vocabulary* in the search box. As you browse the search results (ebooks, games, and so on), narrow your options by determining whether the app will be incorporated into the reading lesson for motivational appeal, reading or literacy area addressed, assessment, extension, or additional practice. In other words, depending on the literacy focus for your lesson, some app features may be distracting for students while others may enhance the learning experience. For instance, an ebook is more engaging with interactive text but might be distracting and hinder reading comprehension with games embedded within the text. After you select an app, determine whether it will be used during the reading minilesson for direct instruction or modeling, during small-group instruction as guided practice, or as independent practice for students. Then download and install the app on the iPad. Second, consider whether the app you select will also impact how many tablets you will need during the lesson: a one-to-one ratio where each student has individual access or a small-group learning center where students work together and share the same iPad. If you are using an Android device rather than an iPad, you can use similar search terms (*literacy phonics*, *literacy vocabulary*, and so on) to access apps on Google Play.

Conclusion

Teachers can use technology to motivate and engage students as readers while scaffolding and guiding students during reading instruction. Motivation is an important aspect of the reading process because "engaged readers are intrinsically motivated to read for a variety of personal goals, strategic in their reading behaviors, knowledgeable in their construction of new understandings from text, and socially interactive about the reading of text" (Gambrell, 2011b, p. 173). The iPad can provide students with access to resources they can use for literacy practices such as repeated reading, fluency development, spelling, and comprehension. With the iPad, their practice and activities are targeted to individualized needs. When teachers are able to identify appropriate literacy-based apps for literacy reading lessons, they can differentiate to provide struggling readers with opportunities to use the apps for independent practice or scaffold learners during guided practice.

PART VIII | Reading Assessment

Assessment in reading may not be the most glamorous of topics. Few people are fond of taking or administering tests or analyzing test results. In fact, for many years, schools did not take advantage of the data they had accumulated through student assessment. Since the early 2000s, however, we have learned the importance of assessment and the fruits of analyzing data for insights into how to improve instruction. Assessment, in our opinion, is best employed in formative ways. We can use assessment to diagnose the source of reading difficulties that some students may experience. We can also use assessment to monitor students' progress in reading. We cannot know if our instruction is having the desired effects unless we periodically assess the gains students made in the various reading competencies described in previous parts. Granted, we tend to assess our students too much and too often. However, targeted assessment used sparingly, intentionally, and wisely can definitely improve reading outcomes for our students.

Formative assessment has plagued teachers as a time-consuming task. Using a traditional informal reading inventory framework, students orally read a set of passages to the teacher then answer a set of comprehension questions that deals with each passage. The teacher would have to manually mark any deviations the student made and, at a later time, tally and analyze them for possible trends. The time it took and complexity involved in completing such assessments often resulted in the teacher not doing them at all. Advances in technology have eased the burden of assessment for teachers. Technological applications provide improved ways to record students' reading of passages. Other applications not only listen to students reading but can also identify any deviations students made. Moreover, these apps can also tally and calculate various statistics required for analyses. Using technology, students can record their understandings of passages in various ways (such as through recorded retellings, blogs, and so on) that the teacher can later access and evaluate. Technology may never replace an informed teacher who makes the final analyses of students' reading behaviors, but it can significantly reduce the burden of assessment that has been an obstacle for years.

In part VIII we offer three tech-related approaches to reading assessment. Jacqueline Love Zeig and her colleague Tara Lee Ronzetti share the Explain Everything app that provides students with a vehicle for demonstrating their comprehension of text and allows teachers to engage in formative assessment of student learning. Next, Jacqueline explores the use of VoiceThread to check students' reading fluency. Finally, Katie Stover and Lindsay Sheronick Yearta describe an approach to blogging that permits teachers to assess comprehension and students to self-assess their learning. The authors provide a useful rubric that can guide teachers and students in the formative assessment process.

We agree that assessment is not necessarily fun. But it is necessary if we want to monitor and guide students' growth in their literacy development. Technological applications, such as the ones described in part VIII, as well as the ones you can develop on your own, can certainly make assessment easier and more productive for teachers, as well as more engaging, authentic, and valuable for students.

Jacqueline Love Zeig, PhD, is a senior literacy associate at Literacy Consultants of Cambridge. She works with the national nonprofit organization City Year, as well as various public, private, and charter education providers. Jacqueline's work spans an array of experiences as an elementary teacher, state-level literacy coach for elementary and secondary turnaround schools, director of America Reads, researcher, lecturer, and educational consultant. Jacqueline's scholarly interests include urban education, at-risk readers, flipped classrooms, and student engagement. She coauthored the chapter "Drawing to Learn: Visual Support for Developing Reading, Writing, and Concepts for Children At-Risk" in *Handbook of Research on Teaching Literacy Through the Communicative and Visual Arts, Volume II*. She's also coauthored articles in *The Elementary School Journal* and in *Reading Research Quarterly*. Jacqueline was co-recipient of the International Reading Association's Albert J. Harris Award in recognition of her work contributing to the understanding of reading and learning disabilities. Visit www.literacyconsultantsofcambridge.com to learn more about Jacqueline's work.

Tara Lee Ronzetti is the literacy coach at Saigon South International School in Ho Chi Minh City, Vietnam. Before moving overseas in 2012, Tara spent eleven years as a literacy coach, reading specialist, and classroom teacher in and around Washington, DC, in high-needs schools. Tara earned her master's degree from the Harvard Graduate School of Education in 2001. She became a Reading Recovery teacher in 2002, and a National Board Certified teacher in early and middle childhood reading in 2011. In 2013, she won an action research grant to study the impact of literacy coaching from the East Asia Regional Council of Schools (EARCOS). Tara's research interests include the impact of coaching on student instruction, boy writers, and the evolving definition of literacy in the 21st century. To learn more about Tara's work, visit www.tararonzetti.com or follow @tararonzetti on Twitter.

CHAPTER 22

Literacy Assessments in the Digital Age

By Jacqueline Love Zeig and Tara Lee Ronzetti

For decades, comprehension assessment consisted of reading a passage and then answering multiple-choice questions (Caldwell, 2008). Historically, this was sufficient for the print-based, single-source texts; however, the demands of 21st century literacy necessitate collecting and synthesizing information from multiple print, digital, and video sources. The need to address these evolving literacy demands can be seen in new standards that emphasize the importance of teaching communication, collaboration, critical thinking, and creativity using multiple texts and technologies (NGA & CCSSO, 2010).

Formative assessments, offered through digital tools, can support students' mastery of the Common Core State Standards (National Education Technology Plan, 2010; NGA & CCSSO, 2010) as well as individual states' standards. Many digital tools, by design, engage students in collaborative experiences that demand the complex and creative use of literacy. Using design features such as recording and storing audio and video files, teachers can track students' learning over time to make meaningful adjustments in teaching and learning.

The International Reading Association's (2009) position statement on new literacies recognizes the need for assessments to match the evolving literacy demands on our students. It calls for teachers to not only address comprehension of the text but also the student's role in creating a multimodal product. Performance-based digital tools offer the opportunity to collect evidence of students' literacy processes (Fountas & Pinnell, 2006) as well as capture their ability to create multimodal products.

As Anne McGill-Franzen and Jacqueline Love Zeig (2008) posit, the multidimensional and complex nature of literacy, new and old, can be well understood through one multimodal response or product.

Teachers can then use these visual and auditory representations of students' thinking (Paquette, Fello, & Jalongo, 2007) as data to inform teaching and learning (Black & Wiliam, 1998). Digital tools can track students' strategic behaviors over time (for instance, over the span of a reading unit) as they talk through their responses with auditory annotations. With these data, teachers and students can make specific goals for next steps that promote continuous learning (Stiggins, 2007).

Certain digital tools make creating a short, text-based multimodal response quick and easy. Through screencast and digital whiteboard functions, students can quickly demonstrate their knowledge and think aloud in creative ways via text, video, and audio functions (Dalton & Grisham, 2013). Coupled with a well-crafted rubric, digital apps offer opportunities for the learner to receive quick feedback from the teacher or through students' self-analysis.

One example of a digital tool for assessing students' literacy knowledge and skills is Explain Everything. This tool allows students to create, collaborate, and share presentations (for our purposes, we call these presentations *responses*). The student can use voiceovers, annotations, video clips, and pictures to create a multimodal response. Apps like Explain Everything are examples of one digital assessment tool that engages and captures students' use of literacy in meaningful ways (Guskey, 2007/2008). Explain Everything layers multiple literacy skills (speaking, reading, synthesizing, presenting) and creates a real-life performance task to show student learning. It integrates new literacies and standards in the way they were intended, and therefore offers an authentic platform to analyze teaching and learning.

How Do I Do It?

Explain Everything must be downloaded to an Android or iOS mobile device. The Explain Everything website (www.explaineverything.com) has pricing for individual devices and bulk purchasing (for schools purchasing multiple apps), as well as links to download the app. To begin using Explain Everything as a formative assessment, a teacher or student selects a text to upload to the app. Explain Everything allows users to upload documents, pdfs, video, and images. Once the selected text is uploaded, the students begin their responses through digital annotation, highlighting, animation, and speech. Students may revise their responses at any time throughout the process. After a student has recorded and digitally saved his or her digital response, the teacher can use the response to assess the student's comprehension. Additionally, student responses may be shared via YouTube, Dropbox, or email, making it easy for teachers and students to access them throughout the unit or school year.

Classroom Example

During the course of a six-week unit on reading and writing nonfiction, we worked with second graders to provide literacy enrichment. We embedded use of Explain Everything in the last four weeks of the unit to assess students' comprehension development. Because this was a pilot, a small group of students was pulled out with Tara, the literacy coach, for the lessons. They met twice a week. Each lesson was forty-five minutes long—the entire reading block—and mimicked the gradual release of responsibility model used in the classroom. Tara also coached in the classroom during the six-week unit.

About two weeks into the unit on informative text, Tara introduced the Explain Everything app using an iPad. Each student had his or her own iPad for the response task. Students viewed a sample response while Tara described why and how the app would be used to represent their understanding of the text. Throughout the explanation, Tara pointed out key design features. Following the visual introduction, students had time to practice using the app. Three minutes into the students' practice time, they were recording their thoughts using the highlighting tool on the screen.

The lessons included a minilesson connected to informative texts, followed by guided practice. The last twelve minutes of each lesson concluded with a response. In these last twelve minutes, the students created and revised 90- to 120-second responses using a text excerpt in Explain Everything. Their responses provided a visual and oral representation of their thinking, which was later analyzed for evidence of how and what they learned. During the next lesson, Tara conferred with students and provided feedback using their most recent responses. Students reflected on their work and made specific goals for the next response.

Tara constructed a teaching continuum (figure 22.1, page 210) and student checklist using the Common Core standards and their performance indicators. Specific standards in the Reading: Informational Text and the Speaking and Listening strands were chosen, and the indicators (or learning targets) of their mastery in K–3 made up the continuum. Using the first two responses as the baseline, each student was placed on the continuum. From there, we could easily identify the skills they needed to master next in order to make progress. Students were given a simple checklist to complete each time they recorded a response: (1) identify what the text was mainly about, (2) recount or summarize what they learned from their chosen text, and (3) explain how the features in the text scaffold their understanding of the content.

Informational Text Reading
1 = Developing, 2 = Approaching, 3 = Meeting, 4 = Exceeding

Key Ideas and Details

1	2	3	4
CCRA.R.1: Read closely to determine what the text says explicitly and to make logical inferences from it; cite specific textual evidence when writing or speaking to support conclusions drawn from the text.			
RI.K.1: With prompting and support, ask and answer questions about key details in the text.	RI.1.1: Ask and answer questions about key details in a text.	RI.2.1: Ask and answer such questions as who, what, where, when, why, and how to demonstrate understanding of key details in a text.	RL.3.1: Ask and answer questions to demonstrate understanding of a text, referring explicitly to the text as the basis for the answers.
CCRA.R.2: Determine central ideas or themes of a text and analyze their development; summarize the key supporting details and ideas.			
RI.K.2: With prompting and support, identify the main topic and retell key details of a text.	RI.1.2: Identify the main topic and retell key details of a text.	RI.2.2: Identify the main topic of a multiparagraph text as well as the focus of specific paragraphs within the text.	RI.3.2: Determine the main idea of a text; recount the key details and explain how they support the main idea.

Craft and Structure

1	2	3	4
CCRA.R.5: Analyze the structure of texts, including how specific sentences, paragraphs, and larger portions of the text (e.g., a section, chapter, scene, or stanza) relate to each other and the whole.			

1	2	3	4
RI.K.5: Identify the front cover, back cover, and title page of a book.	RI.1.5: Know and use various text features (e.g., headings, tables of contents, glossaries, electronic menus, icons) to locate key facts or information in a text.	RI.2.5: Know and use various text features (e.g., captions, bold print, subheadings, glossaries, indexes, electronic menus, icons) to locate key facts or information in a text efficiently.	RI.3.5: Use text features and search tools (e.g., key words, sidebars, hyperlinks) to locate information relevant to a given topic efficiently.
Integration of Knowledge			
1	2	3	4
CCRA.R.7: Integrate and evaluate content presented in diverse media and formats, including visually and quantitatively, as well as in words.			
RI.K.7: With prompting and support, describe the relationship between illustrations and the text in which they appear (e.g., what person, place, thing, or idea in the text an illustration depicts).	RI.1.7: Use the illustrations and details in a text to describe its key ideas.	RI.2.7: Explain how specific images (e.g., a diagram showing how a machine works) contribute to and clarify a text.	RI.3.7: Use information gained from illustrations (e.g., maps, photographs) and the words in a text to demonstrate understanding of the text (e.g., where, when, why, and how key events occur).

Source: Adapted from NGA & CCSSO, 2010.

Figure 22.1: CCSS continuum for comprehending second-grade informational text.

The responses served as a barometer for future teaching points and student revision points. For instance, in the first responses, students attempted to summarize or retell the information they learned, but ultimately they reverted to reading the text aloud to the audience (Ronzetti, 2014b) because they did not understand the content well enough to recount it in their own words. This indicated a need for more explicit instruction and practice identifying the most important information, understanding what it means for them, and learning how to convey it in their own words. We also added scaffolded lessons for determining important ideas and details—skills that the students approximated during guided practice and responses (Ronzetti, 2014a).

These responses also supplied students with the means to reflect and monitor their own speaking and reading performances. Reviewing their ongoing work helped students understand that they could control how well they did and whether they accomplished their goals—what Peter Johnston (2012) refers to as *agency*. Students could immediately play back their responses to reflect on and (if needed) clarify their ideas. They could also view all their previous responses to decide what they needed to improve. With their goals in mind, they started to utilize their own strategies, such as pausing the recording to take a deep breath and think about what they wanted to say next. The students also started to rehearse before recording to adapt their speech appropriately and be sure their descriptions and summaries were clear. For instance, Christopher rehearsed and listened to his response before recording his final piece of the day (Ronzetti, 2014a). Such rehearsal showed that students recognized the importance of considering what they did and did not understand and could choose words that best expressed their ideas. They monitored their own performances and improved them. Thus, agency and metacognition grew in a comfortable, low-stakes way as they moved up the CCSS continuum.

Keeping the brief responses on our tablets enabled us to access them during one-on-one conferences with students. During conferences, Tara and her students watched the responses together and discussed areas of growth and next steps. As a result, students created specific goals for their next response—as they would with a writing piece. The availability of students' responses at the tap of a button allowed us to reflect often and recognize needed differentiation based on students' performance. Essentially, Explain Everything provided quick and consistent formative assessments that became a series of drafts throughout the unit, providing teachers and students a comprehensive picture of growth over time.

Your Turn

The Explain Everything app can be a flexible, formative assessment tool for virtually any content area to assess ELA skills. It is best to play with the app to familiarize yourself with its capabilities before implementing it in the classroom. We recommend creating your own Explain Everything response to learn, as well as to illustrate for students, how to show what you understand about a text. Remind students that if they need time to think, they can pause and resume the recording at any point.

This helps quell students' fear of making a mistake. When using an app as an assessment tool, introduce it early in your unit so that students have multiple opportunities to use it. This provides a series of drafts with revisions for the teacher and the student to track growth throughout the learning process.

Explain Everything's various design features allow assessment of students' reading, writing, listening, and speaking skills within one response. Develop a continuum or rubric of skills that can be assessed through multimodal responses to texts (using the CCSS makes it easy). A continuum such as this can help teachers analyze students' development in a formative manner throughout the unit, so that the assessment can guide further instruction. It also supports students so they know the ultimate goal and where they are in the trajectory.

Conclusion

Performance-based, formative assessments help teachers determine the next steps in teaching and learning and help students build awareness of their learning and thinking (Black & Wiliam, 1998). Students' multimodal digital responses illustrate various skills through an authentic performance task (Dalton & Grisham, 2013). This information helps teachers make decisions specific to an individual learner's needs. The task supports that learner in building agency and metacognition through an authentic low-stakes response. As 21st century educators, we strive to develop critical thinkers. An app-turned-assessment like Explain Everything addresses the text, task, and the complex learning demands facing students.

 **Jacqueline Love Zeig, PhD,** is a senior literacy associate at Literacy Consultants of Cambridge. She works with the national nonprofit organization City Year, as well as various public, private, and charter education providers. Jacqueline's work spans an array of experiences as an elementary teacher, state-level literacy coach for elementary and secondary turnaround schools, director of America Reads, researcher, lecturer, and educational consultant. Jacqueline's scholarly interests include urban education, at-risk readers, flipped classrooms, and student engagement. She coauthored the chapter "Drawing to Learn: Visual Support for Developing Reading, Writing, and Concepts for Children At-Risk" in *Handbook of Research on Teaching Literacy Through the Communicative and Visual Arts, Volume II.* She's also coauthored articles in *The Elementary School Journal* and in *Reading Research Quarterly.* Jacqueline was co-recipient of the International Reading Association's Albert J. Harris Award in recognition of her work contributing to the understanding of reading and learning disabilities. Visit www .literacyconsultantsofcambridge.com to learn more about Jacqueline's work.

CHAPTER 23

Developing and Assessing Fluency Through Web 2.0 Digital Tools

By Jacqueline Love Zeig

Notably, the turn of the 21st century marked several radical social and cultural changes. One markedly radical change was the shift from web 1.0 to web 2.0, where "interactivity went from linking and clicking to creating and sharing" (Solomon & Schrum, 2007, p. 13). This shift to web 2.0 signaled a transition from merely downloading and accessing information in isolation to interconnectedness across continents. The web was no longer just a place to search for and use information; it became a participatory, interactive place where users came together to create, edit, present, share, and collaborate (Solomon & Schrum, 2007). As the function and use of the web evolved, the types of literacy demands required to thrive within this open space also evolved. Thus, the use of the web quickly emerged as an essential tool in education, particularly through web 2.0 tools. These digital tools, by design, facilitate creativity, listening, viewing, collaboration, and sharing (Frey, Fisher, & Gonzalez, 2010)—all vital skills for thriving in today's society. Consequently, making use of these tools within our classrooms is essential to preparing our students to participate fully in this digital world.

Contemporary federal initiatives and educational standards emphasize new ways of reading and writing to prepare students to flourish in today's society. Therefore, teachers' integration and use of digital tools are vital to engage and support students' literacy needs. Innovative uses of digital tools for teaching and learning surface daily.

Yet, the focus of web 2.0 tools as literacy assessments hasn't garnered as much attention as the function and use of the tools.

Although various web-based literacy assessment software and platforms (representing more of the web 1.0 capabilities) exist in some schools, many are static in nature. Web 2.0 tools offer multifaceted design features that allow for student ownership over their learning to practice, record, and assess their literacy development over time within an interactive, collaborative space representing the real-world literacies necessary. Likewise, teachers have opportunities within these web 2.0 platforms to scaffold and assess students' literacy development using a common, flexible assessment. For instance, students can engage in the authentic use of literacy to create multimedia products (involving reading, writing, speaking, viewing, collaborating) as a representation of their learning. These products can then be recorded and reviewed later as a performance-based measure of student learning to make instructional decisions. Performance-based assessments that capture real-world use of literacy can lead to improved student learning (Wiggins & McTighe, 2011). Robert Marzano (2007) further illuminates the power of formative assessments that "begin immediately within a learning episode [i.e. oral reading of a text] and span its entire duration" (p. 106). Formative assessment information collected as students orally engage in the process of reading offers important information to be used as feedback to dramatically augment student learning. Thus, these performance-based, student-centered assessments that make use of web 2.0 tools are essential to 21st century education. As teachers prepare students for college and career demands, digital tools offer innovative ways to observe and collect information about students' literacy development to inform 21st century teaching and learning.

Certainly web 2.0 tools offer opportunities to assess all areas of literacy as well as students' digital-literacy skills; however, the tools discussed here will focus specifically on assessments of fluency. Traditionally, fluency assessments involve a student's oral reading of a passage for one minute while the assessor (preferably the teacher) records miscues (on a digital or print scoring sheet), accuracy rates, and sometimes prosody. Usually, the scoring and analysis of fluency development focus on students' oral-reading accuracy and rate (Allington, 2006), as heard and recorded by the assessor. Prosody, the ability to read with expression to convey meaning, typically relies on the assessor recalling and rating students' expression *after* the reading. Visit **go.solution-tree.com/technology** to see a fluency rubric.

Jerry Zutell and Timothy V. Rasinski (1991) reiterate the importance of teachers listening to their students reading to provide an accurate assessment of fluency. They further posit that these assessments occur in timely and accessible ways. Digital tools offer easy-to-use functions found in older technologies (such as tape recording), but unlike traditional technologies, web 2.0 tools combine text and audio support for the learner all in one virtual space. Leveraging these digital tools decreases the rate in scoring students' errors (missed words) since students' oral readings are available to review whenever necessary. Teachers and students have a digital record, with accompanying text, to listen to, view, and replay as an online portfolio of students' fluency development.

Additionally, web 2.0 tools offer students autonomy over their learning through self-directed and self-assessed practice opportunities. Repeated readings, widely recognized as a high-leverage practice for improving students' fluency development, are easily supported through web 2.0 tools. The production aspect inherent in publishing online reinforces the need to practice reading the selected text multiple times before performing for the online audience. Repeated oral readings lead to improvements in students' fluency—rate, accuracy, and comprehension (NICHD, 2000; Rasinski & Hoffman, 2003; Samuels, 1979). In addition to the inherent practice through repeated readings, Roxanne Hudson, Holly Lane, and Paige Pullen (2005) noticed that students take more ownership over their learning through goal setting and reflecting on their fluency development. Students' fluency improves even further when they can listen to a model of fluent reading (Rasinski, 2003). Fortunately, digital tools' capabilities enable opportunities for students to listen to a model, perform, record, set goals, and assess through authentic tasks that deepen student learning and inform teaching. Our preferred tool for recording and measuring fluency is VoiceThread, a web 2.0 interactive collaboration and sharing tool that enables users to add images, documents, and videos, and allows other users to add voice, text, audio file, or video comments (Bruder, 2011).

A *VoiceThread* refers to one multimedia slideshow of documents, images, or videos that multiple users can comment on. Users are able to create separate VoiceThreads within the VoiceThread interactive platform. Each VoiceThread can be named to represent the text read, the student, or the group. The K–12 network for VoiceThread (www.ed.voicethread.com) provides a secure, collaborative platform to create and access these slideshows. Recognized as a "tool to adopt" by *The New Horizon Report 2009: K–12 Edition* for its collaborative functions (Johnson, Levine, Smith, & Smythe, 2009), VoiceThread is gaining prominence among educators (see Brunvand & Byrd, 2011). Stein Brunvand and Sara Byrd (2011) champion the tool for enhancing student engagement, motivation, and learning. The engaging, multimodal experience of creating, sharing, collaborating, listening, and viewing within one media player makes VoiceThread an ideal digital tool to assess 21st century learners participating in literacy experiences necessary for college and career readiness.

How Do I Do It?

I began by creating a class account on the educator network (www.ed.voicethread .com). Although VoiceThread offers an open platform for any users, the use of the educator network within VoiceThread provides a safe space for students. By creating a classroom account, I can set up multiple identities within that one account. For instance, my classroom account was named "Dr. Z's Class," and within that account I created an identity for students using their first names (you may choose to use initials or other private identifiers, if needed). While I chose to create an identity for each of the students, the intuitive design of the tool makes it easy for students to create their own identity as well.

Once the identities were created, I was ready to begin creating a VoiceThread. To start, I named my project and added text from a document saved to my computer. Using the comment function, I then recorded myself reading the chosen text; this offered students an example of fluent reading to support their fluency development.

Students accessing this VoiceThread could then listen to me reading prior to recording their reading of the text. Once each student had recorded his or her own VoiceThread, the files were accessible as evidence of the student's reading fluency development for both instruction and assessment.

Classroom Example

As a literacy researcher and educator, I wanted to explore how digital tools can shape and support assessing 21st century learners' fluency development. VoiceThread quickly emerged as a promising digital tool. As I began using the tool, I quickly recognized its potential to measure students' fluency development. VoiceThread replicated the functions of the beloved tape recorder or handheld audio recorder (my typical go-to technology to measure students' fluency development—when time and patience allowed) with improved capabilities.

I began by creating a folder of selected poems, collected from Ken Nesbitt's website (www.poetry4kids.com), which has many poems, silly topics, titles, and readability levels available to choose from. One drawback I encountered when using VoiceThread was the time it took to select and format text to be readable when displayed on the screen, making short poems ideal. Consequently, I began with poetry for its supportive features of rhythm and rhyme, brevity, engagement, and prose to support students' fluency development. As an instructional support, I clicked the comment feature within my "My Puppy Likes the Water" VoiceThread and recorded myself reading the poem fluently. My fluent reading of the text was then saved within the VoiceThread, so that when students accessed the "My Puppy Likes the Water" VoiceThread, they could click on my profile image and hear my prerecorded model reading of "My Puppy Likes the Water." Some students tracked print on the screen while listening to the model of me reading, while others just listened. Students then clicked their individual profile images and began recording their own oral reading of the text. Students had the opportunity to read the text from the screen again, with or without my prerecorded model reading, to practice. When students felt ready, they re-recorded themselves reading the text again. Once they were pleased with their reading, they saved the VoiceThread on the MyVoice page, which is your home page within your classroom account that stores the individual VoiceThreads, making access to students' oral readings easy.

I then asked students to complete a self-reflection rubric while reviewing and listening to their completed VoiceThread session. Students' self-reflections revealed areas of growth, goal setting, and engagement. Isabella (a fifth grader) responded during her first self-assessment, "I didn't realize how much my reading changes." Another student, Sal (a first grader), struggled through his initial reading of the poem "My Teacher Took My iPod"; however, after he listened to the model reading twice, he demonstrated improved accuracy, rate, and expression. Overall, students demonstrated enhanced engagement and ownership of their learning, while I benefited from the easy access to students' oral reading captured through VoiceThread.

Your Turn

Integrating a web 2.0 tool into your literacy assessment toolbox takes time and practice. You will want to begin by exploring the tool. What are its features? Are there videos or other resources to learn more about the functions and use? If you are using VoiceThread to assess multiple students, you will need to create a classroom account (be sure to check the website for current pricing). Once signed up, create an identity for each student (or students can create their own through your classroom account). I chose to create multiple identities within my classroom account so students did not have to log in and out of the VoiceThread between their recordings. This allowed multiple students to record themselves reading the same text (such as the "My Teacher Took My iPod" VoiceThread) seamlessly.

Once students are assigned identities, they are ready to create an original Voice-Thread or visit an existing VoiceThread by accessing the MyVoice page. Although I created VoiceThreads ahead of time for students to access, the instinctive features of VoiceThread make it easy for students to upload a self-selected text as well. Once I identified an appropriate text (considering my students' interests, their reading levels, and the length of the poem), I downloaded a copy of the poem in pdf form. Because VoiceThread only allows students to record comments (oral recordings) while viewing one screen (no scrolling down to additional text) and the zoom features don't work while recording, I opened the selected poems as pdf files and took a screenshot of just the title and poem (excluding extraneous text or pictures). If you want students to self-select texts, I recommend creating a folder of poems or other texts that you have already fitted to the screen's size requirements. In those cases, when the teacher-identified or student- selected text can't fit on the digital screen, a print version of the text can be used while students orally read while recording within VoiceThread.

Once VoiceThreads are created and students have recorded their oral reading of a text, students' fluency development can be accessed at any time from home or school by students, peers, and teachers. Consider creating a benchmark text by identifying a grade-specific text to be administered periodically throughout the school year at specified times during a curriculum sequence in order to evaluate students' knowledge and skills relative to an explicit set of longer-term learning goals. The students' oral reading of the benchmark text is then used to inform instructional planning and decision making in the classroom. Students could track their progress reading the same text at the beginning, middle, and end of the year. As students continue to record, reflect, and review their fluency development, VoiceThread could also be used for peer review and feedback. Using a rubric, students listen to their classmates' recordings and score fluency. Students then conference with each other, giving specific feedback using the rubric and VoiceThreads to support the conference. VoiceThread allows for a portfolio of student reading that, when analyzed, provides a rich source of information to inform teaching and learning.

Conclusion

Integrating web 2.0 tools, such as VoiceThread, into the classroom provides endless possibilities for teaching and assessing 21st century learners. Although traditional technologies offered similar functions as web 2.0 tools, new and emerging digital tools combine traditional, static functions (listening, viewing, sharing, and so on) with an interactive multimedia environment. VoiceThread is one example of a digital tool that encourages learners to create and communicate knowledge in divergent, creative ways while simultaneously documenting and tracking students' learning (Kingsley & Brinkerhoff, 2011). In addition to being engaging, VoiceThread allows for quality assessments to inform teaching and learning. Through students' authentic application of literacy skills, coupled with functions available through web 2.0 tools, teachers can tailor instruction to meet the needs of their 21st century learners.

 **Katie Stover** is an assistant professor and coordinator of the Literacy Graduate Program at Furman University in Greenville, South Carolina. Katie's research interests include digital literacy, critical literacy, writing for social justice, and teacher education. To learn more about Katie's work, follow @kstover24 on Twitter.

 **Lindsay Sheronick Yearta** is an assistant professor of literacy at the University of South Carolina Upstate in Spartanburg, South Carolina. A former elementary school teacher, her research interests include digital literacy, vocabulary acquisition and retention, and critical literacy. To learn more about Lindsay's work, follow @Lyearta on Twitter.

CHAPTER 24

Using Blogs as Formative Assessment of Reading Comprehension

By Katie Stover and Lindsay Sheronick Yearta

As Joyce Holt Jennings, JoAnne Schudt Caldwell, and Janet Lerner (2013) write, "comprehension is the essence of the reading act" (p. 12). Yet comprehension is a complex cognitive process that cannot be measured in isolation. Judy Fiene and Susan McMahon (2007) write that educators must be wary of the overreliance on standardized test scores to determine student growth in the area of comprehension. If teachers wait for summative test results regarding comprehension, it is too late to make changes to instruction and remediation. Therefore, it is critical that teachers utilize ongoing formative assessment data to inform instruction (Fiene & McMahon, 2007).

Authentic classroom-based assessments, such as reader response, allow students to apply the skills and strategies being learned in class. When students participate in written discussion to convey their meaning-making process, teachers obtain a window into students' comprehension. Through reader response, students demonstrate their understanding, gain insight into text, and interact with literature in meaningful ways. Stephanie Harvey and Anne Goudvis (2007) discuss the importance of providing opportunities for students to respond in writing. When students write about their reading, instead of merely selecting a multiple-choice option, they are elucidating their thought processes. Therefore, teachers can more effectively assess students' comprehension. Examination of individual responses to text allows teachers to monitor and enhance students' comprehension (Duke & Pearson, 2002), helping teachers gain insight into their students' work, examine students' strengths and areas of need, and tailor instruction for individual learners.

According to Victoria Risko and Doris Walker-Dalhouse (2010), "classroom assessments should represent the multimodal ways students engage in literacy activity both in and out of school" (p. 421). With the nature of reading and writing communication constantly shifting as a result of rapidly developing technology (IRA, 2009; Leu, 2000), it is paramount that teachers incorporate 21st century tools to foster creative, communicative, and collaborative assessment and instructional opportunities (Karchmer-Klein & Shinas, 2012b).

One such digital tool is the blog. Blogs allow users to post content on the web for a wider audience and can enhance students' motivation and engagement in reading and writing practices. Common educational uses for blogs include sharing class news, reflecting, presenting student work, and responding to literature (Zawilinski, 2009). Blogs offer teachers authentic opportunities to assess students' thinking and understanding of what they read, and they can be incorporated as formative assessments in numerous ways. According to Harvey and Goudvis (2007), "it is impossible to know what readers are thinking when they read unless they tell us through conversation or written response" (p. 28). Blogs provide students with just such a digital space to demonstrate their inner conversation through written response and therefore also provide teachers with a glimpse into students' comprehension, allowing them to refine instruction to meet students' individual needs.

How Do I Do It?

First, we create a free account on Kidblog (www.kidblog.org) or a similar child-friendly blog website (visit **go.solution-tree.com/technology** for more examples). Once we established our account, we clicked on Create a Class to generate the class blog page. Next, we chose a URL and added the students. Kidblog requires that we give each student a screen name and a password to protect student privacy on the Internet. With a screen name and a password, students can begin blogging to share their thinking about text.

Once students publish their reader responses, we use the comment feature to provide a thoughtful response that considers students' strengths and areas of need based on their blog posts. We can also extend students' thinking by offering praise, asking critical questions, and engaging students in a dialogue about reading. Responding to students within the blog space allows us to provide strategy instruction and propel students' thinking further.

Blogs serve as excellent evidence of student growth in reading comprehension. Not only can we use this information to supplement student records and inform instructional decisions, but we can also encourage students to self-assess and reflect on their growth as readers. At the onset of the blogging experience, we have students establish two to three goals for themselves as readers and writers and post them on the blog for easy access to monitor and reflect. As the year progresses, students return to their goals and ongoing posts to assess their growth. As they reflect on their progress, they determine if they need to set new goals or continue to work on the established goals. A rubric can help guide their reflective process and provides us with a tool to assess various aspects of the blogging posts.

When developing a rubric for formative assessment of students' comprehension, we begin by narrowing the criteria down to a particular focus. The rubric is designed based on skills we are currently teaching or have previously taught rather than expectations that students have yet to learn. For instance, targeted skills could include making predictions or inferences, asking questions about the text, or summarizing. We might also consider adding writing skills that students have been learning. Criteria listed on the rubric will change as the year progresses and as students become accountable for learned reading and writing skills.

Classroom Example

Kayla Parton, a third-grade teacher, uses blogs to engage her students in meaningful interactions with the text and with their peers. Additionally, Kayla is able to formatively assess her students' reading comprehension within the blog space. In her first unit in the reader's workshop, she focuses on goal setting and establishing a love of reading. Instructional goals include referencing the text to describe the characters and setting, recognizing the theme, and retelling a story. Initial assessment of blog posts reveals that students' answers are short and only surface level. For example, when describing the character in the story, many students write the characters' names or describe their outward appearances rather than the characters' attitudes or character traits. Based on this assessment, Kayla decides to model how to think deeper about characters and guide students to engage in analysis and discussion with peers. During independent reading, she reminds students to record their thinking about the characters, setting, and plot on sticky notes as they read. Kayla encourages her students to use their notes to compose their blog posts. Not only does the blog allow Kayla to assess her students' comprehension, but it also allows her to monitor and adjust her instruction, enabling her to better meet the needs of her students.

As an experienced teacher, Kayla knows that students perform best when they are clear on expectations. Therefore, Kayla provides them with a rubric to develop their awareness and understanding of expectations before blogging began (figure 24.1, page 226). While the blog as a discussion space allows for flexibility, the rubric provides students with clear guidelines and parameters. She also encourages her students to explore the blog posts of their peers to see other examples. Students self-evaluated their posts by highlighting the appropriate criteria within the rubric. This fosters an active stance in the evaluation process. By monitoring their progress using rubrics to evaluate their blogs, students become more aware of their progress and develop a sense of ownership for their learning.

	0	1	2	3
Content	Student posts no blog or comment.	Student types one sentence about the book. Limited discussion on topic and about the book. Discussion has a detail about the story.	Student types two to four sentences about the book. Discussion is on topic and about the book. Discussion has lots of details about the story, and the student provides his or her buddy with questions, comments, or concerns about the story.	Student types five or more sentences about the book. In-depth discussion is on topic and about the book. Discussion has thought-provoking details about the story, and the student provides his or her buddy with questions, comments, or concerns about the story.
Reference to text	Student makes no references to the text.	Student makes few connections between evidence from the text and the discussion and interpretation of text one time by providing the page number, chapter number, paragraph, or uses a direct quote from the story.	Student makes few connections between evidence from the text and the discussion and interpretation of text one time by providing the page number, chapter number, paragraph, or uses a direct quote from the story.	Student makes connections between evidence from the text and the discussion and interpretation of text three or more times by providing the page number, chapter number, paragraph, or uses a direct quote from the story.

	0	**1**	**2**	**3**
Goal setting	Student establishes no goals.	Student establishes goals but goals are vague or unclear.	The student's goal includes general goals, including skills and strategies and the page or chapter he or she plans to read to in the upcoming reading.	Student sets clear goals, including skills and strategies. The student clearly states what page or chapter she or he plans to read to in the coming week.
Capitalization	Student does not capitalize any letters.	Student capitalizes some letters at the beginning of sentences, but not all of them.	Student capitalizes every letter at the beginning of a new sentence.	Student capitalizes every letter at the beginning of a new sentence. Character names and the book title are all capitalized.
Punctuation	Student uses no punctuation.	Student uses some punctuation, but not all sentences contain a sentence stopper.	Student uses a sentence stopper in all sentences, but some are not appropriate for the sentence.	Student uses an appropriate sentence stopper in all sentences.

Figure 24.1: Blogging rubric.

Using students' feedback and the criteria established in the rubric, Kayla regularly reads her students' blog posts and assesses their growth. She also conferences with them to demonstrate ways they could extend their thinking. For instance, when one student continuously asks low-level questions within his blog, she encourages him to create a T-chart in his journal to explore thick and thin questions. Thick, or divergent, questions foster deeper responses and do not have a single correct answer, while thin, or convergent, questions tend to have one acceptable answer and require surface-level thinking. For other students who struggle with character development, she encourages them to divide their journal into four squares and place sticky notes about their characters as they read under appropriate headings such as description of character, theory of character, motivation of character, and attributes of character. They then discuss how these sticky notes and charts can be used to develop blog posts about characters.

Ongoing assessment of students' blogs helps Kayla design a range of minilessons based on areas of needed development, including how to retell a story; how to reference the text; how to make connections, comments, or reactions to the text; and how to make predictions and ask questions about the text. One of Kayla's students responds to his reading by making text-to-text connections but little else. She encourages him to use a highlighter to find the specific elements of the text and see what type of connections he was making. Later blog posts reveal that this strategy enhances this student's understanding, as he includes the following: a retelling of the story ("Harry is scared of the drop of doom"), student-generated questions ("If you were Harry, would you ride the drop of doom?"), references to the text ("On page 56, Song Lee said, 'You had your eyes closed the whole time Sid. You're one cool dude.' Sidney made a face. 'At least I wasn't afraid to go on it like Harry'"), and connections ("If I was Harry, I would not go on the drop of doom").

Another student's initial blog posts are rather simple with no evidence of comprehension. One of her first posts states, "Finished the book today. It was a great book. Stanley was the main character. It was the best book ever." With teacher probing, this student becomes more expressive as she responds to the teacher's comments, as is evident in a more developed later post. She writes, "At the end of the book, Stanley became not invisible anymore. His family was happy and Stanley was happy too and Arthur was happy too with joy." This post suggests that teacher support and guidance foster her development of ideas and deeper comprehension of the text.

Another student focuses solely on summarizing. One of her first blogs reads, "So far, I have learned that she is starting fourth grade and there is a new girl at school. When Ramona sees the new girl, she is polite and asks her what her name is. And they become friends and start doing things together like when they ate lunch together and shared food together." Based on this post, it is evident that the student is creating meaning from the text. However, Kayla encourages her to support her thinking with evidence from the text. As time goes on, the student develops her posts by adding textual evidence to support her summaries: "Ramona was so so mad she almost screamed, but instead she just yelled 'MOM.' Her mom did not answer. Ramona called again, and this time her mom came. She did not like what she saw. 'What happened Ramona?' said her mother. Ramona did not answer. Mrs. Quimby says, 'Just go clean up.'"

These examples show how nudging and probing from the teacher in a digital space can help students to construct meaning and deepen their understanding. Ongoing assessment within the blog allows teachers to provide students with feedback on a regular basis. Evidence of student implementation of feedback and learning becomes clear in subsequent blog posts and provides the teacher with a window into students' overall understanding of text.

Your Turn

To begin using blogs in your own classroom, you will want to determine a focus and a purpose for the blog. For example, the primary purpose might be for students to discuss content with one another, or perhaps the intention is to enhance communication and collaboration with students from other classrooms. Blogging enables students to discuss their reading with peers at the same school or other schools, family members, or bloggers from around the world. There is a myriad of endless possibilities for purposes and audiences for blogging in the classroom.

After you determine a purpose and audience for the use of blogs in your classroom, the next step is to decide on a digital platform. The blogging examples presented in this chapter were established using Kidblog, a free blogging site teachers created for K–12 classroom teachers and students. Kidblog has various safety features in place, which make it appropriate for use in the K–12 classroom. You have the ability to approve all posts and comments before they are posted to the blog.

Once the blog space is established for the class, discuss blogs with students and show them various examples, including the class blog. Using a Promethean board or SMART Board, model how to create a blog post and use the various features offered in Kidblog, such as font, size, the addition of images, how to change the background, and so on. Following a gradual release of responsibility model (Pearson & Gallagher, 1983), we suggest engaging students in shared writing to construct a blog post about a commonly read book or experience. This will provide students with an opportunity to learn how to log in and create posts with support and guidance, as this is a new experience for many students. Like all new technologies, it is necessary to model for students and provide time for exploration.

Next, encourage students to write an "all about me" post to provide them with an opportunity to practice interacting with the blog space. This post serves several purposes. First, it allows students to introduce themselves to their classroom community, inclusive of their peers and teacher. You can model what students should do by first sharing your own "all about me" post as an introduction to the class (figure 24.2).

Welcome!

Categories: Blog   September 5, 2013 @ 9:45 PM   8 Comments   Edit this Post

Welcome to our third grade Kidblog site! I am excited to begin my fourth year teaching. For the past three years I taught Kindergarten and am thrilled to be teaching third grade this year. I am super excited about incorporating this new technology into my students' reading time this year. My students are super excited to share about their readings on this blog. Thank you for taking the time to read our thinking. Happy reading!!

8 Comments

Figure 24.2: Sample teacher introductory blog post.

In addition to allowing students to familiarize themselves with the blogging experience, the "all about me" post fosters a sense of community as students get to know their classmates (figure 24.3).

All About Me

Categories: Blog   September 6, 2013 @ 9:23 AM   3 Comments   Edit this Post

Hi. My name is Alexis. I am in third grade. My favorite subject in school is math! In my free time I like to write stories about animals. I have one sister. My dad loves to play video games, and my mom tells me what to do a lot. I have a dog named Chico.

3 Comments

Figure 24.3: Sample student introductory blog post.

Once students familiarize themselves with the blog in general through a few initial posts, they can begin to blog independently. Again, there are numerous ways to implement blogs in the classroom. However, in this chapter, we describe the use of blogging to respond to independent reading as a form of reader response. As a class, examine some of the exemplary posts and discuss them. Before you begin assessing the blog posts, make sure that the students are aware of the requirements and have access to the scoring guidelines and rubric.

While we have provided some concrete suggestions to implement blogging to assess student comprehension and provide differentiated instruction through the use of authentic reader response, the steps can and should be adapted to meet your learners' specific needs.

Conclusion

The International Reading Association (2013) states that formative assessment should be purposeful, collaborative, and dynamic in order to provide descriptive feedback and support continuous improvement. We hope that the examples included here provide compelling evidence that demonstrates a need for formative assessment that integrates 21st century literacies and technology. This approach offers a way to incorporate formative assessment and individualized instruction beyond the far-too-common whole-class format. As Patricia Cunningham and Richard Allington (2011) suggest, teachers should regularly assess students to determine how they are developing and make instructional decisions accordingly. Blogging, therefore, allows for individualized instruction informed by the assessment of the students' blog posts.

References and Resources

Afflerbach, P. (2012). *Understanding and using reading assessment, K–12* (2nd ed.). Newark, DE: International Reading Association.

Aitken, K., & Dewey, B. (2013). Ecstatic for e-readers. *The Reading Teacher, 66*(5), 390.

Albion, P. R. (2008). Web 2.0 in teacher education: Two imperatives for action. *Computers in the Schools, 25*(3–4), 181–198.

Allington, R. L. (2006). *What really matters for struggling readers: Designing research-based programs* (2nd ed.). Boston: Allyn & Bacon.

Alvermann, D. E. (2001). *Effective literacy instruction for adolescents: Executive summary and paper commissioned by the National Reading Conference.* Chicago: National Reading Conference. Accessed at http://literacyresearchassociation.org/publications/alverwhite2.pdf on January 18, 2014.

Alvermann, D. E. (Ed.). (2002). *Adolescents and literacies in a digital world.* New York: Peter Lang.

Alvermann, D. E. (2003). *Seeing themselves as capable and engaged readers: Adolescents and re/ mediated instruction.* Naperville, IL: Learning Point Associates.

Alvermann, D. E., Marshall, J. D., McLean, C. A., Huddleston, A. P., Joaquin, J., & Bishop, J. (2012). Adolescents' web-based literacies, identity construction, and skill development. *Literacy Research and Instruction, 51*(3), 179–195.

Aronson, E., Blaney, N., Stephan, C., Sikes, J., & Snapp, M. (1978). *The jigsaw classroom.* Beverly Hills, CA: SAGE.

Artino, A. R., Jr. (2008). Promoting academic motivation and self-regulation: Practical guidelines for online instructors. *TechTrends, 52*(3), 37–45.

Attewell, P., Suazo-Garcia, B., & Battle, J. (2003). Computers and young children: Social benefit or social problem? *Social Forces, 82*(1), 277–296.

Baker, E. A. (Ed.). (2010). *The new literacies: Multiple perspectives on research and practice.* New York: Guilford Press.

Bakhtin, M. M. (1981). Forms of time and the chronotope in the novel (C. Emerson & M. Holquist, Trans.). In M. Holquist (Ed.), *The dialogic imagination: Four essays by M. M. Bakhtin* (pp. 84–258). Austin: University of Texas Press.

Barone, D. (2012). Exploring home and school involvement of young children with Web 2.0 and social media. *Research in the Schools, 19*(1), 1–11.

Barone, D., & Wright, T. E. (2008). Literacy instruction with digital and media technologies. *The Reading Teacher, 62*(4), 292–302.

Beach, R. (2012). Constructing digital learning commons in the literacy classroom. *Journal of Adolescent and Adult Literacy, 55*(5), 448–451.

Beach, R. (2013, December). *Understanding and creating digital texts through social practices.* Presidential Address of the 57th Annual Literacy Research Association conference, Dallas, TX. Accessed at www.literacyresearchassociation.org/index.php/component/content/article?id=116 on January 9, 2015.

Beach, R., & O'Brien, D. (2012). Apple iBooks textbooks: What is a textbook? [Web log post]. Accessed at www.appsforlearningliteracies.com/blog/2012/1/23/apple-ibooks-textbooks-what-is-a-textbook.html on August 15, 2014.

Beach, R., & O'Brien, D. (2013). *Using iPad and iPhone apps for learning with literacy across the curriculum.* Author.

Beach, R., & O'Brien, D. (2015). *Using apps for learning across the curriculum.* New York: Routledge.

Bear, D. R., Invernizzi, M., Templeton, S., & Johnston, F. (2012). *Words their way: Word study for phonics, vocabulary, and spelling instruction* (5th ed.). Boston: Pearson.

Beck, I. L., McKeown, M. G., & Kucan, L. (2008). *Creating robust vocabulary: Frequently asked questions and extended examples* (2nd ed.). New York: Guilford Press.

Beck, I. L., McKeown, M. G., & Kucan, L. (2013). *Bringing words to life: Robust vocabulary instruction* (2nd ed.). New York: Guilford Press.

Becker, M., McElvany, N., & Kortenbruck, M. (2010). Intrinsic and extrinsic reading motivation as predictors of reading literacy: A longitudinal study. *Journal of Educational Psychology, 102*(4), 773–785.

Beers, K. (2003). *When kids can't read: What teachers can do—A guide for teachers 6–12.* Portsmouth, NH: Heinemann.

Berenbaum, M. (2005). *The world must know: The history of the Holocaust as told in the United States Holocaust Memorial Museum* (2nd ed.). Baltimore: Johns Hopkins University Press.

Beschorner, B., & Hutchison, A. (2013). iPads as a literacy teaching tool in early childhood. *International Journal of Education in Mathematics, Science and Technology, 1*(1), 16–24.

Biancarosa, G., & Snow, C. E. (2006). *Reading next: A vision for action and research in middle and high school literacy* (2nd ed.). Washington, DC: Alliance for Excellent Education.

Biemiller, A., & Boote, C. (2006). An effective method for building meaning vocabulary in primary grades. *Journal of Educational Psychology, 98*(1), 44–62.

Blachowicz, C. L. Z., & Fisher, P. (2000). Vocabulary instruction. In M. L. Kamil, P. B. Mosenthal, P. D. Pearson, & R. Barr (Eds.), *Handbook of reading research* (Vol. 3, pp. 503–523). Mahwah, NJ: Erlbaum.

Black, P., & Wiliam, D. (1998). Assessment and classroom learning. *Assessment in Education*, 5(1), 7–74.

Bruce, B. C. (2002). Diversity and critical social engagement: How changing technologies enable new modes of literacy in changing circumstances. In D. E. Alvermann (Ed.), *Adolescents and literacies in a digital world* (pp. 1–19). New York: Peter Lang.

Bruder, P. (2011). *VoiceThread—A valuable classroom collaboration tool*. Accessed at www.njea.org/news-and-publications/njea-review/march-2011/voicethread on December 20, 2014.

Brunvand, S., & Byrd, S. (2011). Using VoiceThread to promote learning engagement and success for all students. *Teaching Exceptional Children*, 43(4), 28–37.

Bucolo, J. (2011). "Survivor: Satis House"—Creating classroom community while teaching Dickens in a reality-TV world. *English Journal*, 100(5), 29–32.

Buehl, D. (2011). *Developing readers in the academic disciplines*. Newark, DE: International Reading Association.

Caldwell, J. S. (2008). *Reading assessment: A primer for teachers and coaches* (2nd ed.). New York: Guilford Press.

Caldwell, J. S., & Leslie, L. (2005). *Intervention strategies to follow informal reading inventory assessment: So what do I do now?* Boston: Pearson.

Calkins, L., Ehrenworth, M., & Lehman, C. (2012). *Pathways to the Common Core: Accelerating achievement*. Portsmouth, NH: Heinemann.

Carnegie Council for Advancing Adolescent Literacy. (2010). *Time to act: An agenda for advancing adolescent literacy for college and career success*. New York: Carnegie Corporation of New York.

Cassidy, J., & Grote-Garcia, S. (2013). Common Core State Standards top the 2014 *What's Hot What's Not* survey. *Reading Today*, 31(1), 12–16.

Castek, J., & Beach, R. (2013). Using apps to support disciplinary literacy and science learning. *Journal of Adolescent and Adult Literacy*, 56(7), 554–564.

Castek, J., Beach, R., Cotanch, H., & Scott, J. (2014). Examining middle-school students' uses of Diigo annotations to engage in collaborative argumentative writing. In R. Anderson & C. Mims (Eds.), *Handbook of research on digital tools for writing instruction in K–12 settings* (pp. 80–101). Hershey, PA: IGI Global.

Castek, J., Dalton, B., & Grisham, D. L. (2012). Using multimedia to support generative vocabulary learning. In E. J. Kame'enui & J. F. Baumann (Eds.), *Vocabulary instruction: Research to practice* (2nd ed., pp. 303–321). New York: Guilford Press.

Cazden, C., Cope, B., Fairclough, N., Gee, J., Kalantzis, M., Kress, G., et al. (1996). A pedagogy of multiliteracies: Designing social futures. *Harvard Educational Review*, 66(1), 60–92.

Chall, J. S., Jacobs, V. A., & Baldwin, L. E. (1990). *The reading crisis: Why poor children fall behind*. Cambridge, MA: Harvard University Press.

Chard, D. J., Vaughn, S., & Tyler, B.-J. (2002). A synthesis of research on effective interventions for building reading fluency with elementary students with learning disabilities. *Journal of Learning Disabilities*, 35(5), 386–406.

Chera, P., & Wood, C. (2003). Animated multimedia "talking books" can promote phonological awareness in children beginning to read. *Learning and Instruction*, 13(1), 33–52.

Chomsky, C. (1976). After decoding: What? *Language Arts*, 53(3), 288–296.

City of Chicago TV. (2011, June 2). *Historic Pullman community* [Video file]. Accessed at www.youtube.com/watch?v=ILI4a2JpdWQ on August 15, 2014.

Clarke, L. W., & Besnoy, K. D. (2010). Connecting the old to the new: What technology-crazed adolescents tell us about teaching content area literacy. *Journal of Media Literacy Education, 2*(1), 47–56.

Coiro, J. (2003). Reading comprehension on the Internet: Expanding our understanding of reading comprehension to encompass new literacies. *The Reading Teacher, 56*(5), 458–464.

Coiro, J., Castek, J., & Guzniczak, L. (2011). Uncovering online reading comprehension processes: Two adolescents reading independently and collaboratively on the Internet. In P. J. Dunston, L. B. Gambrell, K. Headley, S. K. Fullerton, P. M. Stecker, V. R. Gillis, & C. C. Bates (Eds.), *60th yearbook of the Literacy Research Association* (pp. 354–369). Oak Creek, WI: Literacy Research Association.

Coiro, J., & Dobler, E. (2007). Exploring the online reading comprehension strategies used by sixth-grade skilled readers to search for and locate information on the Internet. *Reading Research Quarterly, 42*(2), 214–257.

Coiro, J., Knobel, M., Lankshear, C., & Leu, D. J. (Eds.). (2008). *Handbook of research on new literacies*. New York: Erlbaum.

Collins, S. (2008). *The hunger games*. New York: Scholastic.

Colwell, J. (2012). Using a collaborative blog project to introduce disciplinary-literacy strategies in social studies pre-service teacher education. *Journal of School Connections, 4*(1), 25–52.

Copple, C., & Bredekamp, S. (Eds.). (2009). *Developmentally appropriate practice in early childhood programs serving children from birth through age 8* (3rd ed.). Washington, DC: National Association for the Education of Young Children.

Costanzo, W. V. (2004). *Great films and how to teach them*. Urbana, IL: National Council of Teachers of English.

Cox, B. E., Shanahan, T., & Tinzmann, M. B. (1991). Children's knowledge of organization, cohesion, and voice in written exposition. *Research in the Teaching of English, 25*(2), 179–218.

Cuban, L. (2001). *Oversold and underused: Reforming schools through technology, 1980–2000*. Cambridge, MA: Harvard University Press.

Culham, R. (2011). Reading with a writer's eye. In T. V. Rasinski (Ed.), *Rebuilding the foundation: Effective reading instruction for 21st century literacy* (pp. 245–268). Bloomington, IN: Solution Tree Press.

Cunningham, A. E., & Stanovich, K. E. (1998). What reading does for the mind. *American Educator, 22*(1–2), 8–15.

Cunningham, P. M., & Allington, R. L. (2011). *Classrooms that work: They can all read and write* (5th ed.). Boston: Pearson.

Dalton, B. (2012/2013). Multimodal composition and the Common Core State Standards. *The Reading Teacher, 66*(4), 333–339.

Dalton, B., & Grisham, D. L. (2011). eVoc strategies: 10 ways to use technology to build vocabulary. *The Reading Teacher, 64*(5), 306–317.

Dalton, B., & Grisham, D. L. (2013). Love that book: Multimodal response to literature. *The Reading Teacher, 67*(3), 220–225.

Dalton, B., & Proctor, C. P. (2008). The changing landscape of text and comprehension in the age of new literacies. In J. Coiro, M. Knobel, C. Lankshear, & D. J. Leu (Eds.), *Handbook of research on new literacies* (pp. 297–324). New York: Erlbaum.

Dalton, B., Proctor, C. P., Uccelli, P., Mo, E., & Snow, C. E. (2011). Designing for diversity: The role of reading strategies and interactive vocabulary in a digital reading environment for fifth-grade monolingual English and bilingual students. *Journal of Literacy Research, 43*(1), 68–100.

Dalton, B., & Smith, B. E. (2012, December). *"It sounds all dramatic like in a movie": Two middle school males collaboratively design a multimodal digital folktale.* Paper presented at the 62nd annual meeting of the Literacy Research Association, San Diego, CA.

Dalton, B., Smith, B. E., & Renner, N. (2012). [Developing academic vocabulary through student-created vocabulary videos]. Unpublished raw data.

Davis, D., Spraker, J., & Jushman, K. (2005). *Improving adolescent reading: Findings from research.* Portland, OR: Northwest Regional Educational Laboratory.

de Jong, M. T., & Bus, A. G. (2002). Quality of book-reading matters for emergent readers: An experiment with the same book in a regular or electronic format. *Journal of Educational Psychology, 94*(1), 145–155.

Denlinger, K. (n.d.) *Overview.* Accessed at https://sites.google.com/site/ormsmodel on August 15, 2014.

Dewey, J. (1933). *How we think: A restatement of the relation of reflective thinking to the educative process.* Boston: Heath.

DiCamillo, K. (2006). *The miraculous journey of Edward Tulane.* Somerville, MA: Candlewick Press.

Diigo Help. (n.d.). *FAQ.* Accessed at http://help.diigo.com/teacher-account/faq on August 15, 2014.

Dorfman, L. R., & Cappelli, R. (2007). *Mentor texts: Teaching writing through children's literature, K–6.* Portland, ME: Stenhouse.

Duke, N. K. (2000). 3.6 minutes per day: The scarcity of informational texts in first grade. *Reading Research Quarterly, 35*(2), 202–224.

Duke, N. K. (2004). The case for informational text. *Educational Leadership, 61*(6), 40–44.

Duke, N. K., Bennett-Armistead, S., & Roberts, E. M. (2003). Filling the great void: Why we should bring nonfiction into the early-grade classroom. *American Educator, 27*(1), 30–34.

Duke, N. K., & Pearson, P. D. (2002). Effective practices for developing reading comprehension. In A. E. Farstrup & S. J. Samuels (Eds.), *What research has to say about reading instruction* (3rd ed., pp. 205–242). Newark, DE: International Reading Association.

Duke, N. K., Pressley, M., & Hilden, K. (2004). Difficulties with reading comprehension. In C. A. Stone, E. R. Silliman, B. J. Ehren, & K. Apel (Eds.), *Handbook of language and literacy: Development and disorders* (pp. 501–520). New York: Guilford Press.

Duke, N. K., & Purcell-Gates, V. (2003). Genres at home and at school: Bridging the known to the new. *The Reading Teacher, 57*(1), 30–37.

Dwyer, B. (2010). *Scaffolding Internet reading: A study of a disadvantaged school community in Ireland.* Unpublished doctoral dissertation, University of Nottingham, Nottingham, England.

Dwyer, B. (2013). Developing online reading comprehension: Changes, challenges, and consequences. In K. Hall, T. Cremin, B. Comber, & L. C. Moll (Eds.), *International handbook of research on children's literacy, learning and culture* (pp. 344–358). Chichester, West Sussex, England: Wiley-Blackwell.

Dwyer, B., & Larson, L. (2014). The writer in the reader: Building communities of response in digital environments. In K. E. Pytash & R. E. Ferdig (Eds.), *Exploring technology for writing and writing instruction* (pp. 202–220). Hershey, PA: IGI Global.

Ebner, R. J., & Ehri, L. C. (2012). *Using the Internet for vocabulary development.* Unpublished manuscript.

Ebner, R. J., & Ehri, L. C. (2013). Vocabulary learning on the Internet: Using a structured think-aloud procedure. *Journal of Adolescent and Adult Literacy, 56*(6), 480–489.

Ebner, R. J., & Ehri, L. C. (2014). *Teaching students how to self-regulate their online vocabulary learning by using a structured think-to-yourself procedure.* Manuscript submitted for publication.

Expeditionary Learning. (n.d.). *Preparing to record your VoiceThread PSA script: Using peer feedback to speak fluently in an engaging manner.* Accessed at http://commoncoresuccess.elschools.org/curriculum/grade-3/module-4/unit-3/lesson-11 on August 15, 2014.

Fahser-Herro, D., & Steinkuehler, C. (2009/2010). Web 2.0 literacy and secondary teacher education. *Journal of Computing in Teacher Education, 26*(2), 55–62.

Fang, Z. (2008). Going beyond the Fab Five: Helping students cope with the unique linguistic challenges of expository reading in intermediate grades. *Journal of Adolescent and Adult Literacy, 51*(6), 476–487.

Fang, Z. (2012). The challenges of reading disciplinary texts. In T. L. Jetton & C. Shanahan (Eds.), *Adolescent literacy in the academic disciplines: General principles and practical strategies* (pp. 34–68). New York: Guilford Press.

Fang, Z. (2013/2014). Disciplinary literacy in science: Developing science literacy through trade books. *Journal of Adolescent and Adult Literacy, 57*(4), 274–278.

Fang, Z., & Schleppegrell, M. J. (2010). Disciplinary literacies across content areas: Supporting secondary reading through functional language analysis. *Journal of Adolescent and Adult Literacy, 53*(7), 587–597.

Fang, Z., Schleppegrell, M. J., & Cox, B. E. (2006). Understanding the language demands of schooling: Nouns in academic registers. *Journal of Literacy Research, 38*(3), 247–273.

Farrell, E. J. (1966). Listen, my children, and you shall read . . . *English Journal, 55*(1), 39–45.

Fiene, J., & McMahon, S. (2007). Assessing comprehension: A classroom-based process. *The Reading Teacher, 60*(5), 406–417.

Fisher, D., Frey, N., & Lapp, D. (2012). *Teaching students to read like detectives: Comprehending, analyzing, and discussing text.* Bloomington, IN: Solution Tree Press.

Florida State Board of Education. (2012). *Digital learning: Harnessing the power of technology to transform education for the 21st century economy.* Accessed at www.fldoe.org/board/meetings/2012_07_17/digitalplan.pdf on August 15, 2014.

Foster, K. C., Erickson, G. C., Foster, D. F., Brinkman, D., & Torgeson, J. K. (1994). Computer administered instruction in phonological awareness: Evaluation of the DaisyQuest program. *Journal of Research and Development in Education, 27*(2), 126–137.

Fountas, I. C., & Pinnell, G. S. (2006). *Teaching for comprehending and fluency: Thinking, talking, and writing about reading, K–8*. Portsmouth, NH: Heinemann.

Frey, N., Fisher, D., & Gonzalez, A. (2010). *Literacy 2.0: Reading and writing in 21st century classrooms*. Bloomington, IN: Solution Tree Press.

Friedman, T. L., & Mandelbaum, M. (2011). *That used to be us: How America fell behind in the world it invented and how we can come back*. New York: Farrar, Straus and Giroux.

Fuchs, D., & Fuchs, L. S. (2009). Responsiveness to intervention: Multilevel assessment and instruction as early intervention and disability identification. *The Reading Teacher, 63*(3), 250–252.

Furger, R. (2002, January 21). *Take a deeper look at assessment for understanding*. Accessed at www .edutopia.org/performance-assessment-math on August 15, 2014.

Gainer, J. (2008). Who is DeAndre? Tapping the power of popular culture in literacy learning. *Voices From the Middle, 16*(1), 23–30.

Gambrell, L. B. (2011a). Motivation in the school reading curriculum. In T. V. Rasinski (Ed.), *Rebuilding the foundation: Effective reading instruction for 21st century literacy* (pp. 41–65). Bloomington, IN: Solution Tree Press.

Gambrell, L. B. (2011b). Seven rules of engagement: What's most important to know about motivation to read. *The Reading Teacher, 65*(3), 172–178.

Gamse, B. C., Bloom, H. S., Kemple, J. J., Jacob, R. T., Boulay, B., Bozzi, L., et al. (2008). *Reading First impact study: Interim report*. Washington, DC: U.S. Department of Education.

Ganske, K. (2000). *Word journeys: Assessment-guided phonics, spelling, and vocabulary instruction*. New York: Guilford Press.

Gee, J. P. (2008). *Logging into the playground: How digital media are shaping children's learning* [Video file]. Accessed at www.youtube.com/watch?v=jwouueYlwGo on January 8, 2012.

Gee, J. P. (2010). A situated-sociocultural approach to literacy and technology. In E. A. Baker (Ed.), *The new literacies: Multiple perspectives on research and practice* (pp. 165–193). New York: Guilford Press.

Glaubke, C. (2007). *The effects of interactive media on preschoolers' learning: A review of the research and recommendations for the future*. Oakland, CA: Children Now.

Golden, J. (2001). *Reading in the dark: Using film as a tool in the English classroom*. Urbana, IL: National Council of Teachers of English.

Graham, S., & Perin, D. (2007). *Writing next: Effective strategies to improve writing of adolescents in middle and high schools—A report to Carnegie Corporation of New York*. Washington, DC: Alliance for Excellent Education.

Graves, M. F., & Watts-Taffe, S. (2008). For the love of words: Fostering word consciousness in young readers. *The Reading Teacher, 62*(3), 185–193.

Greene, B. A., & Land, S. M. (2000). A qualitative analysis of scaffolding use in a resource-based learning environment involving the World Wide Web. *Journal of Educational Computing Research, 23*(2), 151–179.

Gregg, M., & Sekeres, D. C. (2006). Supporting children's reading of expository text in the geography classroom. *The Reading Teacher, 60*(2), 102–110.

Griffith, L. W., & Rasinski, T. V. (2004). A focus on fluency: How one teacher incorporated fluency with her reading curriculum. *The Reading Teacher, 58*(2), 126–137.

Grisham, D. L., & Smetana, L. (2011). Generative technology for teachers and teacher educators. *Journal of Reading Education, 36*(3), 12–18.

Guskey, T. R. (2007/2008). The rest of the story. *Educational Leadership, 65*(4), 28–35.

Guthrie, J. T., & Alao, S. (1997). Designing contexts to increase motivations for reading. *Educational Psychologist, 32*(2), 95–105.

Guthrie, J. T., Wigfield, A., Humenick, N. M., Perencevich, K. C., Taboada, A., & Barbosa, P. (2006). Influences of stimulating tasks on reading motivation and comprehension. *The Journal of Educational Research, 99*(4), 232–245.

Haggard, M. R. (1982). The vocabulary self-collection strategy: An active approach to word learning. *Journal of Reading, 26*(3), 203–207.

Hall, M., & Stahl, K. A. D. (2012). Devillainizing video in support of comprehension and vocabulary instruction. *The Reading Teacher, 65*(6), 403–406.

Hancock, M. R. (2004). *A celebration of literature and response: Children, books, and teachers in K–8 classrooms* (2nd ed.). Upper Saddle River, NJ: Prentice Hall.

Harrison, C., Dwyer, B., & Castek, J. (2014). *Using technology to improve reading and learning.* Huntington Beach, CA: Shell Education.

Harvey, S., & Goudvis, A. (2007). *Strategies that work: Teaching comprehension for understanding and engagement* (2nd ed.). Portland, ME: Stenhouse.

Hassett, D. D., & Curwood, J. S. (2009). Theories and practices of multimodal education: The instructional dynamics of picture books and primary classrooms. *The Reading Teacher, 63*(4), 270–282.

Herman, P., Gomez, L. M., Gomez, K., Williams, A., & Perkins, K. (2008). Metacognitive support for reading in science classrooms. In P. A. Kirschner, F. Prins, V. Jonker, & G. Kanselaar (Eds.), *Proceedings of the 8th International Conference of the Learning Sciences* (Vol. 1, pp. 342–349). Utrecht, the Netherlands: International Society of the Learning Sciences.

Herman, P., & Wardrip, P. (2012). Reading to learn. *Science Teacher, 79*(1), 48–51.

Hew, K. F., & Brush, T. (2007). Integrating technology into K–12 teaching and learning: Current knowledge gaps and recommendations for future research. *Educational Technology Research and Development, 55*(3), 223–252.

Hillman, M., & Moore, T. J. (2004). The web and early literacy. *Computers in the Schools, 21*(3–4), 15–21.

Horrigan, J. B. (2010). *Broadband adoption and use in America* (OBI Working Paper Series No. 1). Washington, DC: Federal Communications Commission. Accessed at http://hraunfoss .fcc.gov/edocs_public/attachmatch/DOC-296442A1.pdf on February 25, 2010.

Hudson, R. F., Lane, H. B., & Pullen, P. C. (2005). Reading fluency assessment and instruction: What, why, and how? *The Reading Teacher, 58*(8), 702–714.

Hull, G. A., & Stornaiuolo, A. (2010). Literate arts in a global world: Reframing social networking as cosmopolitan practice. *Journal of Adolescent and Adult Literacy, 54*(2), 85–97.

Hundley, M., & Holbrook, T. (2013). Set in stone or set in motion? Multimodal and digital writing with preservice English teachers. *Journal of Adolescent and Adult Literacy, 56*(6), 500–509.

Hutchison, A. (2013). *NYC movie: Made with Explain Everything* [Video file]. Accessed at www .youtube.com/watch?v=q5kaOEPiWHk&feature=youtu.be on August 15, 2014.

Hutchison, A., Beschorner, B., & Schmidt-Crawford, D. (2012). Exploring the use of the iPad for literacy learning. *The Reading Teacher, 66*(1), 15–23.

Hutchison, A., & Reinking, D. (2011). Teachers' perceptions of integrating information and communication technologies into literacy instruction: A national survey in the United States. *Reading Research Quarterly, 46*(4), 312–333.

Hutchison, A., & Woodward, L. (2014). A planning cycle for integrating digital technology into literacy instruction. *The Reading Teacher, 67*(6), 455–464.

International Reading Association. (2009). *New literacies and 21st-century technologies: A position statement of the International Reading Association.* Newark, DE: Author. Accessed at www .reading.org/Libraries/position-statements-and-resolutions/ps1067_NewLiteracies21stCentury .pdf on August 15, 2014.

International Reading Association. (2013). *Formative assessment: A position statement of the International Reading Association.* Newark, DE: Author. Accessed at www.reading.org /Libraries/position-statements-and-resolutions/ps1080_formative_assessment_web.pdf on August 15, 2014.

International Society for Technology in Education. (2007). *ISTE Standards: Students.* Accessed at www.iste.org/docs/pdfs/20–14_ISTE_Standards-S_PDF.pdf on January 12, 2015.

International Society for Technology in Education. (2008). *ISTE Standards: Teachers.* Accessed at www.iste.org/docs/pdfs/20–14_ISTE_Standards-T_PDF.pdf on January 12, 2015.

Ito, M., Baumer, S., Bittanti, M., Boyd, D., Cody, R., Herr-Stephenson, B., et al. (2010). *Hanging out, messing around, and geeking out: Kids living and learning with new media.* Cambridge, MA: MIT Press.

Ivey, G., & Broaddus, K. (2001). "Just plain reading": A survey of what makes students want to read in middle school classrooms. *Reading Research Quarterly, 36*(4), 350–377.

Ivey, G., & Johnston, P. (2011, November). *Engagement with young adult literature: Processes, consequences and limits.* Paper presented at the annual meeting of the Literacy Research Association, Jacksonville, FL.

Jenkins, H. (2006). *Confronting the challenges of participatory culture: Media education for the 21st century* [White paper]. Accessed at www.digitallearningmacfound.org on September 1, 2011.

Jennings, J. H., Caldwell, J. S., & Lerner, J. W. (2013). *Reading problems: Assessment and teaching strategies* (7th ed.). Boston: Pearson.

Jewish Holocaust Centre. (2013). *StoryPod JHC* [Mobile application]. Accessed at https://itunes .apple.com/vg/app/storypod-jhc/id620265487?mt=8 on September 15, 2014.

Jewitt, C. (2005). Multimodality, "reading," and "writing" for the 21st century. *Discourse: Studies in the Cultural Politics of Education, 26*(3), 315–331.

Jewitt, C. (Ed.). (2009). *The Routledge handbook of multimodal analysis.* New York: Routledge.

Jewitt, C. (2011). An introduction to multimodality. In C. Jewitt (Ed.), *The Routledge handbook of multimodal analysis* (pp. 14–27). New York: Routledge.

Jocius, R. (2013). Exploring adolescents' multimodal responses to *The Kite Runner*: Understanding how students use digital media for academic purposes. *Journal of Media Literacy Education, 5*(1), 310–325.

Johnson, L., Levine, A., Smith, R., & Smythe, T. (2009). *The 2009 Horizon report: K–12 edition.* Austin, TX: The New Media Consortium.

Johnston, P. H. (2012). *Opening minds: Using language to change lives*. Portland, ME: Stenhouse.

Jones, S. (2002). *The Internet goes to college: How students are living in the future with today's technology*. Washington, DC: Pew Internet and American Life Project. Accessed at www.pewinternet.org/files/old-media/Files/Reports/2002/PIP_College_Report.pdf.pdf on August 15, 2014.

Kalantzis, M., Cope, B., & Cloonan, A. (2010). A multiliteracies perspective on the new literacies. In E. A. Baker (Ed.), *The new literacies: Multiple perspectives on research and practice* (pp. 61–87). New York: Guilford Press.

Kame'enui, E. J., & Baumann, J. F. (Eds.). (2012). *Vocabulary instruction: Research to practice* (2nd ed.). New York: Guilford Press.

Kamil, M. L., Borman, G. D., Dole, J., Kral, C. C., Salinger, T., & Torgesen, J. (2008). *Improving adolescent literacy: Effective classroom and intervention practices* (NCEE #2008–4027). Washington, DC: National Center for Education Evaluation and Regional Assistance.

Kamil, M. L., Pearson, P. D., Moje, E. B., & Afflerbach, P. P. (Eds.). (2011). *Handbook of reading research* (Vol. 4). New York: Routledge.

Kanuka, H., & Anderson, T. (1998). Online social interchange, discord, and knowledge construction. *The Journal of Distance Education*, *13*(1), 57–74.

Karchmer, R. A., Mallette, M. H., Kara-Soteriou, J., & Leu, D. J., Jr. (Eds.) (2005). *Innovative approaches to literacy education: Using the Internet to support new literacies*. Newark, DE: International Reading Association.

Karchmer-Klein, R., & Layton, V. (2006). Literature-based collaborative Internet projects in elementary classrooms. *Reading Research and Instruction*, *45*(4), 261–294.

Karchmer-Klein, R., & Shinas, V. (2012a). 21st century literacies in teacher education: Investigating multimodal texts in the context of an online graduate-level literacy and technology course. *Research in the Schools*, *19*(1), 60–74.

Karchmer-Klein, R., & Shinas, V. H. (2012b). Guiding principles for supporting new literacies in your classroom. *The Reading Teacher*, *65*(5), 288–293.

Kingsley, K. V., & Brinkerhoff, J. (2011). Web 2.0 tools for authentic instruction, learning, and assessment. *Social Studies and the Young Learner*, *23*(3), 9–12.

Kintsch, W. (1992). A cognitive architecture for comprehension. In H. L. Pick Jr., P. van den Broek, & D. C. Knill (Eds.), *Cognition: Conceptual and methodological issues* (pp. 143–163). Washington, DC: American Psychological Association.

Kirkland, D. E. (2013). *A search past silence: The literacy of young Black men*. New York: Teachers College Press.

Kist, W. (2000). Beginning to create the new literacy classroom: What does the new literacy look like? *Journal of Adolescent and Adult Literacy*, *43*(8), 710–718.

Kist, W. (2008). Film and video in the classroom: Back to the future. In J. Flood, S. B. Heath, & D. Lapp (Eds.), *Handbook of research on teaching literacy through the communicative and visual arts* (Vol. 2, pp. 521–527). New York: Routledge.

Kleiman, G. M., Winograd, P. N., & Humphrey, M. M. (1979). *Prosody and children's parsing of sentences* (Tech. Rep. No. 123). Urbana-Champaign, IL: Center for the Study of Reading.

Korat, O., & Shamir, A. (2008). The educational electronic book as a tool for supporting children's emergent literacy in low versus middle SES groups. *Computers and Education*, *50*(1), 110–124.

Krathwohl, D. R. (2002). A revision of Bloom's Taxonomy: An overview. *Theory Into Practice*, *41*(4), 212–218.

Kress, G. (2003). *Literacy in the new media age*. New York: Routledge.

Kress, G. (2010). *Multimodality: A social semiotic approach to contemporary communication*. New York: Routledge.

Kress, G., & van Leeuwen, T. (2001). *Multimodal discourse: The modes and media of contemporary communication*. New York: Oxford University Press.

Labbo, L. D. (2005). From morning message to digital morning message: Moving from the tried and true to the new. *The Reading Teacher*, *58*(8), 782–785.

Labbo, L. D., & Reinking, D. (1999). Negotiating the multiple realities of technology in literacy research and instruction. *Reading Research Quarterly*, *34*(4), 478–492.

Langer, J. A. (2011). *Envisioning knowledge: Building literacy in the academic disciplines*. New York: Teachers College Press.

Lankshear, C., & Knobel, M. (2011). *New literacies: Everyday practices and social learning* (3rd ed.). New York: Open University Press.

Lapp, D., & Fisher, D. (2009). It's all about the book: Motivating teens to read. *Journal of Adolescent and Adult Literacy*, *52*(7), 556–561.

Lapp, D., Fisher, D., & Johnson, K. (2010). Text mapping plus: Improving comprehension through supported retellings. *Journal of Adolescent and Adult Literacy*, *53*(5), 423–426.

Lapp, D., Moss, B., & Rowsell, J. (2012). Envisioning new literacies through a lens of teaching and learning. *The Reading Teacher*, *65*(6), 367–377.

Larson, L. C. (n.d.). *Thoughtful threads: Sparking rich online discussions* [Lesson plan]. Accessed at www.readwritethink.org/classroom-resources/lesson-plans/thoughtful-threads-sparking -rich-1165.html?tab=1#tabs on August 15, 2014.

Larson, L. C. (2009). Reader response meets new literacies: Empowering readers in online learning communities. *The Reading Teacher*, *62*(8), 638–648.

Larson, L. C. (2010). Digital readers: The next chapter in e-book reading and response. *The Reading Teacher*, *64*(1), 15–22.

Lau, K.-L. (2009). Reading motivation, perceptions of reading instruction and reading amount: A comparison of junior and senior secondary students in Hong Kong. *Journal of Research in Reading*, *32*(4), 366–382.

Leach, J. M., Scarborough, H. S., & Rescorla, L. (2003). Late-emerging reading disabilities. *Journal of Educational Psychology*, *95*(2), 211–224.

Lee, C. D., & Spratley, A. (2010). *Reading in the disciplines: The challenges of adolescent literacy*. New York: Carnegie Corporation of New York.

Lefever-Davis, S., & Pearman, C. (2005). Early readers and electronic texts: CD-ROM storybook features that influence reading behaviors. *The Reading Teacher*, *58*(5), 446–454.

Lenhart, A., Simon, M., & Graziano, M. (2001). *The Internet and education: Findings of the Pew Internet & American Life Project*. Washington, DC: Pew Internet and American Life Project. Accessed at www.pewinternet.org/2001/09/01/the-internet-and-education on August 15, 2014.

Leu, D. J., Jr. (2000). Literacy and technology: Deictic consequences for literacy education in an information age. In M. L. Kamil, P. B. Mosenthal, P. D. Pearson, & R. Barr (Eds.), *Handbook of reading research* (Vol. 3, pp. 743–770). Mahwah, NJ: Erlbaum.

Leu, D. J., Jr., Kinzer, C. K., Coiro, J. L., & Cammack, D. W. (2004). Toward a theory of new literacies emerging from the Internet and other information and communication technologies. In R. B. Ruddell & N. J. Unrau (Eds.), *Theoretical models and processes of reading* (5th ed., pp. 1570–1611). Newark, DE: International Reading Association.

Leu, D. J., Kinzer, C. K., Coiro, J., Castek, J., & Henry, L. A. (2013). New literacies: A dual-level theory of the changing nature of literacy, instruction, and assessment. In D. E. Alvermann, N. J. Unrau, & R. B. Ruddell (Eds.), *Theoretical models and processes of reading* (6th ed., pp. 1150–1181). Newark, DE: International Reading Association.

Leu, D. J., McVerry, J. G., O'Byrne, W. I., Kiili, C., Zawilinski, L., Everett-Cacopardo, H., et al. (2011). The new literacies of online reading comprehension: Expanding the literacy and learning curriculum. *Journal of Adolescent and Adult Literacy, 55*(1), 5–14.

Leu, D. J., Jr., O'Byrne, W. I., Zawilinski, L., McVerry, J. G., & Everett-Cacopardo, H. (2009). Comments on Greenhow, Robelia, and Hughes: Expanding the new literacies conversation. *Educational Researcher, 38*(4), 264–269.

Lubans, J. (1998). *How first-year university students use and regard Internet resources.* Accessed at www.lubans.org/docs/1styear/firstyear.html on December 30, 2014.

Lubans, J. (1999). *Key findings on Internet use among students.* Accessed at www.lubans.org/docs/key/key.html on December 30, 2014.

Lubliner, S., & Grisham, D. L. (2012). Cognate strategy instruction: Providing powerful literacy tools to Spanish-speaking students. In J. Fingon & S. Ulanoff (Eds.), *Learning from culturally and linguistically diverse K–12 classrooms: Promoting success for all students* (pp. 105–123). New York: Teachers College Press.

Luckin, R., Connolly, D., Plowman, L., & Airey, S. (2003). With a little help from my friends: Children's interactions with interactive toy technology. *Journal of Computer Assisted Learning, 19*(2), 165–176.

Luke, C. (2003). Pedagogy, connectivity, multimodality, and interdisciplinarity. *Reading Research Quarterly, 38*(3), 397–403.

Madden, M., Lenhart, A., Duggan, M., Cortesi, S., & Gasser, U. (2013). *Teens and technology 2013.* Washington, DC: Pew Internet and American Life Project. Accessed at www.pewinternet.org/Reports/2013/Teens-and-Tech.aspx on August 15, 2014.

Manderino, M., & Wickens, C. (2014). Addressing disciplinary literacy in the Common Core State Standards. *Illinois Reading Council Journal, 42*(2), 28–39.

Martinez, M., Roser, N. L., & Strecker, S. (1998/1999). "I never thought I could be a star": A Readers Theatre ticket to fluency. *The Reading Teacher, 52*(4), 326–334.

Marzano, R. J. (2004). *Building background knowledge for academic achievement: Research on what works in schools.* Alexandria, VA: Association for Supervision and Curriculum Development.

Marzano, R. J. (2007). Designing a comprehensive approach to classroom assessment. In D. Reeves (Ed.), *Ahead of the curve: The power of assessment to transform teaching and learning* (pp. 103–125). Bloomington, IN: Solution Tree Press.

Mayer, R. E. (2001). *Multimedia learning.* New York: Cambridge University Press.

Mayer, R. E. (2008). Multimedia literacy. In J. Coiro, M. Knobel, C. Lankshear, & D. J. Leu (Eds.), *Handbook of research on new literacies* (pp. 359–376). New York: Erlbaum.

McConachie, S., & Petrosky, A. (Eds.). (2010). *Content matters: A disciplinary literacy approach to improving student learning.* San Francisco: Jossey-Bass.

McEneaney, J. E. (2006). Agent-based literacy theory. *Reading Research Quarterly, 41*(3), 352–371.

McGill-Franzen, A., & Zeig, J. L. (2008). Drawing to learn: Visual support for developing reading, writing, and concepts for children at-risk. In J. Flood, S. B. Heath, & D. Lapp (Eds.), *Handbook of research on teaching literacy through the communicative and visual arts* (Vol. 2, pp. 399–411). New York: Routledge.

McKenna, M. C. (1998). Electronic texts and the transformation of beginning reading. In D. Reinking, M. C. McKenna, L. D. Labbo, & R. D. Kieffer (Eds.), *Handbook of literacy and technology: Transformations in a post-typographic world* (pp. 45–59). Mahwah, NJ: Erlbaum.

McVerry, J. G., Belshaw, D., & O'Byrne, W. I. (in press). Guiding students as they explore, build, and connect online. *Journal of Adolescent and Adult Literacy.*

Media Education Lab. (n.d.). *Code of best practices in fair use for media literacy education.* Accessed at http://mediaeducationlab.com/sites/mediaeducationlab.com/files/CodeofBestPracticesinFairUse.pdf on August 25, 2014.

Media Education Lab. (2012). *Copyright.* Accessed at http://mediaeducationlab.com/copyright on August 15, 2014.

Melekoglu, M. A. (2011). Impact of motivation to read on reading gains for struggling readers with and without learning disabilities. *Learning Disability Quarterly, 34*(4), 248–261.

Metiri Group. (2008). *Multimodal learning through media: What the research says* [White paper]. Accessed at www.cisco.com/web/strategy/docs/education/Multimodal-Learning-Through-Media.pdf on October 20, 2010.

Metzger, M. J. (2007). Making sense of credibility on the web: Models for evaluating online information and recommendations for future research. *Journal of the American Society for Information Science and Technology, 58*(13), 2078–2091.

Miner, K. (2013). Writing Readers Theatre scripts. In T. V. Rasinski & N. Padak (Eds.), *From fluency to comprehension: Powerful instruction through authentic reading* (pp. 103–111). New York: Guilford Press.

Miranda, T., Johnson, K. A., & Rossi-Williams, D. (2012). E-readers: Powering up for engagement. *Educational Leadership, 69*, 1–3.

Miranda, T., Williams-Rossi, D., Johnson, K. A., & McKenzie, N. (2011). Reluctant readers in middle school: Successful engagement with text using the e-reader. *International Journal of Applied Science and Technology, 1*(6), 81–91.

Moje, E. B. (2008). Foregrounding the disciplines in secondary literacy teaching and learning: A call for change. *Journal of Adolescent and Adult Literacy, 52*(2), 96–107.

Monte-Sano, C., & De La Paz, S. (2012). Using writing tasks to elicit adolescents' historical reasoning. *Journal of Literacy Research, 44*(3), 273–299.

Moore, R. (2000, August 20). Ray Bradbury can still burn through paper. *Orlando Sentinel.* Accessed at http://articles.orlandosentinel.com/2000–08–20/entertainment/0008190011_1_ray-bradbury-science-fiction-science-fiction on January 12, 2015.

MorrisCooke Interactive. (2014). *Explain Everything* [Mobile application]. Accessed at www.morriscooke.com/applications-ios/explain-everything-2 on September 17, 2014.

Mozilla Webmaker. (n.d.). *Web literacy map* (1.1.0). Accessed at https://webmaker.org/standard on August 15, 2014.

mr6n8. (2013, December 7). *Best free children's ebooks online.* Accessed at www.techsupportalert.com/best-free-childrens-ebooks-online.htm on August 15, 2014.

Nagy, W. E., & Scott, J. A. (2000). Vocabulary processes. In M. L. Kamil, P. B. Mosenthal, P. D. Pearson, & R. Barr (Eds.), *Handbook of reading research* (Vol. 3, pp. 269–284). Mahwah, NJ: Erlbaum.

National Education Technology Plan. (2010). *Transforming American education: Learning powered by technology.* Washington, DC: U.S. Department of Education.

National Governors Association Center for Best Practices & Council of Chief State School Officers. (2010). *Common Core State Standards for English language arts and literacy in history/ social studies, science, and technical subjects.* Washington, DC: Authors. Accessed at www .corestandards.org/ELA-Literacy on August 15, 2014.

National Institute of Child Health and Human Development. (2000). *Report of the National Reading Panel: Teaching children to read—An evidence-based assessment of the scientific research literature on reading and its implications for reading instruction* (NIH Publication No. 00–4769). Washington, DC: U.S. Government Printing Office.

Naughton, V. M. (2008). Picture it! *The Reading Teacher, 62*(1), 65–68.

Nettles, D. H. (2006). *Comprehensive literacy instruction in today's classrooms: The whole, the parts, and the heart.* Boston: Pearson.

New Literacies Essentials. (n.d.). *Examples of VoiceThreads for education.* Accessed at https:// sites.google.com/site/voicethreadliteracyessentials/home/voicethread-basics/examples-of-voicethreads-for-education on August 15, 2014.

The New London Group. (1996). A pedagogy of multiliteracies: Designing social features. *Harvard Educational Review, 66*(1), 60–92.

Nine Square. (2014). DocAS Lite (Version 6.3) [Mobile application software]. Accessed at https:// itunes.apple.com/us/app/docas-lite-pdf-converter-annotate/id451036875?mt=8 on August 15, 2014.

Northrop, L., & Killeen, E. (2013). A framework for using iPads to build early literacy skills. *The Reading Teacher, 66*(7), 531–537.

O'Brien, T. (1990). *The things they carried.* Boston: Houghton Mifflin.

O'Byrne, W. I. (2013). Online content construction: Empowering students as readers and writers of online information. In K. Pytash & R. Ferdig (Eds.) *Exploring technology for writing and writing instruction* (pp. 276–297). Hershey, PA: Information Science Reference.

Pachtman, A. B., & Wilson, K. A. (2006). What do the kids think? *The Reading Teacher, 59*(7), 680–684.

Paige, D. D., Rasinski, T. V., & Magpuri-Lavell, T. (2012). Is fluent, expressive reading important for high school readers? *Journal of Adolescent and Adult Literacy, 56*(1), 67–76.

Palincsar, A. S., & Brown, A. L. (1986). Interactive teaching to promote independent learning from text. *The Reading Teacher, 39*(8), 771–777.

Paquette, D. (2013, January 5). Kindle e-readers have had big impact at Clearwater High. *Tampa Bay Times.* Accessed at www.tampabay.com/news/education/k12/kindle-e-readers-have-had -big-impact-at-clearwater-high/1269193 on August 15, 2014.

Paquette, K. R., Fello, S. E., & Jalongo, M. R. (2007). The talking drawings strategy: Using primary children's illustrations and oral language to improve comprehension of expository text. *Early Childhood Education Journal, 35*(1), 65–73.

Patall, E. A. (2013). Constructing motivation through choice, interest, and interestingness. *Journal of Educational Psychology, 105*(2), 522–534.

Paterson, W. A., Henry, J. J., O'Quin, K., Ceprano, M. A., & Blue, E. V. (2003). Investigating the effectiveness of an integrated learning system on early emergent readers. *Reading Research Quarterly, 38*(2), 172–207.

Pearson, P. D. (2013, January 25). *Research and the Common Core: Can the romance survive?* [Webinar]. Accessed at www.textproject.org/assets/library/powerpoints/PDPearson-webinar -Research-and-the-Common-Core.pdf on August 15, 2014.

Pearson, P. D., & Gallagher, M. C. (1983). The instruction of reading comprehension. *Contemporary Educational Psychology, 8*(3), 317–344.

Pecjak, S., & Kosir, K. (2008). Reading motivation and reading efficiency in third and seventh grade pupils in relation to teachers' activities in the classroom. *Studia Psychologica, 50*(2), 147–168.

Pew Research Center. (2010). *Millennials: A portrait of Generation Next.* Accessed at http:// pewresearch.org/millennials on March 1, 2010.

Pitcher, S. M., Albright, L. K., DeLaney, C. J., Walker, N. T., Seunarinesingh, K., Mogge, S., et al. (2007). Assessing adolescents' motivation to read. *Journal of Adolescent and Adult Literacy, 50*(5), 378–396.

Prensky, M. (2001). Digital natives, digital immigrants. *On the Horizon, 9*(5), 1–6.

Prensky, M. (2005). Listen to the natives. *Educational Leadership, 63*(4), 8–13.

Pressley, M., & Afflerbach, P. (1995). *Verbal protocols of reading: The nature of constructively responsive reading.* Hillsdale, NJ: Erlbaum.

Pritchard, R., & O'Hara, S. (2009). Vocabulary development in the science classroom: Using hypermedia authoring to support English learners. *The Tapestry Journal, 1*(1), 15–29.

Project Tomorrow. (2011). *The new 3 E's of education: Enabled, engaged, empowered—How today's educators are advancing a new vision for teaching and learning.* Irvine, CA: Author. Accessed at www.tomorrow.org/speakup/pdfs/SU10_3EofEducation_Educators.pdf on August 15, 2014.

Pullinger, K., & Joseph, C. (2012). *Inanimate Alice* [Web novel]. Accessed at www.inanimatealice .com on August 15, 2014.

Putman, S. M., & Kingsley, T. (2009). The atoms family: Using podcasts to enhance the development of science vocabulary. *The Reading Teacher, 63*(2), 100–108.

RAND Reading Study Group. (2002). *Reading for understanding: Toward an R&D program in reading comprehension.* Accessed at www.rand.org/pubs/monograph_reports/MR1465.html on December 24, 2014.

Rasinski, T. V. (n.d.). Fluency rubric. Accessed at www.timrasinski.com/presentations /multidimensional_fluency_rubric_4_factors.pdf on August 15, 2014.

Rasinski, T. V. (1990). Effects of repeated reading and listening-while-reading on reading fluency. *The Journal of Educational Research, 83*(3), 147–150.

Rasinski, T. V. (2003). *The fluent reader: Oral reading strategies for building word recognition, fluency, and comprehension.* New York: Scholastic.

Rasinski, T. V., & Hoffman, J. V. (2003). Oral reading in the school literacy curriculum. *Reading Research Quarterly, 38*(4), 510–522.

Rasinski, T. V., Homan, S., & Biggs, M. (2009). Teaching reading fluency to struggling readers: Method, materials, and evidence. *Reading and Writing Quarterly, 25*(2–3), 192–204.

Rasinski, T. V., Padak, N. D., McKeon, C. A., Wilfong, L. G., Friedauer, J. A., & Heim, P. (2005). Is reading fluency a key for successful high school reading? *Journal of Adolescent and Adult Literacy, 49*(1), 22–27.

Rasinski, T. V., Reutzel, D. R., Chard, D., & Linan-Thompson, S. (2011). Reading fluency. In M. L. Kamil, P. D. Pearson, E. B. Moje, & P. P. Afflerbach (Eds.), *Handbook of reading research* (Vol. 4, pp. 286–319). New York: Routledge.

ReadWriteThink. (2005). *Script guidelines.* Accessed at www.readwritethink.org/files/resources/lesson_images/lesson863/script.pdf on August 15, 2014.

Reinking, D. (1992). Differences between electronic and printed texts: An agenda for research. *Journal of Educational Multimedia and Hypermedia, 1*(1), 11–24.

Reinking, D. (1997). Me and my hypertext:) A multiple digression analysis of technology and literacy (sic). *The Reading Teacher, 50*(8), 626–643.

Reinking, D., Labbo, L. D., & McKenna, M. (1997). Navigating the changing landscape of literacy: Current theory and research in computer-based reading and writing. In J. Flood, S. B. Heath, & D. Lapp (Eds.), *Handbook of research on teaching literacy through the communicative and visual arts* (Vol. 1, pp. 77–92). New York: Macmillan.

Resnick, L. B., Salmon, M., Zeitz, C. M., Wathen, S. H., & Holowchak, M. (1993). Reasoning in conversation. *Cognition and Instruction, 11*(3–4), 347–364.

Richardson, W. (2010). *Blogs, wikis, podcasts, and other powerful web tools for classrooms* (3rd ed.). Thousand Oaks, CA: Corwin Press.

Rideout, V. (2011). *Zero to eight: Children's media use in America.* San Francisco: Common Sense Media. Accessed at www.commonsensemedia.org/sites/default/files/research/zerotoeightfinal2011.pdf on August 15, 2014.

Rideout, V. J., Foehr, U. G., & Roberts, D. F. (2010). *Generation M2: Media in the lives of 8- to 18-year-olds.* Menlo Park, CA: Henry J. Kaiser Family Foundation. Accessed at www.kff.org/entmedia/mh012010pkg.cfm on February 1, 2010.

Risko, V. J., & Walker-Dalhouse, D. (2010). Making the most of assessments to inform instruction. *The Reading Teacher, 63*(5), 420–422.

Risko, V. J., Walker-Dalhouse, D., Bridges, E. S., & Wilson, A. (2011). Drawing on text features for reading comprehension and composing. *The Reading Teacher, 64*(5), 376–378.

Robinson, E., & Robinson, S. (2003). *What does it mean? Discourse, text, culture—An introduction.* Sydney, New South Wales, Australia: McGraw-Hill.

Rolfe, G., Freshwater, D., & Jasper, M. (2001). *Critical reflection for nursing and the helping professions: A user's guide.* Basingstoke, Hampshire, England: Palgrave Macmillan.

Ronzetti, T. (2014a). *Chris Terns1* [Video file]. Accessed at www.youtube.com/watch?v=vIOyV8GH8H8&feature=youtu.be on August 15, 2014.

Ronzetti, T. (2014b). *Hannah Whale1* [Video file]. Accessed at www.youtube.com/watch?v=Idi92I1qArE&feature=youtu.be on August 15, 2014.

Rose, D. H., & Meyer, A. (2002). *Teaching every student in the digital age: Universal design for learning.* Alexandria, VA: Association for Supervision and Curriculum Development.

Rosenblatt, L. M. (1985). Viewpoints: Transaction versus interaction—A terminological rescue operation. *Research in the Teaching of English, 19*(1), 96–107.

Rosenblatt, L. M. (1995). *Literature as exploration* (5th ed.). New York: Modern Language Association of America.

Sadoski, M., & Paivio, A. (2007). Toward a unified theory of reading. *Scientific Studies of Reading, 11*(4), 337–356.

Samuels, S. J. (1979). The method of repeated readings. *The Reading Teacher, 32*(4), 403–408.

Schön, D. A. (1987). *Educating the reflective practitioner.* San Francisco: Jossey-Bass.

Schreiber, P. A. (1980). On the acquisition of reading fluency. *Journal of Reading Behavior, 12*(3), 177–186.

Schulten, K. (2013a). Student contest: 15-second vocabulary videos [Web log post]. Accessed at http://learning.blogs.nytimes.com/2013/10/31/student-contest-15-second-vocabulary-videos on August 15, 2014.

Schulten, K. (2013b). Words gone wild: The student winners of our 15-second vocabulary video contest [Web log post]. Accessed at http://learning.blogs.nytimes.com/2013/12/19/words -gone-wild-the-student-winners-of-our-15-second-vocabulary-video-contest/?_php=true&_ type=blogs&_r=0 on August 15, 2014.

Schwartz, A. (1981). *Scary stories to tell in the dark.* New York: HarperCollins.

Scott, J. A., Jamieson-Noel, D., & Asselin, M. (2003). Vocabulary instruction throughout the day in twenty-three Canadian upper-elementary classrooms. *The Elementary School Journal, 103*(3), 269–286.

Shackelford, J., Thompson, D. S., & James, M. B. (1999). Teaching strategy and assignment design: Assessing the quality and validity of information via the web. *Social Science Computer Review, 17*(2), 196–208.

Shanahan, C. (2009). Disciplinary comprehension. In S. E. Israel & G. G. Duffy (Eds.), *Handbook of research on reading comprehension* (pp. 240–260). New York: Routledge.

Shanahan, T., & Shanahan, C. (2008). Teaching disciplinary literacy to adolescents: Rethinking content-area literacy. *Harvard Educational Review, 78*(1), 40–59.

Shanahan, T., & Shanahan, C. (2012). What is disciplinary literacy and why does it matter? *Topics in Language Disorders, 32*(1), 7–18.

Sherer, J. Z., Gomez, K., Herman, P., Gomez, L., White, J., & Williams, A. (2009). Literacy infusion in a high school environmental science curriculum. In K. R. Bruna & K. Gomez (Eds.), *The work of language in multicultural classrooms: Talking science, writing science* (pp. 93–114). New York: Routledge.

Shinas, V. H. (2012). *Reading path and comprehension: An investigation of eighth-grade skilled readers' engagement with online, multimodal texts.* Unpublished doctoral dissertation, University of Delaware, Newark.

Shuler, C. (2009). *Pockets of potential: Using mobile technologies to promote children's learning.* New York: Joan Ganz Cooney Center.

Siegle, D. (2012). Embracing e-books: Increasing students' motivation to read and write. *Gifted Child Today, 35*(2), 137–143.

Smagorinsky, P. (2008). *Teaching English by design: How to create and carry out instructional units.* Portsmouth, NH: Heinemann.

Smith, B. E. (2013). *Composing across modes: Urban adolescents' processes responding to and analyzing literature.* Unpublished doctoral dissertation, Vanderbilt University, Nashville, TN.

Smith, B. E. (2014). Beyond words: A review of research on adolescents and multimodal composition. In R. E. Ferdig & K. E. Pytash (Eds.), *Exploring multimodal composition and digital writing* (pp. 1–19). Hershey, PA: IGI Global.

Smith, F. (1994). *Writing and the writer* (2nd ed.). Hillsdale, NJ: Erlbaum.

Smolkin, L. B., & Donovan, C. A. (2001). The contexts of comprehension: The information book read aloud, comprehension acquisition, and comprehension instruction in a first-grade classroom. *The Elementary School Journal, 102*(2), 97–122.

Snow, C. E. (2002). *Reading for understanding: Toward an R&D program in reading comprehension.* Santa Monica, CA: RAND.

Snow, C. E., & Biancarosa, G. (2003). *Adolescent literacy and the achievement gap: What do we know and where do we go from here?* New York: Carnegie Corporation of New York. Accessed at http://olms1.cte.jhu.edu/olms/data/resource/2029/class9_snow_biancarosa.pdf on August 15, 2014.

Snow, C. E., Burns, M. S., & Griffin, P. (Eds.). (1998). *Preventing reading difficulties in young children.* Washington, DC: National Academies Press.

Solomon, G., & Schrum, L. (2007). *Web 2.0: New tools, new schools.* Eugene, OR: International Society for Technology in Education.

Spires, H. A., Hervey, L. G., Morris, G., & Stelpflug, C. (2012). Energizing project-based inquiry: Middle-grade students read, write, and create videos. *Journal of Adolescent and Adult Literacy, 55*(6), 483–493.

Stauffer, R. G. (1969). *Directing reading maturity as a cognitive process.* New York: Harper & Row.

Stauffer, R. G. (1970). *The language/experience approach to the teaching of reading.* New York: Harper & Row.

Steinbeck, J. (1937). *Of mice and men.* New York: Penguin.

Stiggins, R. (2007). Assessment through the student's eyes. *Educational Leadership, 64*(8), 22–26.

Swandby, M. (n.d.). *Home.* Accessed at https://sites.google.com/site/swandby/home on August 15, 2014.

Tomlinson, C. A. (1999). *The differentiated classroom: Responding to the needs of all learners.* Alexandria, VA: Association for Supervision and Curriculum Development.

Torres, M., & Mercado, M. (2006). The need for critical media literacy in teacher education core curricula. *Educational Studies, 39*(3), 260–282.

Tracey, D. H., & Young, J. W. (2007). Technology and early literacy: The impact of an integrated learning system on high-risk kindergartners' achievement. *Reading Psychology, 28*(5), 443–467.

Unsworth, L. (2006). Towards a metalanguage for multiliteracies education: Describing the meaning-making resources of language-image interaction. *English Teaching: Practice and Critique, 5*(1), 55–76.

Unsworth, L. (2009). Multiliteracies and metalanguage: Describing image/text relations as a resource for negotiating multimodal texts. In J. Coiro, M. Knobel, C. Lankshear, & D. J. Leu (Eds.), *Handbook of research on new literacies* (pp. 377–405). New York: Erlbaum.

Varrato, T. (2013). *Teaching with technology: There's no time like real-time.* Newark, DE: International Reading Association. Accessed at www.reading.org/Libraries/members-only/ira-e-ssentials-8041-immediate-formative-assessments-secondary-classrooms.pdf on October 15, 2013.

Vasinda, S., & McLeod, J. (2011). Extending Readers Theatre: A powerful and purposeful match with podcasting. *The Reading Teacher, 64*(7), 486–497. Accessed at www.readingrockets.org /article/52140 on August 15, 2014.

Vasinda, S., & McLeod, J. (2013). Powerful pairing: Podcasting and readers theatre. In T. V. Rasinski & N. Padak (Eds.), *From fluency to comprehension: Powerful instruction through authentic reading* (pp. 91–102). New York: Guilford Press.

Vygotsky, L. S. (1978). *Mind in society: The development of higher psychological processes.* Cambridge, MA: Harvard University Press.

Wade, S. E., & Moje, E. B. (2001). The role of text in classroom learning: Beginning an online dialogue. *Reading Online, 5*(4).

Wainwright, A. (2013, May 3). 10 facts show growth of iPads in the classroom as learning tools [Web log post]. Accessed at www.securedgenetworks.com/secure-edge-networks-blog /bid/89862/10-Facts-Show-Growth-of-iPads-in-the-Classroom-as-Learning-Tools on August 15, 2014.

Walsh, M. (2006). Reading visual and multimodal texts: How is 'reading' different? *Australian Journal of Language and Literacy, 29*(1), 24–37.

Weaver, C. A., & Kintsch, W. (1991). Expository text. In R. Barr, M. L. Kamil, P. B. Mosenthal, & P. D. Pearson (Eds.), *Handbook of reading research* (Vol. 2, pp. 230–244). New York: Longman.

Wiggins, G., & McTighe, J. (2005). *Understanding by design* (Expanded 2nd ed.). Alexandria, VA: Association for Supervision and Curriculum Development.

Wiggins, G., & McTighe, J. (2011). *The understanding by design guide to creating high-quality units.* Alexandria, VA: Association for Supervision and Curriculum Development.

Wilfong, L. G. (2008). Building fluency, word-recognition ability, and confidence in struggling readers: The Poetry Academy. *The Reading Teacher, 62*(1), 4–13.

Wineburg, S. (1991). On the reading of historical texts: Notes on the breach between school and academy. *American Educational Research Journal, 28*(3), 495–519.

Wineburg, S. (2001). *Historical thinking and other unnatural acts: Charting the future of teaching the past.* Philadelphia: Temple University Press.

Wineburg, S., Martin, D., & Monte-Sano, C. (2011). *Reading like a historian: Teaching literacy in middle and high school history classrooms.* New York: Teachers College Press.

Wisecrack. (n.d.). *Wisecrack.* Accessed at www.youtube.com/user/wisecrack on January 15, 2015.

Wohlwend, K. E. (2010). A is for avatar: Young children in literacy 2.0 worlds and literacy 1.0 schools. *Language Arts, 88*(2), 144–152.

Wolf, M., & Barzillai, M. (2009). The importance of deep reading. *Educational Leadership, 66*(6), 32–37.

Wolsey, T. D. (2010). Complexity in student writing: The relationship between the task and vocabulary uptake. *Literacy Research and Instruction, 49*(2), 194–208.

Wolsey, T. D., & Grisham, D. L. (2007). Adolescents and the new literacies: Writing engagement. *Action in Teacher Education, 29*(2), 29–38.

Xin, J. F., & Rieth, H. (2001). Video-assisted vocabulary instruction for elementary school students with learning disabilities. *Information Technology in Childhood Education Annual, 2001*(1), 87–103.

Young, C. J. (2013, April 19). *The bad news: A student produced movie* [Video file]. Accessed at www.youtube.com/watch?v=qMy-zQpYJds on August 15, 2014.

Young, C. J., & Rasinski, T. V. (2009). Implementing Readers Theatre as an approach to classroom fluency instruction. *The Reading Teacher, 63*(1), 4–13.

Young, C. J., & Rasinski, T. V. (2011). Enhancing author's voice through scripting. *The Reading Teacher, 65*(1), 24–28.

Young, C. J., & Rasinski, T. V. (2013). Student-produced movies as a medium for literacy development. *The Reading Teacher, 66*(8), 670–675.

Zammit, K. (2007). Popular culture in the classroom: Interpreting and creating multimodal texts. In R. Whittaker, M. O'Donnell, & A. McCabe (Eds.), *Advances in language and education* (pp. 60–76). New York: Continuum.

Zammit, K., & Downes, T. (2002). New learning environments and the multiliterate individual: A framework for educators. *Australian Journal of Language and Literacy, 25*(2), 24–36.

Zawilinski, L. (2009). HOT blogging: A framework for blogging to promote higher order thinking. *The Reading Teacher, 62*(8), 650–661.

Zhao, Y., Pugh, K., Sheldon, S., & Byers, J. L. (2002). Conditions for classroom technology innovations. *Teachers College Record, 104*(3), 482–515.

Zickuhr, K., & Rainie, L. (2014). *E-reading rises as device ownership jumps.* Washington, DC: Pew Internet and American Life Project. Accessed at http://pewinternet.org/Reports/2014/E-Reading-Update.aspx on January 28, 2014.

Zimmerman, B. J. (2008). Investigating self-regulation and motivation: Historical background, methodological developments, and future prospects. *American Educational Research Journal, 45*(1), 1–18.

Zucker, T. A., & Invernizzi, M. (2008). My eSorts and digital extensions of word study. *The Reading Teacher, 61*(8), 654–658.

Zucker, T. A., Moody, A. K., & McKenna, M. C. (2009). The effects of electronic books on pre-kindergarten-to-grade 5 students' literacy and language outcomes: A research synthesis. *Journal of Educational Computing Research, 40*(1), 47–87.

Zutell, J., & Rasinski, T. V. (1991). Training teachers to attend to their students' oral reading fluency. *Theory Into Practice, 30*(3), 211–217.

Index

A

abc PocketPhonics, 14–15, 30
agency, 212
Airey, S., 11
Albion, P., 12
Allington, R., 231
Ambling Books, 55
apps, 13
    annotation, for informational texts, 101–109
    classroom example of using, 105–108
    ereaders and, 157–163
    how to use, 102–104, 108–109
    for informational texts, 95–98, 101–109
    for letter identification and letter sounds, 30
    for motivation and iPads, 197–202
    for phonics practice, 30, 200
    selecting, 32–34
    for sight word recognition, 31, 200
    tablets and matching, to student needs,
        25–34
    See also name of
assessment. *See* reading assessment
Attewell, P., 12
Audacity, 44, 59
audio-assisted reading
    benefits of, 54
    classroom example, 57–59
    fluency rubric, 56–57
    implementation of, 54–57
    reading fluency and, 36, 53–59
    resources on, 55

B

Barzillai, M., 20
Battle, J., 12
Beach, R., 157
Beers, K., 89
Beschorner, B., 158
Besnoy, K., 158
Biteslide, 126
Blackboard, 123
Blogger, 154

blogs
    disciplinary literacy and use of, 149–154
    examples of introductory posts, 230
    informational text and use of, 106–108
    online literature circles and response options
        and use of, 125
    reading assessment and use of, 223–231
    rubric, 226–227
Bob Books, 31
Bradbury, R., 189
Brunvand, S., 217
Bush, G. W., 1
Byrd, S., 217

C

Caldwell, J. S., 223
Castek, J., 157
CCSS (Common Core State Standards), 7
    digital texts and, 18–19
    foundational skills and, 19
    literary text and, 131
Clarke, L., 158
classroom blogs, disciplinary literacy and use of
    classroom example, 151–153
    implementation of, 150–151, 154
    role of, 149
close reading
    digital resources, close reading and use of
    See also defined, 131
Cloud, 194
coding and connecting complex literature,
    131–135
Coleman, D., 131
collaborative writing platforms, 125–126
Coming of Age, 160
common language, 20–21
computers, literacy skills and use of, 14
Connolly, D., 11
Council of Chief State School Officers, 157, 165
Cunningham, P., 231
Cute CUT, 183

D

Dalton, B., 22
Dewey, J., 117
digital language experience, 14
digital learning hub, 115
digital morning message, 14
digital natives, 8, 18
digital resources, close reading and use of
    classroom example, 167–168
    how to use, 166–167, 169
    role of, 165–166
digital texts
    classroom example, 21
    common language, 20–21
    how to use, 19–21
    multimodality, 20
    reading path, 20
    standards and, 18–19
digital tools, role of, 215–217
Diigo, 102, 103, 108, 109
Directed Reading-Thinking Activity, 70
disciplinary literacy
    blogs, use of, 149–154
    defined, 145
    digital resources, use of, 165–170
    ereaders and apps, use of, 157–163
DocAS, 102, 105, 108, 109
Doodle Buddy, 200
Dropbox, 183, 209
Duke, N., 53

E

ebooks, 12–13, 122, 128
    See also ereaders
e-dictionary pages, generating, 67–68
Edublogs, 45, 125
engagement. *See* motivation and engagement
ePals, 129
ereaders
    popularity of, 189–190
    types of, 158, 190
ereaders, disciplinary literacy and
    classroom example, 159–162
    how to use, 159, 162
    research on, 158
    role of, 158–159, 163
ereaders, motivation and engagement and
    classroom example, 192–193
    how to use, 191–192, 194
Explain Everything
    classroom example, 209–212
    how to use, 208–209, 212–213
    informational texts, 95–98
    reading assessment, 95–98, 207–213

F

FarFaria, 13
Fiene, J., 223
filmmaking
    classroom example, 183–184
    implementation of, 177–183, 184–186
    motivation and engagement and, 175–186
    steps required before, 176
Fisher, D., 117, 171
Folger Shakespeare Library, 55, 57
foundational competencies, 7

foundational skills, 19
    tablets and, 25–34
Freshwater, D., 116
Fry Words, 31

G

Gizmo's Freeware, 13
GlobalSchoolNet, 129
Glogster, 68, 126
Google Books, 194
Goudvis, A., 223, 224

H

Harvey, S., 223, 224
Hilden, K., 53
Hillman, M., 12
Hudson, R., 217
Hutchison, A., 158
hypertexts
    classroom example, 140–141
    how to use, 138–139, 141–143
    role of, 137–138
Hypothesis, 133

I

iBrainstorm, 162
iCardSort, 31
iMovie, 50, 183
Inanimate Alice (Pullinger and Joseph), 21
informational text, improving comprehension of
    apps for, 101–109
    Multimodal Explanatory Composition, 93–99
    Online Research and Media Skills model, 111–116
International Reading Association, 207, 231
Internet, vocabulary building and use of the
    classroom example, 85–86
    how to use, 83–85, 86, 88
    pros and cons of, 81–82
    structured think-alouds, 82–83
    vocabulary learning checklist, 84
    worksheet for online actions, 87
Internet Archive, 194
iPad apps, motivation and
    benefits of, 197–199
    classroom example, 200–201
    how to use, 199, 201–202
    list of, 200
    One Minute Reader, 199, 200–201
    VocabularySpellingCity, 199, 200, 201
iPods, 40
iTunes, 180
Ivey, G., 171
iWriteWords, 13, 30

J

Jasper, M., 116
Jennings, J. H., 223
Johnson, K., 117, 158
Johnston, P., 171, 212
Joseph, C., 21

K

Kidblog, 125, 150, 154, 224
Knobel, M., 166
Kress, G., 94, 166

L

Labbo, L., 14
Lane, H., 217
Lankshear, C., 166
Lapp, D., 117, 171
Lefever-Davis, S., 21
Lerner, J., 223
LibriVox, 55
Licking Letters, 200
literacy skill acquisition, technology and
    apps, 13
    classroom example, 14–15
    computers, 14
    ebooks, 12–13
    research on, 12
literary text, improving comprehension of
    coding and connecting complex literature,
        131–135
    discussions, 118
    hypertexts, 137–143
    online literature circles and response options,
        121–129
    strategy instruction, 117
Lit Genius, 133
Little Matchups ABC, 30
Lit2Go, 55
Luckin, R., 11
Luke, C., 137

M

Martinez, M., 39
Marzano, R., 216
McGill-Franzen, A., 208
McKenna, M., 12
McKenzie, N., 158
McMahon, S., 223
message/discussion boards, asynchronous,
    123–124
MindMeister, 162
Miranda, T., 158
MixedInk, 126
Moje, E. B., 145
Montessori Crosswords, 30, 31–32
Moodle, 123
Moody, A., 12
Moore, T., 12
motivation and engagement
    defined, 171
    ereaders and ebooks and, 189–194
    filmmaking and, 175–186
    iPad apps and, 197–202
    peer interaction and, 171
    reading relevancy and, 171
    self-selection and, 171
Mozilla Web Literacy Map, 113
Multimodal Explanatory Composition
    classroom example, 96–98
    Explain Everything app, 95–98
    how to use, 94–95
    role of, 93–94, 99
multimodality, 20
multimodal posters, 126–127

N

National Governors Association Center for Best
    Practices, 157, 165

National Institute of Child Health and Human
    Development (NICHD), 1
National Reading Panel, 20
NewHive, 126

O

One Minute Reader, 199, 200–201
online literature circles and response options
    blogs, 125
    classroom example, 127–128
    collaborative writing platforms, 125–126
    digital thinkmarks, 122, 123
    ebooks, 122, 128
    how to use, 122–127, 128–129
    message/discussion boards, asynchronous,
        123–124
    role of, 121–122
    web-based multimodal posters, 126–127
Online Research and Media Skills (ORMS)
    model, 112
    background information, 112–113
    classroom example, 114–115
    how to use, 113, 115–116

P

Pearman, C., 21
phonemic awareness
    apps for, 30, 200
    defined, 7
    tablets and matching apps to student needs,
        25–34
phonics
    apps for, 30, 200
    defined, 7
    tablets and matching apps to student needs,
        25–34
Plowman, L., 11
Pocket WavePad, 44
podcasts
    benefits of, 40
    classroom example, 42–43
    how to use, 41
    posting, 44–45
    practice schedules, 44
    public domain stories, 43–44
    recording, 44
    repeated reading and, 39–45
    scripts, finding, 43–44
poetry slams, 48
Popplet, 162
posters, web-based multimodal, 126–127
PowerPoint, 67–68, 137–143, 162
Pressley, M., 53
Prezi, 68, 162
PrimaryPad, 125–126
Project Gutenberg, 133, 194
Project Tomorrow, 166
Pullen, P., 217
Pullinger, K., 21

R

RAND Reading Study Group, 111
Rasinski, T., 216
readers theater, 39–45, 48
reading, audio-assisted, 36, 53–59
reading, repeated
    podcasting and, 39–45

rehearsal and, 36
student-produced movies and, 47–51
reading assessment
    blogs and, 223–231
    digital tools, role of, 215–217
    Explain Everything, 95–98, 207–213
    importance of, 207–208
    VoiceThread, 55, 68, 217–220
Reading A–Z, 200
Reading First, 1
reading fluency
    audio-assisted reading, 36, 53–59
    constructs of, 35
    methods for improving, 36
    podcasting and, 39–45
    student-produced movies and, 47–51
reading path, 20
reading vocabulary. *See* vocabulary
response to intervention
    matching apps to student needs, 25–34
    tablets and, 25–26
    tracking progress, 27–29
Risko, V., 224
Rolfe, G., 116
Rosenblatt, L., 117
Roser, N., 39

S

Schmidt-Crawford, D., 158
script treatment, 49
self-regulated learning, 81–82
Shepherd, A., 43
Shinas, V. H., 21
Siegle, D., 190
Sight Word Bingo, 200
sight word recognition
    apps for, 31, 200
    defined, 7–8
    tablets and matching apps to student needs,
        25–34
Sight Words, 31
SimpleMind, 162
Smore, 126, 127
SoundBible, 180
SoundCloud, 45
SpellingCity, 200
Starfall, 13
Starfall ABCs, 30, 31
Starfall Learn to Read, 30, 200
Stauffer, R., 14
Stonewashed, 180
storyboards, 49, 50, 180, 183
StoryPod JHC, 160
Strecker, S., 39
student-produced movies
    classroom example, 50–51
    implementation of, 48–50
    reading fluency and, 47–51
student-produced vocabulary videos, 73–74
    classroom examples, 76–77
    implementation of, 75–76, 77–79
student technology use, research on, 11–12
Suazo-Garcia, B., 12
Subtext, 133, 134, 135
Super Why!, 30

T

tablets
    classroom example, 31–32
    how to use, 26–31
    response to intervention and use of, 25–26
Technology Integration Planning Cycle for Literacy and Language Arts, 99
text annotation/analysis
    classroom example, 133–134
    hypertexts, 137–143
    implementation of, 133, 134–135
    purpose of, 132–133
think-alouds, 70
    structured, 82–83
ThingLink, 67, 68
Touch and Write Phonics, 30

V

videos. *See* filmmaking; vocabulary videos
Videoshop, 183
Visual Thesaurus, 75
vocabulary
    Internet to build, 81–88
    rote-memory approach, 61
    technology, role of, 66
    videos, 73–79
Vocabulary Self-Selection Strategy Plus
    (VSSPlus)
    classroom example, 68–69
    e-dictionary pages, generating, 67–68
    how to use, 66–68, 70–71
VocabularySpellingCity, 30, 199, 200, 201
vocabulary videos, 73–74
    classroom examples, 76–77
    implementation of, 75–76, 77–79
VoiceThread, 55, 68
    classroom example, 218–219
    how to use, 218, 219–220
    reading assessment and use of, 217–220
    role of, 217

W

Walker-Dalhouse, D., 224
web-based multimodal posters, 126–127
web literacy, 113
web 2.0 digital tools, role of, 215–217
Weebly for Education, 125
Williams-Rossi, D., 158
Windows Movie Maker, 50, 183
Wolf, M., 20
Wordle, 200
Word Wizard, 31

Y

YouTube, 167, 209

Z

Zeig, J. L., 208
zone of proximal development, 26
Zucker, T., 12
Zutell, J., 216

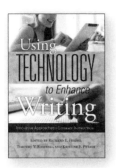

Using Technology to Enhance Writing
Edited by Richard E. Ferdig, Timothy V. Rasinski, and Kristine E. Pytash
Sharpen your students' communication skills while integrating digital tools into writing instruction. Loaded with techniques for planning and organizing writing, this handbook troubleshoots issues students face when writing in a printed versus digital context and teaches them how to read in multiple mediums.
BKF607

Rebuilding the Foundation
Edited by Timothy V. Rasinski
Teaching reading is a complex task without a simple formula for developing quality instruction. Rather than build on or alter existing models, this book considers how educators and policymakers might think about rebuilding and reconceptualizing reading education, perhaps from the ground up.
BKF399

Contemporary Perspectives on Literacy series
Edited by Heidi Hayes Jacobs
Today's students must be prepared to compete in a global society in which cultures, economies, and people are constantly connected. The authors explain three "new literacies"—digital, media, and global—and provide practical tips for incorporating these literacies into the traditional curriculum.
BKF441, BKF235, BKF236, BKF415

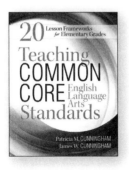

Teaching Common Core English Language Arts Standards
By Patricia M. Cunningham and James W. Cunningham
Explore twenty lesson frameworks to help teach the Common Core State Standards for English language arts. Discover targeted lessons to help students master critical skills, including how to organize ideas from informational texts, identify similarities and differences, and write with grade-appropriate language.
BKF617

Solution Tree | Press

a division of
Solution Tree

Visit solution-tree.com or call 800.733.6786 to order.

Wait! Your professional development journey doesn't have to end with the last pages of this book.

We realize improving student learning doesn't happen overnight. And your school or district shouldn't be left to puzzle out all the details of this process alone.

No matter where you are on the journey, we're committed to helping you get to the next stage.

Take advantage of everything from **custom workshops** to **keynote presentations** and **interactive web and video conferencing**. We can even help you develop an action plan tailored to fit your specific needs.

Let's get the conversation started.

Call 888.763.9045 today.

solution-tree.com